Everyday pornography

At a time when pornography is more ubiquitous than ever before, *Everyday Pornography* offers a specifically feminist intervention to the field. Taking an anti-pornography stance, this book repositions the textual study of pornography within a broader political and cultural frame.

Everyday Pornography focuses on the 'everyday' of pornography by addressing both the 'pornification' of mainstream culture and pornography's own mainstream – its predominantly heterosexual male audience and the commercial materials produced for that audience. This edited collection brings together new work from established and emerging scholars, introducing fresh methodologies whilst reflecting on the ongoing value of older approaches. The book is organized in two parts:

- Content and context
- Address, consumption, regulation.

Drawing on the experiences of activists alongside academics, *Everyday Pornography* offers the opportunity to explore the intellectual and political challenges of anti-pornography feminism and consider its relevance for contemporary academic debate. The editor, Karen Boyle, contextualizes the arguments developed within and across each chapter in relation to existing debates. *Everyday Pornography* is a comprehensive, accessible text which will be highly relevant to students approaching pornography from a wide range of humanities and social science disciplines.

Karen Boyle is Senior Lecturer in Film and Television Studies at the University of Glasgow, and is a Director of the Women's Support Project, a feminist anti-violence organization. She is author of *Media and Violence* (2005) and has published widely on gendered violence and feminist media studies.

Everyday pornography

Edited by
Karen Boyle

 Routledge
Taylor & Francis Group

LONDON AND NEW YORK

First published 2010
by Routledge
2 Park Square, Milton Park, Abingdon, Oxon. OX14 4RN

Simultaneously published in the USA and Canada
by Routledge
270 Madison Ave, New York, NY 10016

Routledge is an imprint of the Taylor & Francis Group, an informa business

Editorial selection and material © 2010 Karen Boyle
Individual chapters © 2010 the Contributors

Typeset in Galliard by Taylor & Francis Books
Printed and bound in Great Britain by
TJ International Ltd, Padstow, Cornwall

British Library Cataloguing in Publication Data
A catalogue record for this book is available from the British Library

Library of Congress Cataloging in Publication Data
A catalog record for this book has been requested

ISBN 10: 0-415-54378-9 (hbk)
ISBN 10: 0-415-54379-7 (pbk)
ISBN 10: 0-203-84755-5 (ebk)

ISBN 13: 978-0-415-54378-1 (hbk)
ISBN 13: 978-0-415-54379-8 (pbk)
ISBN 13: 978-0-203-84755-8 (ebk)

Contents

Figures and tables

Figures

Tables

Notes on the contributors

Karen Boyle is Senior Lecturer in Film and Television Studies at the University of Glasgow. She is author of *Media and Violence: Gendering the Debates* (2005) and has published widely on pornography, gendered violence and feminist media studies. She is a Director of the Women's Support Project, a feminist anti-violence organization.

Ana J. Bridges is an Assistant Professor of Clinical Psychology at the University of Arkansas, Fayetteville. Since 1999 she has been investigating the effects of explicit sexual media on women and couples. Her research has been featured in both the academic and the popular press, including *Psychology Today*.

Gerry Carlin is Senior Lecturer in English at the University of Wolverhampton. He has published articles on British Modernism critical theory and is researching 1960s fiction.

Gail Dines is a Professor of Sociology and Women's Studies at Wheelock College in Boston, MA. She has written and lectured widely on the impact of pornography on women and men, and has worked with numerous anti-violence organizations to develop educational programmes. Her latest book is *Pornland: How Porn has Hijacked our Sexuality* (2010).

Michael Flood is a Research Fellow at La Trobe University's Australian Research Centre in Sex, Health and Society. Michael's current research focuses on the primary prevention of violence against women, while he has also published on men and masculinities, heterosexuality, sexual and reproductive health and fathering. Michael is also a community educator and activist.

Robert Jensen is a journalism professor at the University of Texas at Austin. He is the author of numerous books, including *All My Bones Shake: Seeking a Progressive Path to the Prophetic Voice* (2009); *Getting Off: Pornography and the End of Masculinity* (2007) and *The Heart of Whiteness: Confronting Race, Racism and White Privilege* (2005).

Jennifer A. Johnson is an Assistant Professor of Sociology at Virginia Commonwealth University in Richmond. Her research focuses on using social network analysis to map the online commercial pornography industry as well as in the crime analysis procedures of local and federal law enforcement agencies.

Mark Jones is Senior Lecturer in English at the University of Wolverhampton. He has published articles on J. G. Ballard and popular music. He is researching 1960s fiction and contemporary horror films.

Clare McGlynn is Professor of Law at the University of Durham. She has published widely on the extreme pornography laws in England and Wales, with her work being discussed in political debates. She is the editor of *Rethinking Rape Law* (with Vanessa Munro, 2010) and *Feminist Judgements* (with Erika Rackley and Rosemary Hunter, 2010) and author of *The Woman Lawyer: Making the Difference* (1998) and *Families and the European Union* (2006).

Lisa Jean Moore, a medical sociologist, has published *Sperm Counts: Overcome by Men's Most Precious Fluid* (2007), *Missing Bodies: The Politics of Invisibility* with Monica Casper (2007) and *The Body Reader: Essential Readings in the Social and Cultural Studies of the Body* with Mary Kosut (2010).

Sarah Neely is a member of the Stirling Media Research Institute and a Lecturer in the department of Film, Media and Journalism at the University of Stirling. She is writing a book on the Orcadian film maker Margaret Tait. The chapter in this book is related to her growing research interest in gender and online identities.

Susanna Paasonen is a researcher at the Collegium for Advanced Studies, University of Helsinki. She is the author of *Figures of Fantasy: Internet, Women and Cyberdiscourse* (2005) and co-editor of *Pornification: Sex and Sexuality in Media Culture* (2007) and *Working with Affect in Feminist Readings: Disturbing Differences* (2010).

Linda Thompson is a Development Worker at the Women's Support Project Glasgow, funded by the Scottish government to develop work challenging all forms of commercial sex. Her background is in community development, youth work and HIV/sexual health promotion with priority groups.

Meagan Tyler completed her Ph.D. in Political Science at the University of Melbourne in 2009. Her thesis was entitled 'Active Service: The Pornographic and Sexological Construction of Women's Sexuality in the West'. She has published on these themes in *Women's Studies International Forum* and *Women and Therapy*.

Juliana Weissbein is a senior at SUNY Purchase, majoring in sociology and gender studies. She lectures to graduate classes and multiple national conferences. She has worked with Gender Public Advocacy Coalition and Teach for America, and is a future leader with the Center for Progressive Leadership.

Rebecca Whisnant is Associate Professor of Philosophy and Director of Women's and Gender Studies at the University of Dayton, OH. She is the co-editor of *Not for Sale: Feminists Resisting Prostitution and Pornography* (2004) and *Global Feminist Ethics* (2008), and a co-founder of Stop Porn Culture.

Acknowledgements

First, my thanks to all of the contributors who have made the process of collating and editing this collection an exciting one and have been extremely patient and generous in their responses to my e-mails, questions and comments. I have had the good fortune to work with excellent editors at Routledge: thanks, in particular, to Emily Laughton for all her help in the final stages of preparing the manuscript.

The Wheelock anti-pornography conference in April 2007 reminded me why feminist anti-pornography work remains essential – both within the academy and outside it – and provided a sense of community to enable me to take this work forward. My sincere thanks to the organizers – Gail Dines, Rebecca Whisnant and Robert Jensen – whose work, energy and commitment are genuinely inspirational. Linda Thompson generously shared her experience working across Scotland on issues of commercial sexual exploitation and has been a sounding board for many of the ideas in this book. Linda and her colleagues at the Women's Support Project – Jan MacLeod, Janette de Haan and Isabell Robertson – give me the grounding which makes feminist academic work in this field possible. Their achievements are too many to list here, but women across Scotland owe them a huge debt for their amazing work in the feminist anti-violence sector stretching back twenty-five years.

The two Sarahs – Neely and Smith – have debated many of the issues in this book and provided much needed support at times when being an anti-porn feminist in academia has been particularly challenging. My colleagues in Film and Television Studies at the University of Glasgow generously supported the study leave which made completion of the book possible. Susan Berridge and Kat Hughes helped me amass material for Chapter 9 and Katharina Lindner offered valuable comments on the Epilogue.

Finally, my love and thanks to Ian and Alec Garwood: anti-porn work is never easy, without their love and support it would be unimaginably bleak.

Introduction

Everyday pornography

Karen Boyle

After a fallow period in the mid-1990s to early 2000s, the academic study of pornography has experienced something of a revival. For many, this new work represents an important re-focusing after the divisive 'sex wars' of the 1980s and early 1990s. In her introduction to *Porn Studies*, for instance, Linda Williams writes:

> The porn studies of this volume diverge markedly from the kind of agonizing over sexual politics that characterized an earlier era of the study of pornography. Where once it seemed necessary to argue vehemently against pro-censorship, anti-pornography feminism for the value and importance of studying pornography ... today porn studies addresses a veritable explosion of sexually explicit materials that cry out for better understanding. Feminist debates about whether pornography should exist at all have paled before the simple fact that still and moving-image pornographies have become fully recognizable fixtures of popular culture.
>
> (Williams 2004a: 2)

For Williams it is the quantity of pornographic materials and their mainstreaming that obviates the need for 'agonizing over sexual politics'. She does not suggest that the questions which prompted such agonizing have been answered, but rather that the expansion and mainstreaming of pornography renders them redundant. Yet, the fact remains: the success of the porn industry largely depends upon the willingness of heterosexual men to buy its products, to enter into a contract which provides them with (vicarious) use of a female body for their arousal or amusement. How can sexual politics be irrelevant?

Williams' claim about the mainstreaming of pornography is less contestable: critics of all persuasions agree on this point.[1] But two rather different processes are at times conflated in such arguments. On one hand, as suggested by Williams, at stake in these debates is the new position pornography has come to occupy: thanks to technological advances, hard-core pornography can be accessed more easily and in greater variety than ever before. As a result, hard-core has become more familiar (even to those who choose not to consume it) as well as more profitable. Its massive revenues have demanded attention and, apparently, respect not only within porn studies but in the culture more generally. At the same time, the mainstream has increasingly and explicitly borrowed (from) pornography, whether by making porn and porn performers the object of mainstream representation (in Hollywood movies or reality TV shows, for instance) or by quotation and allusion in the codes, conventions, language and fashions of popular culture. Through such quotation, pornography achieves a mainstream currency and visibility, but whilst popular culture may be 'pornified' (Paul 2005) as a result, it does not *become* pornography. To properly understand how pornographic quotation of this kind functions depends on understanding the *differences* as well as *similarities* between these pop culture examples and the hard-core they reference. Equally, whilst analysing 'pornification' (Paasonen *et al.* 2007b) is important and relevant, this does not obviate careful and considered scholarship of pornography itself: something that, despite Williams' claims, has long been a concern of anti-pornography feminists as well as those of different political persuasions.

Everyday Pornography conceptualizes the 'everyday' in relation to both of these processes and with the assumption that sexual politics *are* still relevant to an analysis and understanding of how they function.[2] The everyday *of* pornography is here defined primarily by audience: heterosexual men remain the largest group of porn consumers and it is this audience that drives the commercial industry. In this sense, the everyday in 'everyday pornography' refers to the commercial industry's own mainstream. Other anthologies take a different approach, focusing on the margins of pornography and on texts or practices which demonstrate the slippery and amorphous status of 'pornography'. This is the approach of many of the essays in Williams' *Porn Studies*, for instance, which analyse texts as diverse as the *Starr Report* into the Clinton/Lewinsky affair, Japanese comics for girls, World War II pin-ups and the Pamela Anderson/Tommy Lee sex tape.

'Everyday pornography' also refers to the way in which pornography itself is represented in mainstream contexts. To use 'everyday pornography' in this second sense is to note one specific aspect of pornography's incursions into the mainstream: the representation of something which is recognized *as* pornography in a context which is not itself pornographic. This is not shorthand for analysing representations of sex *per se*: rather, this collection retains an understanding of pornography as *both* a genre of representation *and* a distinct form of industrial practice. This is worth reiterating because in much contemporary writing pornography is framed, first and foremost, relative to sex. Such a framing is implicit in the labelling of the 1980s feminist debates as *sex* wars as well as the apparent interchangeability of labels such as pro-porn, pro-sex and sex-positive and the ensuing caricature of anti-pornography positions as anti-sex.

In an edited collection – entitled *Mainstreaming Sex* – Feona Attwood (2009a: xiii) takes this a step further, conflating sex with pornography. She opens by noting that the 'study of *sex* has been an academic concern for many years', before situating her collection relative to more recent scholarship on 'the mainstreaming of *sex* – or what some writers have called a 'pornified' or 'striptease culture' (emphasis mine). There is no distinction made between the main-streaming of *sex* and specific forms of *commercial* sex (pornography and stripping). A little later Attwood writes:

> today the places, products and performances associated with sex for its own sake are becoming more visible. Commercial sex is gaining a toehold in the high street and being gentrified. Strip joints have become gentlemen's clubs. The Rampant Rabbit vibrator is now almost as well known as that much older sign for sex, the Playboy bunny girl, signifying a new interest in women as sexual consumers. Porn shops have been joined by the cheap and cheerful sexual paraphernalia of the Ann Summers empire and by elegant and expensive boutiques selling lingerie, toys and erotica. Pole dancing is being repackaged as a form of keep-fit, and burlesque is undergoing a revival, producing new stars such as Dita von Teese.
>
> (Attwood 2009a: xiv–xv)

Here Attwood allies pornography and other forms of commercial sex with a hedonistic pursuit of sexual pleasure ('sex for its own sake'). Whilst this definition of porn consumption may chime with some consumers' experiences (although this cannot be taken for granted), it is certainly not how the sex *of* pornography is experienced by those who perform it. Sex for its own sake suggests an activity (sex) which is enjoyable and satisfying in itself, engaged in freely and for pleasure. Whatever else it is or is not, commercial sex is – by definition – not 'sex for its own sake'. It is sex for money.

Moreover, the eclectic range of places, products and performances listed by Attwood have little more than a bottom line in common involving, as they do, fundamentally different processes of production and consumption. Quite obviously, buying and using a vibrator is not equivalent to attending a strip club (or performing in one). Both may involve sexual pleasure for the consumer, but the 'products' and 'experiences' at their heart are very different: one depends upon purchasing sexual access to the bodies of other human beings, the other does not. Similarly, whilst the marketing of 'sexy' lingerie and pole-dancing clas-ses may be influenced by the commercial sex industry, these activities align their consumers with the 'objects' to be bought (the *performer*) and not with the buyer of commercial sex. For this reason, it is important to distinguish between the commercialization of sex (the invitation to buy products to enhance our sex lives) and commercial sex (purchasing access to the bodies of others for our own gratification and independent of theirs).

Certainly, there is work to be done following the money to see how/whether the commercialization of sex is tied in to the business of commercial sex. But the casual equation of these activities appears to be a way of making commercial sex appear less misogynistic by suggesting that women are also consumers of sexual products.[3] Whilst this broader context can be a provocative one in which to situate contemporary pornography, it is not of central concern in *Everyday Pornography*. Rather, this collection is concerned with 'pornography' as a category in itself, a category which is still recognized, and sometimes embraced, by performers, producers, distributors and consumers, despite critical hesitation over its undefinability (Jensen 1998a: 3–4).[4]

In short, *Everyday Pornography* is about pornography's mainstream (sexually explicit material for the heterosexual male consumer, widely recognized as pornography): it is not fundamentally about sex, nor is it more generally about the sexualization of culture. The 'mainstream' of pornography is further determined by local legislation and practice regarding the regulation of the commercial sex industry as well as attitudes and cultural norms related to the media, the market, gender, sexuality and sexualization. As a response to a particular Anglo-American debate about pornography and its position relative to the mainstream, *Everyday Pornography* is primarily concerned with pornographies in English and the debates which surround their production and consumption. Although some reference is made to other contexts (e.g. Chapters 4 and 11) and there is some discussion of the commonalities and differences between the UK and US in particular (Chapter 1), this collection is not genuinely *international* and the claims made in and for *Everyday Pornography* must be understood in light of this.

Within these parameters, the contributors take a variety of approaches and employ a range of methodologies, which I outline below. For some contributors, pornographic texts, their marketing, distribution and consumption – as well as their place in the curriculum – are the object of study. Others are concerned with how pornography is represented in mainstream media, policy and public debate. Not all of the contributors share a political position on pornography and, indeed, Susanna Paasonen questions the value of taking 'sides' (Chapter 4). However, all of the contributors offer analyses which are relevant to the concerns of anti-pornography feminists and are critically engaged with contemporary debates about pornography in the broadest sense. Sadly, this can by no means be taken for granted in academic debate, where Andrea Dworkin and Catharine MacKinnon are still often referred to as the beginning (and end) of academic anti-pornography feminism. Nadine Strossen (1999), for instance, condescendingly defines anti-pornography feminists as 'MacDworkinites', as though we are incapable of thinking for ourselves. To speak personally, whilst I admire Dworkin and MacKinnon immensely, I also understand that they were/are writing particular kinds of texts, with particular audiences and goals in mind. Dworkin, in particular, was a polemicist. This is not to dismiss her considerable insights but to understand that they are a *starting point* for political organization and a spur to research. To take these writers as the *only* word on anti-porn feminism is hugely problematic, not least because they were/are writing in a particular national, historical and disciplinary context.

Of course, like other contributors to this book, I don't agree with everything that is or has been written by other feminists using the anti-pornography label; nor are my arguments accepted by everyone I would ally myself with politically.

This would go without saying in relation to other intellectual frameworks – we wouldn't expect Marxist feminists to agree with each other all of the time, for instance. That it needs stating here is further evidence of the enduring influence of the 'sex wars': in much academic debate there remains a perception that if you are on 'a side' you are following a party line. In the diversity of approaches and arguments gathered in this volume I hope to offer something of a corrective to this perception. Each of the chapters presents material that is important for anti-pornography feminism – but, as will become apparent, the authors do not speak with one voice.

As such, the on-going usefulness and relevance of labels like 'anti-pornography feminism' must be open to debate. To the extent that they hark back to the binary thinking of the 1980s, they can seem unhelpful. Labelling myself an 'anti-pornography feminist' might lead to assumptions about my work which I would be uncomfortable with. I am certainly not pro-censorship or anti-sex, for instance: though such categorizations have never been an easy fit for the diversity of anti-pornography feminist research and activism. The main reason I have continued to define myself as an anti-pornography feminist is that – particularly in the current climate – it seems important to give visibility to the possibility of resistance. Intellectually, it is also more honest, as it allows readers to understand where I am coming from and to engage critically with my writings with that knowledge. Politically, it also allies me with activist organizations working to challenge the demand from men to buy commercial sex in various forms and it makes my work accessible to them as well as vice versa (though, like other readers, activists are critical respondents). This also defines the questions which are liable to be of most interest to me in relation to pornography; not least this book's emphasis on its 'mainstream'.

To summarize, then, *Everyday Pornography* is a book edited by an anti-pornography feminist, whose contributors – though they may not all share that position – are engaged with questions about pornographic texts, contexts, practices and consumers which are of importance to contemporary anti-pornography feminist thinking and organizing. It deals with pornography's mainstream – and the mainstream representation of pornography – and brings a variety of disciplinary perspectives and methodological approaches to bear on the objects of study.

Part I, Content and context

Part I brings together six chapters dealing with pornographic texts and the contexts in which they are produced, distributed, debated and (pre-empting the concerns of Part II) consumed.

Part I opens with a round-table discussion on anti-pornography feminism which I chaired in June 2009 and which brings together Gail Dines, Rebecca Whisnant and Linda Thompson. Dines and Whisnant are US-based academics who define themselves as anti-pornography feminists, a position which – they argue – mandates an analysis of pornography that is more than an intellectual exercise in textual analysis but that, rather, understands pornography as a specific industrial practice. They are clear that their analyses of pornography are not intended to remain in academia but are to be engaged with more widely. A tool long used by anti-pornography feminists to engage a wider public (particularly women) is the anti-pornography slide show, and in this chapter Dines and Whisnant discuss its contemporary use in a climate where pornography is, in many ways, taken for granted. Their aim is to provide a critical language with which to analyse pornography and they also discuss the way this work has been received, both within and outside of academic settings.

The slide show developed by Dines and Whisnant (along with Robert Jensen) has been picked up and adapted by activists outside of the US. The third contributor to this discussion is Linda Thompson, who works for a feminist anti-violence organization in Scotland, focusing specifically on commercial sexual exploitation. Thompson reflects on the differences – as well as on the similarities – between the ways in which these debates are played out in the US and Scottish contexts.

Unlike Dines and Whisnant, Thompson does not have formal links with the academy and, indeed, finds that the considerable knowledge of activists is too often dismissed by those of us in academia. As academics *and* activists, Dines and Whisnant occupy a privileged (if fraught) position and their considerable experience of delivering public lectures on pornography over a number of years provides them with a wealth of 'anecdotal' evidence about the changing role(s) of pornography in the lives of their audiences. To really get to grips with the complexity of these accounts would – as Dines acknowledges – require a more formal capturing of the evidence. Nonetheless, Dines, Whisnant and Thompson have undoubtedly accessed a range of responses which more conventional means of academic research may struggle to elicit. For example, Thompson's work has brought her into discussion with people from a diverse cross-section of the population: student and youth groups, professionals in the anti-violence sector, police officers, social workers, relationship counsellors, sexual health workers, women working in the commercial sex industry, and community groups in rural and urban areas with varying socio-economic and ethnic identities. Thompson's evidence may not have been gathered according to social-scientifically approved methods, but she has had access to a more diverse audience than academic researchers have often reached. For instance, much of the existing academic work on pornography consumption is qualitative and small in scale (with the problems of generalizability that entails)[5] or, within the effects tradition, has emphasized the experiences of a very select demographic (often male students) (Boyle 2000). This chapter offers an opportunity to consider what we might learn if we used the insights of activists as jumping-off points for future research.

In Chapter 2, Ana Bridges focuses more specifically on the content of contemporary pornographic film produced in the US. A clinical psychologist, Bridges approaches pornographic content through debates about its putative effects.

As she notes, such debates demand an understanding of that content, but selecting, codifying and analysing audio-visual texts is far from straightforward and ideological framing and methodological choices define what it is possible to find out. In this chapter, Bridges presents findings from her own co-authored content analysis of fifty best-selling/top-rented pornographic films (Wosnitzer and Bridges 2007), which found significantly higher levels of violence and degradation than others in the field. Bridges explores the differences in sampling, definition and methods which may have led to such divergent results, presenting a reanalysis of her own data alongside a critique of other studies. As such, this chapter not only provides a 'snapshot' of the content of contemporary film pornography in the US, it also contextualizes those findings in order that future work can better understand the results and replicate the analysis in other contexts.

The approach taken by Bridges is, in some ways, quite dissimilar from that taken in the following two chapters, which use content analysis in different disciplinary contexts and as part of the research projects of single scholars (a model far more common in humanities). Read alongside Bridges, Meagan Tyler (political science) and Susanna Paasonen (media studies) offer a useful opportunity to think through the different assumptions, methodologies and approaches which characterize some of the disciplines which have had a stake in pornography research. Rather than suggesting that one approach is inherently 'better' than the other, in publishing these three chapters together I am interested in what they can *collectively* tell us about different aspects of contemporary commercial pornography aimed at heterosexual men – as well as what they reveal about what we still do not know, or could be more rigorous in finding out.

Tyler and Paasonen do not approach the text through debates about its effects but both are, nonetheless, using texts as a way of working through broader arguments about what pornography might mean for consumers. The consumer is particularly present for Tyler and Paasonen because the texts they examine – promotional materials produced by the porn industry – are instrumental in extracting the most salient, saleable features of porn texts for distributors (Tyler) and potential consumers (Paasonen). Collectively, these three chapters reveal that acts that may have seemed unimaginable, extreme or too specialist in earlier periods of the industry's growth are now far more 'mainstream' as the industry openly and explicitly caters to ever-proliferating 'niches' even within the heterosexual male market.

Like Bridges, Tyler uses *Adult Video News* as a source of information about the kinds of pornographic material which are most popular and profitable. Echoing Bridges' arguments that pornography is often invested in an ideological reframing of violence as sex, Tyler finds that pornographers are more than willing to acknowledge the violence and degradation in their texts and, indeed, understand the marketability of these themes. There is a disturbing pornographic double-speak at play here: industry insiders describe how dirty, filthy, disgusting women are degraded, abused, humiliated and hurt in their films – but they call it sex. This pornographic double-speak makes critiques of the industry extremely difficult as there is no language that has not been colonized and rebranded as sex. In this context, not only has the 'extreme' become increasingly mainstream but the physical demands on performers have also changed considerably.

Paasonen's chapter focuses on another marketing tool of the porn industry, but, whilst Tyler is concerned with how the industry speaks to itself, Paasonen's focus is spam e-mail sent to (potential) consumers as 'tasters' of online porn. By focusing on spam messages sent to her e-mail address over a seventeen-month period from 2002 to 2004 (overlapping the periods studied by Tyler and Bridges), Paasonen provides an interesting response to the problems of sampling and questions about representability that have often stymied analyses of the vast and ever-proliferating online industry. In the context of this book's focus on pornography's everyday, Paasonen's work is particularly significant, as she identifies a corpus that is absolutely quotidian: delivered, every day, to her e-mail account without her solicitation or consent. Again, she demonstrates the presence of the extreme within the everyday: although relatively small in number, Paasonen did not have to seek out sites about fetishism, urophilia and bestiality, they were simply delivered to her in-box. In other ways, her findings are perhaps less surprising: pornography continues to provide textual evidence of gendered inequalities, inequalities which are magnified and simplified in these e-mails whose 'messages', at one level, could not be clearer.

Whilst this is, in itself, important evidence about the content of contemporary pornography, Paasonen cautions against (only) taking these representations at face value. Rather, by situating these messages in the context of a wider online industry where 'extreme' examples of women's sexual degradation have a particular currency, she insists on the importance of thinking through the varying affective responses to such texts. Such responses have, in themselves, become part of the online meta-pornographic discourse through the display and circulation of 'reaction videos', emphasizing the physical and emotional responses of viewers to extreme clips. Paasonen suggests that focusing on sexual arousal as the *raison d'être* of pornography may result in an oversimplification of its contemporary functions which may be more complexly affective as well as fundamentally social.

The final two chapters in Part I offer analyses of more participatory pornographies. Lisa Jean Moore and Juliana Weissbein consider the various ways in which male ejaculation and ejaculate function in consumer/producers' pornographic narratives. Moore and Weissbein focus on amateur videos posted on X-Tube alongside calls placed to an adult phone fantasy provider, where one of the authors worked as an operator. The meanings ascribed to semen – and its role in the pornographic narrative – are, on the whole, remarkably similar to those in commercial porn. The fascination with 'cum' betrays the genre's emphasis on male pleasure whilst the targeting of the ejaculate (typically at women) becomes part of a narrative of ownership and, often, explicit degradation.

Sarah Neely, writing about Second Life, similarly argues that commercial pornography has shaped representations and activities in the virtual world. Here, as in the amateur examples analysed by Moore and Weissbein, consumers are also producers of pornographic narratives, but what is particularly striking about Second Life is the extent to which sex *per se* is both commercial and representational. And yet, pornography – and other forms of commercial sex such as prostitution and lap dancing – retain a distinct presence. Neely's chapter unravels the different ways in which sexual – and commercial sexual – possibilities are framed and delimited within Second Life and also points to the relevance of 'real world' analyses of these practices in the virtual world. Bringing Part I full circle, she notes that anti-pornography slide shows have been mobilized by activists within Second Life to challenge the modes of representation and action they encounter as 'residents' of the virtual world.

Part II, Address, consumption, regulation

In Part II the emphasis is more squarely on the consumer: how he is addressed by pornography, represented within the mainstream, understood by academics and contained by legislation. Mirroring the focus on pornography aimed at heterosexual men in Part I, it is heterosexual male consumers who are of primary concern.

In the chapter which opens Part II, Robert Jensen recounts the emotional impact of his research on pornography and suggests that such affective responses can be valuable tools in helping us to unravel what pornography means for our societies. The disjunction Jensen describes between his physical 'trained' response to pornographic texts and his developing political analysis of them is a useful reminder of the complexity of understanding responses to porn and the inadequacies of our critical vocabulary. As Whisnant also notes (Chapter 8), feminists need to develop our own language to describe experiences which are otherwise unspeakable, and 'dysrotic' is the term proposed to capture such conflicted responses to physical arousal. For Jensen, one of the most worrying aspects of contemporary pornography is the extent to which it depends on a lack of empathy, and he reminds us of the importance of keeping in focus the entire pornographic 'circuit' (production, distribution, representation, consumption) as we theorize and research in this field.

Rebecca Whisnant is concerned with how pornography speaks to men, and specifically with how the industry works to erode men's ethical objections to the mistreatment of women. Echoing Jensen's concern that the success of contemporary pornography depends on a lack of empathy, Whisnant argues that men have to be 'groomed' to accept material that they might otherwise object to. She highlights the role that communities of porn users play in this process: user forums have proliferated on line and offer important reinforcement for individual men, normalizing and rationalizing their existing pleasures whilst suggesting new avenues of exploration. As with Tyler's discussion of *Adult Video News* in Part I, here the porn industry – and its consumers – are remarkably candid about the appeal of violence and degradation. Whilst it would be a mistake to generalize from these studies to argue that this is always and for all consumers the appeal of contemporary pornographies, such evidence nonetheless demonstrates that the 'agonizing over sexual politics' of which Williams is so dismissive remains important and, indeed, urgent. Whisnant's chapter provides ample evidence of why *men* – as well as women – should be angry about what pornography says about them, often very explicitly, and what their peers say about the women (and men) in pornography.

In Chapter 9 I am also concerned with particular representations of consumption, although my examples are from mainstream media. Like Whisnant, I am interested in the frameworks which these texts provide for understanding porn consumption and I argue that a range of imaginative identifications are possible: both through the presumptive address of certain men's genres and via representations in a range of generic contexts. Having identified a range of 'types' – the lonely, unemployed addict, the cult fan, the wealthy connoisseur, the hedonistic man-boy, the sex-obsessed teen, the sex criminal and the sexualized female-consumer – I conclude that, in certain genres at least, it is the possibility of non-engagement with pornography which is consistently marginalized.

Although coming from a very different disciplinary perspective, this is also the context for Jennifer Johnson's analysis of the functioning of the online porn industry. Johnson brings a new method to porn studies – social network analysis – which she uses to investigate the connections between different aspects of the industry. Highlighting these connections allows Johnson to demonstrate the functionality of the industry and the multiple sites for extracting profit from consumers: as paying customers, audiences for advertising and online 'traffic'. Like Whisnant, Johnson sees the consumer as exploit*ed* (as well as exploiting) and argues that such exploitation serves the joint interests of patriarchy and capitalism.

In Chapter 11, Michael Flood reviews the evidence of research which has focused on male consumers or the act of consuming pornography (e.g. in laboratory situations). Flood synthesizes existing quantitative and qualitative studies (the latter notably thin on the ground), arguing that pornography plays an increasingly significant role in boys' and young men's sociosexual relations and that the research evidence about the potential 'effects' of pornography should give us pause in considering the possible ramifications of this. Flood outlines a range of potential 'effects', ranging from the apparently pro-social (sex education, normalization of marginalized sexualities) to the contested evidence linking pornography with sexual violence against women. However, Flood is concerned to think through the implications of even these more 'positive' functions in light of the kind of evidence presented in Part I: what are young people learning about sex from pornography? This isn't (or doesn't have to be) a *moral* question which passes judgement about the desirability of certain acts or relationships. Instead, questions can be – and, to an extent, have been – asked about users' self-perceptions of their sex lives and bodies relative to what they learn from porn, as well as about consumers' attitudes towards others (in particular, women) and sexual relationships in general. In his conclusion, Flood discusses where this evidence might lead us in terms not only of argument and research but, more fundamentally, in terms of sex education in the broadest possible sense.

The final two chapters in Part II deal with public debates about porn consumption in the UK, demonstrating the limited (and limiting) framing of these debates in the media and policy-making. Mark Jones and Gerry Carlin focus on a local 'moral panic' that was generated by a press story in a regional newspaper about their university teaching of pornography as part of the English Literature curriculum. Having analysed the unfolding of this story – and discussed the various players who claimed a role in it – Jones and Carlin are prompted to reflect on their practice. Whilst, they suggest, their teaching was both ethical and in line with practice elsewhere, the debate in which they became embroiled revealed the enduring *un*critical appeal of pornographic quotation. There is, they note, 'a complex interdependence between the academic and media meta-discourses on pornography, together with a further reticulation of both with the thing-in-itself'.

This interdependence means that certain frameworks for understanding pornography remain under-explored. As academic debate has increasingly been guided by popular culture – as in the refocusing on pornification rather than pornography within this field – the possibilities for resistance of an intellectual or political kind begin to recede. As Clare McGlynn's discussion in Chapter 13 demonstrates, in relation to pornography this means that neither 'side' in the 'sex wars' is actually being heard on its own terms. So whilst themes such as sexual diversity and the harms of pornography were paid a certain lip service in the media and Westminster Parliament in debates about the extreme pornography legislation (McGlynn's focus), they were presented in ways that would be anathema to most feminists.

Unsurprisingly, perhaps, the vexed question of 'effects' also dominated much of the debate about the extreme pornography measures in a familiar – and familiarly stultifying – way. As a result, McGlynn sounds a cautionary note about the use of research within the effects tradition: at least as a basis for public policy, debate and legislation. Although this might seem to contradict Michael Flood's rather more positive assessment of 'effects' research (Chapter 11), Flood does not argue that this research can provide a robust basis for legislation. Rather, he identifies its suggestive value as a jumping-off point for thinking about social and educational strategies for mitigating the multi-layered harms of pornography. Careful evaluation of such strategies would offer a far more compelling contribution to public debate that may, genuinely, offer the opportunity to move beyond the cause-and-effect debates which have dominated public discourse for too long with little reference to feminist analyses of pornography.

Indeed, McGlynn argues that what feminists on both 'sides' of the pornography debates share – as far as public policy and media representation are concerned – is their marginalization. For a variety of reasons – some alluded to in this Introduction, others discussed in more detail in the Epilogue – I am less optimistic that feminists on different 'sides' in this debate will find common ground. However, there is – in the academy at least – always the possibility of a *middle* ground, where we engage, intellectually and critically, with research (and researchers) from all perspectives and from none. The possibility of *not* taking an explicit position 'pro' or 'anti' does not have to be disingenuous. Certainly I am concerned that there are times when scholars claim to 'transcend' this binary logic whilst firmly locating their work relative to existing 'pro' scholarship, masking the ideological framing of their approach.[6] However, I also recognize that there are many scholars (including some of the contributors to this book) who *genuinely* move between sides as, dependent in part on the object of study, their position will change. That is, they recognize and value the insights from both 'sides' and suggest that both are – in different contexts – *right*. This chimes with my long-held view that those on different sides are often talking about different objects and processes of production. Although I continue to read widely on both 'sides' and none, my anti-porn politics drive what I think are the significant questions to be asked about/of pornography. These politics shape how I define pornography and have influenced the emphasis of this collection on its *everyday* manifestations and *industrial* character. This is not to preclude the possibility of ethical audio-visual pornography, but I wonder whether 'pornography' is (or will be) the term best used to describe such representation?

I hope that by being explicit in this introduction about how both 'pornography' and its 'everyday' are operationalized in this book, you will work your way through to your own conclusions about the broader implications of these arguments for understanding the contemporary scene.

Notes

1 See, for example, McNair (2002), Williams (2004b), Paul (2005), Levy (2006), Hall and Bishop (2007), Paasonen *et al.* (2007b), Sarracino and Scott (2008), Attwood (2009b), Reist (2009).

2 Jane Caputi (2003) also uses the term 'everyday pornography' although in a narrower sense than it is used here. For Caputi, 'everyday pornography' is mainstream advertising which uses the conventions of pornography. She does not use the term to discuss hard-core pornography's mainstreaming. Caputi notes that it is not the sexually explicit *per se* which concerns her, but – following Dworkin and MacKinnon (e.g. 1988) – that she is interested in material showing sexually explicit subordination, exploitation and degradation of women. Like other radical feminists, Caputi's definition of pornography (in the everyday) is intended to expand the category and recognize how the values of hard-core seep into the culture more generally. Whilst this can be useful in understanding pornography on a continuum, the danger is that the specificity of pornography as an industrial practice is lost.

3 Williams (2004a: 2) and Smith (2007a: 167) list 'sex toys' for women alongside examples of pornography in this way.

4 As Jensen (1998a: 3) argues, whilst such a definition does not provide absolute precision, it is sufficiently clear to make conversation possible. Defining pornography for legal purposes may require a different approach (McGlynn, Chapter 13 in the present volume).

5 For example, Clarissa Smith's (2007b) book-length study of women readers of *For Women* magazine is based on correspondence with fourteen women and two men; Simon Hardy (1998) interviewed twenty-four readers of *Men Only* magazine; and Z. Fareen Parvez (2006) interviewed thirty women who enjoy porn films. That these samples are relatively small and do not enable us to consider other demographic factors (e.g. class, race, age) does not mean they have nothing to offer. However, bringing this work together with the insights of key workers in relevant fields can expand our knowledge of the ways in which porn use is understood in the complex and varied conditions of contemporary life.

6 It is not my own 'bias' which leads me to the conclusion that this is less prevalent on the other 'side': for anti-pornography feminists, labelling their position and politics has an important function in making visible the possibility of dissent in a pornified culture. Without the label we do not exist.

Part 1

Content and context

Chapter I

Arresting images

Anti-pornography slide shows, activism and the academy

Gail Dines, Linda Thompson and Rebecca Whisnant, with Karen Boyle

This chapter presents a round-table discussion with Gail Dines (G.D.), Linda Thompson (L.T.) and Rebecca Whisnant (R.W.), chaired by Karen Boyle (K.B.) and recorded in Leeds in June 2009. Gail and Rebecca are US-based academics, anti-pornography activists and founders of Stop Porn Culture. In 2007, they – together with Robert Jensen – launched a new anti-pornography slide show at a two-day anti-pornography conference at Wheelock College, Boston.[1] Linda Thompson is a Development Worker with the Women's Support Project (a feminist anti-violence organization) and works against all forms of commercial sexual exploitation across Scotland. Members of Linda's organization attended the Wheelock conference and have since brought Gail and Rebecca to Scotland to speak at events challenging the demand from men for commercial sex, including pornography.

K.B. Gail and Rebecca, why did you decide to reinvent the anti-porn slide show at this point in time?

G.D. The anti-porn slide show produced in the 1980s had a huge impact on me. It shifted the way I thought about men, masculinity and sexual violence because it showed me, in stark detail, how porn users think about women. It delivered, in a succinct form, just what it means to be a woman in a male-supremacist society. So I've always thought that slide shows are hugely important tools, because a lot of women – even a lot of feminists – really don't know what's in pornography, especially in the age of the internet, and that makes it too easy to conduct abstract intellectual arguments about the empowering possibilities of porn.

R.W. Every feminist anti-pornography activist I know came to the issue through seeing a slide show. Especially for women, many of whom haven't seen much if any pornography, there is simply no substitute for encountering the material itself in a reflective and critical context. In my experience, the vast majority of women who see these slide shows recognise immediately that they are looking at raw, visceral contempt for women.

The slide shows that many of us used in the 1980s and 1990s were showing their age; new images and some new analysis were needed to speak to a younger generation, for whom porn has become 'normal', and to address changes in the industry over the last couple of decades. So Gail and I decided to collaborate on a new slide show along with Bob Jensen. The goal was not to produce something that we would own and control, in the traditional way that academics 'own' their scholarship, but rather to provide a tool that people could take, adapt and use in their own communities. We wanted the slide show to help people move beyond powerlessness and despair into action – to help reignite a movement.

K.B. What is in the slide show?

G.D. The slide show takes you on a journey through porn culture. It starts with fairly mainstream images[2] in order to get us thinking about the sexualization of women in the culture more generally and the kind of 'pornified' sexuality that is being sold to women. This leads us into what is actually in pornography today. The pornographic images we use were all obtained easily and for free through internet searches, accessed within thirty seconds from Google. They are from the mainstream of the porn industry. We give a sense of the different genres within pornography and the different kinds of 'acts' and 'characters' that are now routinely depicted.[3] But it's not just about showing the images, it's about providing the feminist analysis of them so that audiences can develop a critical understanding of the ways that porn shapes our reality and our cultural practices.

R.W. Yes, the analysis places the images into context. These images exist as part of an industry within capitalism and as part of an ideological system within patriarchy. They can't be understood independently of these systems. If it was just about seeing shocking images, we could send people out to surf internet porn on their own!

This is why not only women, but many men too, are upset by the slide show. For the men, it's not (usually) that they haven't seen these kinds of images before, but that they are being cued to see them differently. Often, what disturbs them most is that similar images *haven't* disturbed them in the past. They realise that they've been manipulated in the service of the industry's profits and that their involvement with pornography has kept them from developing an authentic sexuality in accordance with their own values.

K.B. But this material is designed to be arousing. How do you deal with the possibility of that response – of arousal – in the slide show?

R.W. We say at the beginning of the slide show that these images are very carefully designed and choreographed to produce arousal, especially in men but also in women, so people may experience that along with other responses. We front-load that message, so that if people are experiencing arousal they won't feel like they are freaks. It's what pornography is designed to do, and it's important that we give people permission to think about how pornography shapes all of our sexuality, without feeling guilt or shame about their physical responses.

We do need to develop better ways to talk about the idea that sexual arousal is not necessarily and always a pleasant experience for the person who's having it.

Some feminists have coined the term 'dysrotic' to describe sexual arousal that is experienced as disturbing, or traumatic, or unpleasant, or scary, or confusing … [4]

G.D. Or against your will, basically.

R.W. … and that's something we need to think about more.

K.B. How do you deal with the criticism that by reproducing these images you are further exploiting the women in them?

R.W. This is something we struggled with. If we could have traced each of the women and asked their permission we would have, but realistically it's not possible. We did think about pixellating the women's faces to conceal their identities, but hiding their faces can disguise what's going on: there's a whole genre built around ejaculating into women's eyes for instance, and women's facial expressions are essential to understanding the images. Is she bored, jaundiced, sad, confused, afraid, even when the text says how much she loves it? So while we recognize that there is a moral down side to this, we ultimately decided that the slide show needs to exist and that it cannot work without the images. I hope that we succeeded in treating the women with respect and dignity.

G.D. The key thing is to remind the audience that the women in pornography are real people, they're human. Because pornography isn't just a representation, it's a documentation: this was really done to someone's body.

K.B. But it is also a representation: it's not a documentation of women's sexual desires.

G.D. It's a documentation (these things are actually being done by and to the people on screen), but it's not a reflection of reality (so just because she says she likes it doesn't make it so). If you read the threads on discussion boards where guys are talking about porn,[5] they have a real investment in the idea that porn is depicting some kind of reality and will go to quite elaborate lengths to protect that. I came across a 'gang bang' discussion forum where the guys were discussing a supposedly 'amateur' film. One of them had recognized the woman from another porn film and was outraged by what he saw as an attempt to fool him. The other posters came back suggesting that the amateur film might be what she did in her free time when she wasn't working. The story these men tell themselves is that she's on a porn set all day having body-punishing sex but, because she loves sex, she then goes to film a 'gang bang' at night for fun. Incredible!

K.B. Moving on, a criticism often levelled at anti-porn work is that it uses the 'extreme' as paradigmatic. How do you respond to this?

R.W. Every image in our slide show represents a major porn genre, and no act or practice is depicted that would be unfamiliar to the average porn consumer. The porn world contains many images and acts that I wouldn't dream of putting into this or any other slide show, both because they do not represent the mainstream of the industry and because they would be too disturbing to audiences. Our slide show addresses everything from *Playboy* and feature porn to mainstream gonzo – including the points of connection among these apparently disparate genres – while stopping well short of anything truly extreme.

G.D. To show just how routine hard-core porn is, take Max Hardcore.[6] We didn't include his porn in the slide show because we thought it may be too much for the audience. His violent and abusive movies used to be considered beyond the pale by people within the industry, but now he's embraced and celebrated – he was on *The Howard Stern Show,* which is an indicator of just how mainstream he has become.[7] When we went to the Adult Expo [in January 2008][8] he was so popular that there was a long line of men queuing up for his autograph. While Hardcore still represents the most violent and cruel of porn, his movies now look a lot more like regular gonzo.

L.T. The most distressing material I've come across in doing this work has actually been via mainstream sites which are supposedly not pornography. For example, on *Zoo* magazine's website I found a series of pictures of a young woman being fisted and having bottles inserted into her.[9] There was no warning or notion that this material may not be appropriate on a high-street magazine site. The images had supposedly been sent in by readers and were offered to other readers to rate. I see some pretty extreme stuff but what was so distressing about that was that it was so mainstream. There's nothing in the slide show that surprises me now.

K.B. What about porn by and for women? How do you deal with that?

R.W. 'By women' and 'for women' are very different. The vast majority of pornography, whether produced by men or women, is produced for a male audience and it is primarily that audience that dictates the content. What do men want to see? What are they willing to buy? So it's not surprising that a recent content analysis found that there is very little difference in content between porn films directed by men and those directed by women [Sun *et al.* 2008].

G.D. My experience with porn produced by women is that it uses the same codes and conventions adopted in mainstream porn, even when they try to market it as something different, and that it's not necessarily any more ethical in its production than porn produced by men. Take the Australian company Abby Winters as an example. It claims to be woman-friendly because it features happy, healthy, natural amateurs doing girl-on-girl scenes. At the Adult Expo we'd been talking to one of the women on the Abby Winters stall about the feminist anti-porn position and it clearly resonated with her. But, not surprisingly, putting her personal choice in a broader context was also unsettling for her. It meant she felt less able to perform porn sexuality on demand, which meant we were bad for business. So we were banned from the stand. There was no way for us to check in with her or have a genuinely open discussion about porn. And that's supposed to be women-friendly porn. By the last day the Abby Winters women were indistinguishable from everyone else, offering live sex shows for the male customers. If you listen to what the industry is saying – in publications like *Adult Video News* and *X-Biz* – they acknowledge that there really isn't much of a women's market.

L.T. Something similar happened with Suicide Girls:[10] they present themselves as an alternative community, yet when some of the women involved started criticizing how the site operated in their posts they were taken down, censored. When fans asked what was going on, all dissent was removed and quashed. This strategy of saying that because the women have tattoos, piercings and step outside the supposed norm of a porn appearance it is all empowering and equal falls down somewhat when you realise that it still operates in the same limited and controlled way. In reality, women in these sites rarely have any more power and control over their images and identity than others in the industry.

K.B. I've heard you say in the past that the feminist analysis of porn developed in the 1970s and 1980s still holds and that the current slide show owes a clear debt to that earlier work. But are there any differences in the new work?

G.D. In the 1970s the analysis was brand new and it was important to develop a theoretical understanding of the role of porn in producing and reproducing gender inequality. Porn was mainly discussed as a single unified entity because the industry was much smaller and its products more standardized. Today, with product diversification, sophisticated marketing practices and the need to find niche markets, the industry is more developed so we need to expand our understanding of both the content of porn and the ways it works as an industry located within a wider capitalist system.

R.W. And this is a different cultural moment. Precisely because porn has taken over the culture to such an extent it's getting to the point where a lot of people have had enough. I used to get a good bit of resistance from slide show audiences in the early to mid-1990s and now I get almost none. Porn has gotten so bad and so pervasive that it's pretty hard to argue with our analysis! So there is a new receptivity, even from many men, because they are starting to recognize what porn has done to their sexuality and relationships.

L.T. After one slide show I had two men come up to talk to me saying that they wouldn't let someone take their sons into a room and talk to them about sex in the way pornography does. They talked about the importance of allowing their sons to find out for themselves what they liked, disliked, what turned them on – not having that predetermined for them and having possibilities shut down by pornography, like they had been for them. The new work has to acknowledge the rough deal men are getting and how porn is shaping relationships *per se*.

K.B. So why did your organization get involved in bringing the slide show to Scotland?

L.T. The Women's Support Project has been involved in working against male violence against women in all its forms for the past twenty-five years. Pornography is a form of violence against women itself and also helps create the culture in which sexual violence is eroticized. In Scotland – amongst the women's sector – there is an understanding that you cannot take a stance that male violence is unacceptable and then give the green light to materials sexualising inequality, power and control. It's contradictory to be working against male violence against women and still be pro-porn.

K.B. What have been the challenges in adapting the slide show for use in the Scottish context?

L.T. It's the pop culture examples that we've had to adapt rather than the pornography. In the age of the internet, pornography doesn't know geographical boundaries, but it does change quickly, and it's a real challenge – particularly when I'm working with younger audiences – to make sure my examples are up to date.

K.B. Is there evidence of the slide show being used outside of the US and Scotland?

R.W. We have heard from activists who have used it in Russia, Ukraine, Belgium, the Netherlands, England, Spain, Canada and Congo as well as all over the US. It's fairly widespread considering that it's just two years since we made the show available. But of course we don't hear from everyone who uses the slide show – we have put it out there for people to take and adapt to their own contexts and audiences.

K.B. One of the key themes in contemporary writing about pornography is the extent to which porn is now both ubiquitous and widely accepted – and that mainstream culture has become increasingly 'pornified'. How does this relate to your experience of presenting the slide show: are these images familiar to your audiences?

R.W. What's familiar, to women at least, is the feature film, it's Jenna Jameson,[11] it's *Playboy* – and, even more than that, it's mainstream media representations of pornography and the sex industry, like *The Girls Next Door* [*E!* 2005–?] and HBO's *Cathouse* [2002–8].

L.T. It depends on the age of the audience. When I'm working with students it's often familiar, and what I get is 'Oh, I could show you much worse.' For older audiences it's different because their experiences of porn are more dated and it comes as a shock to realise what is in contemporary porn.

G.D. What our audiences usually don't have, what's been kept from them, is the critical language to understand how the pornified culture shapes their relationships, sexuality and reality. When I'm working with mixed age-range groups the older women often have some language because they were brought up at a time when feminist ideas were circulating in the culture. This group, however, is usually appalled by what they see because they have never looked at porn. With younger groups it's the other way around: all they've had access to is a caricature of anti-porn feminism, but they've seen these images, or images like them.

L.T. I've found that it's often the language that women react most strongly to.[12] There's something in seeing it written down, seeing how pornography categorizes women – all women – that makes it more personal because there's that sense of wondering where you fit, recognizing that this could be about you.

K.B. What about the way pornography talks about men?

G.D. In porn men are virtually invisible as human beings. They are reduced to a life support machine for an erect penis. Porn tells men that they have no sexual boundaries, morality or compassion for women. It strips them of their humanity and in its place offers them an image of themselves as a robotic fucker of women's orifices. Not all men are treated the same in porn: black men are hypermasculinized as sexual monsters who defile white women, while Asian men are generally ignored but when shown – especially in gay porn – they appear feminised and sexually inexperienced.

R.W. It's also instructive to look at the ways that other media sources talk to men about pornography.[13] The December 2008 issue of *Details* magazine included an article titled 'Welcome back, asshole' [Dumenco 2008] about how, after decades of being cowed by feminism, 'the sensitive male is getting back in touch with his inner pig'. A number of the examples involved men using pornography, going to strip clubs and using women in prostitution. It's a very sly approach, because at the same time that it's calling men 'assholes' for doing these things, it's also telling them that they are entitled to be assholes, that it's just their 'sad little insurgency' against the growing power of women.

K.B. How do people respond to the slide show?

R.W. Again, my experience, especially more recently, is that audiences are open and interested. For the most part the women are pretty shocked; they tend to ask things like 'How is this possible?' 'How is this legal?' 'What can we do?' And, usually, even male students – and it is generally students I'm presenting to – are pretty receptive.

L.T. I've done it in different settings and I'm coming from a violence-against-women agenda, so maybe that influences the response. But it varies. Some women feel that they've been really naïve and wonder how they could not know about this. And some women have said, 'I had bought into the idea that porn was empowerment, but actually that was based on my experience as a young woman in the 1980s, not really with what's going on now.' And it's that sense of 'Is that out there? Is that what it is?' I've not really had any negative reactions, but I have had people asking for more evidence, for statistics. There's a certain distancing involved: 'Yeah, the images are like this, but then show me the *other* evidence.'

G.D. You've just shown them the evidence!

L.T. That's it. But some people are of the mind-set that everything must be backed up by academic research with statistical evidence otherwise it's not valid. But overall, I think people are really receptive, and a lot of what I get is people saying, 'Everybody needs to see this, so you need to go and do this everywhere.' And that's great, but my role is then to empower *them* to go out and do things with it.

G.D. In the last two years it's changed. First of all, the crowds at my lectures have been much bigger (on average between 500 and 700). I get a lot of men coming up to me confessing their compulsive use: that never happened before.

I get a lot of hopelessness from women because they're trying to date men and they can't find men who haven't used pornography. And I always say, 'You're not likely to find a man who hasn't used pornography. That's not the issue. The issue is whether he continues to use it once you've given him the analysis.' Another response I've had is women coming up to me crying and saying, 'Thank you. I thought I was going mad, I thought I was the only one who felt that way.'

R.W. I'd say the major responses from women fall into two categories. One is 'I had no idea, and I feel like I've been duped by *The Girls Next Door* and all these glamorizing messages.' And the other is 'I did know, or at least I had an inchoate sense that something was seriously wrong, but I was told I was wrong, I was crazy, I was frigid.' And these women leave feeling unbelievably validated. Which is very rewarding for me as an educator, particularly because we don't have a lot of big victories in this movement.

L.T. I've also had women feeling really angry and saying, 'I'm going home right now and I'm going through every cupboard. There's going to be a porn bonfire in the garden, and I'm checking all through the computer.' It can crystallize a need to take action. But I'm really conscious that I don't want to send women home with a sense of anger and home's not necessarily a safe place. So I'll suggest that, instead of going home and binning it all, maybe it's about starting a conversation and saying how they felt like as a result of a slide show. It's not about asking women to manage *away* that anger, but thinking about how they can turn it into action that's not going to make them more vulnerable.

G.D. I often meet married women who say, 'He's been using pornography for years. I've never told anybody. I don't know what to do about it. He won't stop.' And some of them, they were confused: they didn't understand why he wanted to do A, B and C sexually; why suddenly he'd changed sexually; why he didn't want sex. (That's a big thing, that some men don't want sex after they get into pornography.) And the women carry this mantle of shame, you can see it written all over them, that somehow this is because they're not good enough sexually, they're not hot enough. The feminist analysis of pornography takes that away. It validates them because what we are saying is 'You know what, this is not you. It's not about you. It's a bigger issue than you.' I do think that really changes the way they feel.

This anger and rage that you see, and that I see too, is the reason we need a movement. I often feel guilty when I give a lecture because I'm going to change the way they see the world, and then I leave. This is one of the reasons we started Stop Porn Culture. We have a website, we have the slide show, we run training programmes and we have many resources on our site. I feel very strongly that if you're going to build rage then it's incumbent upon you to have somewhere for people to take it. For some women, they come to the lecture and they are enraged, and they have to go home to a man who's going to fight with them. And they are just beside themselves, and a lot of women tell me that that they just go home and weep because they feel this anger and rage, and the boyfriend is mocking them or he refuses to listen.

R.W. Or the women can't articulate what it is they've seen.

G.D. Yeah, that's a big one, that they can't articulate it – which goes back to what we were saying earlier about the feminist analysis of pornography just not being familiar or available to young people. So all of this is about movement politics and that the answer is never on an individual level.

L.T. You need to inform people of what you can do with this anger, this frustration, where you can go with it because if we don't have activism we won't have big cultural change. The slide shows are a really important way of encouraging people, but you must have something concrete they can do afterwards: in the UK, Object, the Women's Support Project and the Front Page campaign offer some ways of taking this forward.[14] Julia Long [2009] talked about how younger women who got involved in activism suddenly had an opportunity for discussion. Whereas before they'd been met with 'Oh, here she goes again with this anti-porn message', whenever they got involved in activism there was this sense of solidarity and connection. And for me it really struck home, how much we need opportunities for women to be involved at different levels.

R.W. That's a really good point. We need to work towards having more advice and resources for people to do forms of activism other than present the slide show, because it's not for everybody. Not everybody wants to do it, and not everybody is equipped to do it.

L.T. Sheila Jeffreys [2009a] gave a great example of a really simple form of activism: don't book into a hotel that has porn and tell them why you don't. That's activism: 'I choose not to stay in your hotel and give you money because you show porn.' Or challenging your local newsagent about stocking porn and not shopping there if they continue to do so. These are relatively straightforward forms of activism people can take on in their own communities and – particularly if done *en masse* – they can communicate a strong message to businesses that there can be a *cost* to their porn profits, that they might lose other business as a result.

K.B. At the Wheelock conference where the slide show was premiered one of the things that struck me was that there was quite an outpouring afterwards and a lot of personal testimony. How do you manage that?

G.D. That outpouring of testimony took us by surprise. It makes sense, though: a good percentage of the women who came to that conference had been struggling, trying to do activism alone and the years of isolation and frustration just kind of blew up after this. It's very rare that you are in a room of 500 people who feel like you do, where you feel completely welcomed. When you're anti-pornography you're so used to battling and being by yourself and feeling isolated. That's what you saw, the raw emotion of 'Thank God I'm not the only person who feels this way.'

R.W. I agree. That's not normally my experience of doing slide shows: the conference was atypical, as it was a very rare space for people to vent and to articulate their own pain around these issues.

L.T. For me there hasn't been that outpouring of personal testimonies – at least in public. People choose an opportunity to do it whilst it's not in a public forum – at the coffee break, helping me tidy up afterwards, etc.

R.W. That would be more normal for us too; usually if someone is going to disclose something they come up to you afterwards.

L.T. It's important to think about how we set the conditions for that kind of discussion: it's not about constraining people or putting boundaries on their emotions or what they need to say, but thinking about how we manage this.

R.W. That's really important, because on the occasions when something does get out of control emotionally in the room when you're doing a slide show – whether it's someone talking about their experience or things getting loud and adversarial – it's enormously important for the presenter to project control. I don't mean dominance, but you need to be in control of your own emotions and in charge of the room. What I tell people at trainings is that part of being in control and being a trustworthy leader or facilitator is saying when you don't know something. Admitting complexity and our own fallibility helps the audience feel safe in exploring the issues.

K.B. In much of the recent academic writing on porn – particularly explicitly pro-porn work – there is a slippage between being anti-porn and anti-sex. How do you deal with that?

L.T. I come from a sexual health background and I use the World Health Organization [2006: 5] definition of sexual health, which is about individuals being free to express their sexuality and develop their sexuality without fear or pressure or coercion. I am very pro-sex, but I am pro-people being sexually healthy. I am operating with a global definition of what it means to be sexually healthy and porn does not fit into that.

K.B. Is it the same for academics?

G.D. When this comes up I think it shows just how successful a PR job the porn industry has done, because now people see sex and porn as interchangeable. If I was critiquing McDonald's people would understand that I am criticising an industrial product (hamburgers) and not food in general. No one would accuse me of being anti-eating. But here, people often don't differentiate between the product, pornography, and the actual human experience of sex. So to say you're anti-sex if you're anti-porn is just ludicrous, because what you're saying is the only vision of sex you have is pornography. Just think of the lack of creativity there, that you can only think of sex in terms of the way pornography represents it. Don't tell me that's the only sex we can think of as a society.

R.W. This is one of those questions that depends on what kind of audience you have. It's one that Gail gets a lot more than I do, because she's often dealing with audiences in more elite institutions, where people are steeped in certain kinds of theory: they know that this is a standard criticism you throw at anti-pornography feminists. Whereas a lot of the audiences I present to have never really thought about the issue one way or the other. They've just sat through the slide show, which in a number of ways heads off this criticism, so usually it doesn't occur to them to charge me with being anti-sex. So that's a reflection of the way that particular kinds of academic environments have been primed to almost robotically generate certain kinds of objections, when, quite honestly, in other environments basic common sense, and having listened to what someone just said, heads that off.

L.T. In doing this kind of work it's useful to come from a point of personal confusion at times, to say, 'I don't understand how this is arousing?'

R.W. How has this become 'sex'?

G.D. We *are* confused. All of us who do this work look at images and we say, you know, we know about pornography and we understand it but on one level we are confused. How did this get fused with sex? How does shoving a woman's head down a toilet bowl as she is being anally penetrated get defined as hot sex?

K.B. Do you think we need to be able to offer alternatives? The argument that's often made is that porn has been around forever and if you're going to take it away you need to be able to offer something in its place.

G.D. I get that a lot and I think, 'Hello, what about your creativity? What about an authentic sexuality that has grown out of your experiences as a human being, that makes sense to you, who you are, your relationships?' What's sad about this is that pornography has killed creativity. It's what all industrial products do, they kill creativity, they kill authenticity and in their place they hand back to you a generic, plasticized, formulaic version that hardly resembles the real thing. And then in pornography that generic, plasticized, formulaic version of sex has become the sex people know about and when they think you're threatening to take that away they're left with nothing.

L.T. They feel exposed. Young women have said to me, 'Porn is really positive because it shows me how to have an orgasm.' And when we talk some more it usually becomes clear that what they mean is that it shows them how to *look* and *sound* when they have an orgasm, not that it increases their sexual knowledge in any direct way.

K.B. Yes, if you're learning about sex from pornography you're learning about a kind of sex that is performed to be *looked* at. The sex in porn is performed so that the viewer gets the best view, not to enhance the performers' physical sensations.

L.T. But if that's what you've grown up with, and that's how you're told people should and do act, if you strip that away there is a sense of vulnerability, an uncertainty about how to act, look and perform, which pose to strike.

G.D. That shows you what an image-based culture looks like. Students (particularly female students) tell me regularly that when they have sex all they can think about is what they look like. Are their stomachs looking too big, do their breasts look good and so on? This is what's going on. And women internalize that plasticized look from the media. What options do they have, given that pornified images have crowded out other images of femininity? Women need never look at porn to be affected by it because they get porn ideology 'lite' delivered to them via women's media too. They are socialised into believing that being a desired object – not a desiring subject – is what makes them worthy. Girls don't talk about their own desire. This is what it means to live in a pornified image-based society.

K.B. Ariel Levy [2006] makes that point really clearly. That for all these expressions of women's desire their desire is never an expression of physical, bodily sensation, but about being desired.

L.T. Problem pages reinforce this. Young women are writing in saying, 'I don't like having sex with the lights on because I detest my body,' and instead of acknowledging where that comes from, one response I read was 'Have you thought of draping a scarf over your stomach?' I also read a suggestion that women put lip plumper on their nipples to make them swell up, look erect and aroused: 'You'll look aroused and he won't know you're not aroused and he'll think he's doing his job well.'

G.D. Women are increasingly having to deal with men who have got their sex education from pornography. This begs the question: how are they going to know how to arouse real women? In pornography he just has to have an erection for her to have an orgasm. In porn women have no sexual agency because they want what he wants, so if he likes gagging her, then she too loves it. This is a massive misinformation campaign.

K.B. One of the criticisms that's been levelled at anti-porn feminism, particularly in the US, is to do with the way that anti-porn discourse has been adopted and used by the Christian right. What do you think are the challenges of reinvigorating anti-porn feminism against that backdrop?

G.D. We've had very little contact with the Christian right, they stay away from us.

R.W. Every now and then some conservative anti-porn organisation has approached us, and we've always said, 'The first thing you should understand is that we're feminist, we're anti-capitalist, we're pro-choice and we're pro-gay.'

G.D. That's usually enough. We never hear from them again. What they have done, though, is adopt some of our language, and that's not a terrible thing, because we've got them thinking about harm to women. Prior to that, the Christian right only ever thought in terms of harm to the man and the family, so now they do actually recognize that women's lives matter. Well, some of them do. But the main focus at the moment seems to be pornography addiction, and one of the reasons is that there are so many religious men who are addicted. I was speaking to someone whose husband runs an addiction group for Mormons – for addictions to any substance or behaviour – and yet the room is full of men wanting to talk about their addictions to pornography.

K.B. Does this have much resonance in the Scottish context?

L.T. No, but it's important in Scotland to look at the influence of the Churches more broadly. If we think about the need to educate young people about pornography, schools have very clearly said that they do not want anybody in to talk about pornography: the religious groups very much directed what happened with the new curriculum for sexual health, and in fact a new curriculum was developed for Catholic schools.[15] So that's where some of the influence is: acting as a gatekeeper.

K.B. More generally, how do you manage dissent and disagreement?

G.D. One thing I find useful after giving a slide show is to let the women speak first. For ten to fifteen minutes it's a women-only space, and that way if there is a man who's going to be hostile he's not going to hi-jack the conversation immediately. The slide show has just introduced women to a feminist analysis of the porn culture, and it's a shock to the system. They're not thinking about questions, they're just thinking about what the images are telling them about the world they live in and what men consume. The real skill is not letting angry men hi-jack the conversation.

K.B. What about angry women?

G.D. In my experience, women tend to get angry when the men get angry. The women jump to the defence of men and accuse me of being a man-hater. Few women in my experience – and that includes those who disagree with me – get angry and hostile.

R.W. That's mostly true, but I've had occasional exceptions, mostly situations where women were there who were self-consciously identified as sadomasochists and they see me as attacking their sexuality. But recently – I don't want to pick too rosy a picture – but I've had very few hostile responses at all.

L.T. I don't necessarily get it after slide shows but I have had comments posted about me as an individual on web sites.

K.B. How do you deal with that?

L.T. The first time I was aware of it, it really did shock me. It was after a press release went out about our position on the Extreme Porn legislation[16] and I wasn't aware it had happened until someone else asked, 'Are you OK with what's been written about you?' It ranged from accusing me of being anti-women right down to 'She must need a good fucking and I'm the man to fuck her.' So I'm very conscious that if we're asking women to become activists and to become involved we need to have good support systems.

K.B. When you developed the slide show it was a tool that was developed for activist use, but you've developed it as academics. How well do you think contemporary academic debates about pornography translate into activism?

G.D. We do activism on the ground with women whose lives are often harmed or ruined by pornography. We get out of the academy and into the real world where people live their lives. A lot of the pro-porn academics aren't really interested in activism. They're interested in bringing out books that won't make waves in the academy. Those of us in the academy who are anti-porn have to deal with a lot of abuse thrown at us, bad reviews and insults from other academics.

The biggest thing they do to insult you is ignore your work altogether. It's as if you don't exist and they quote each other. The only anti-porn feminists they usually quote are Dworkin and MacKinnon, and even then it's usually only a caricature of their work. Dworkin's and MacKinnon's work was, and is, incredibly important, but they ignore the last twenty to thirty years of work generated by the rest of us.

R.W. The other side don't need to be activists. They've won, the culture is theirs. What is there for them to be activists about? It's an intellectual game for them.

L.T. I sometimes feel that academics don't actually take activists seriously enough.

G.D. Activism is not how you get Brownie points in academia, you get it through publishing books and peer-reviewed articles. And of course we do that too, but what matters most for anti-porn feminists is that our work can be used as an activist tool. We're not just interested in doing things for ourselves. We're not interested in talking to the pro-porn academics, because we're not going to move them. We're interested in going out into the real world and speaking to women and men whose lives are being affected by pornography. Rebecca's comment about the pro-porn side winning reminds me of an interview I did with Nina Hartley at Adult Expo.[17] I opened the interview by saying, 'The radical feminist analysis of porn was correct. It has gotten much more violent over the years. I was right and you were wrong, and you won and I lost, because look around you: everything that we said was going to happen *is* happening.' And she had absolutely nothing to say. And I said to her, 'Did you ever think that pornography would get this bad?' and she refused to acknowledge how body-punishing it had become, although she's now in a position where she has to do double penetration and double anal to get work.

R.W. Which she says is her sexuality.

G.D. It's evolved. She says her sexuality has evolved.

R.W. Remarkably, right alongside the porn industry.

L.T. If you give examples of what women at slide shows say, or feel, or think, academics will say, 'That can't be true, because it hasn't been researched,' or 'Show me the evidence of that,' which minimizes women's feelings and reactions.

R.W. Which is astonishing, because they are the ones whose entire position is based on 'My personal experience is that I like this' or 'It liberates me' or whatever, so when the anecdote is just about 'me and my own personal feelings and unique interpretations', that's fine from their point of view.

K.B. So, Linda, as someone who's working on the ground, what is it you're looking for from academic research?

L.T. There aren't close enough links between what is being studied and how that applies to public policy or funding priorities. I'd like to see more research done on how women in communities really feel about commercial sexual exploitation, and about porn in particular, because my sense is that a lot of women are very unhappy and concerned, but don't have the space and chance to have their voice heard.

G.D. I'd like to see more qualitative work. We really need more information on the meanings that men make from gonzo pornography.[18]

K.B. That's so much more important than thinking simply in terms of 'effects'. My problem with effects is that the minute you use that language people seize on it in particular ways. What Robert Jensen says about this is really helpful – why do we need science to tell us this?[19]

R.W. I completely agree. It's all very well to look at laboratory studies but we all are sitting here with our common sense. We can look at the material, think about the messages it's sending, and reason our way through to at least some tentative conclusions.

K.B. So we need more qualitative research?

G.D. Absolutely. One of the ways we learned about the effects of pornography on women was through the hearings for the anti-pornography law. It was all collected in this huge volume of testimony [Everywoman 1988; MacKinnon and Dworkin 1997], and that was such an insight for us: we learned things just by listening to women. We need to do this with men now. I've heard thousands of men speak and I can tell you what they tell me. But I'd like to see something more systematic.

K.B. What are the main themes in what they tell you?

G.D. Men talk about their compulsive use and how difficult it is to stop. Men are telling me that all they know about sex they learned from pornography, because they started using it at such an early age – it's almost like it's encoded into their sexual DNA. Some want to bring porn into their intimate relationships, others need to conjure up porn images to ejaculate with partners, and still others have lost interest in sex with real women. To show just how porn destroys creativity, men have told me that once they stopped using porn they didn't know how to masturbate. Men who've developed a critique of pornography tell me they find they can't be around their friends that much, they feel alone and isolated because they've got to the point where they realise pornography isn't a joke any more.

L.T. I'm seeing organizations who haven't taken an anti-porn approach before having to take this stance because of what they are seeing in their practice. For example Relationships Scotland (an organization which supports couples with issues in their relationships) told me pornography is increasingly coming up in their counselling. So because this is a problem for their clients they are having to recognize this as a problem. And young people's organizations that might have been porn-neutral before are telling me they're increasingly dealing with young women talking about the pressure they're under to have sex they don't want to have, and young men talking about worries about their bodies, their penis size, that they don't ejaculate enough, that they're worried they can't have sex the way it's shown in pornography. So that's an example of the broader impacts and reaches of pornography. In terms of research, we need longitudinal studies with people who are now much more immersed in a porn culture than other generations have been.

K.B. So what next in terms of your own work? What are the priorities?

L.T. In terms of the slide show it's about broadening the base of facilitators and how we support women taking on this work, and linking work in different parts of the UK. And capturing the evaluation of what we know, anecdotally, happens for women attending the slide shows.

G.D. I have just finished writing a book on porn [Dines 2010] and now want to devote time to activism. My energies will go into Stop Porn Culture and building it up into a viable movement so that we can train more people to do this work and become activists. This way they can feel that they are doing something real in the world rather than just feeling overwhelmed or paralysed. And we want to develop a slide show specifically targeting youth, because you can't show actual porn to adolescents. We want to find a way to talk to young people so we need to work with experts in child and adolescent development.

K.B. So for anyone reading this who wants to take the work forward what would you advise?

G.D. If you want to give the slide show get yourself to a training because you will find a community of activists and that's so important.[20] You've got to be prepared for all the difficulties that get thrown at you doing this work. You become a public figure in a very controversial subject so you need to be well prepared.

R.W. One of the things we encourage for anyone wanting to use the slide show is to start small. Present in a supportive environment to start with.

L.T. And co-facilitate if possible.

K.B. So it's all about building connections and building a movement?

G.D. Absolutely, that's so vital.

Notes

1 The slide show (*Who Wants to be a Porn Star? Sex and Violence in Today's Pornography Industry*), together with the presenter's toolkit and videos from the Wheelock conference, can be accessed via <www.stoppornculture.com> (accessed 29 September 2009).

2 Mainstream images are taken from MTV, mainstream women's and men's magazines, adverts for toys and clothing aimed at pre-pubescent girls, computer games and celebrity images.

3 The slide show (in its original form) deals with features (produced by companies like Vivid and Wicked) and 'gonzo'. The features and their contracted 'stars' provide a bridge between the mainstream and gonzo, providing performers with a degree of mainstream visibility, legitimacy and wealth whilst presenting content that – like gonzo – is 'body-punishing' for performers. In discussing gonzo, the industry's own publicity – as well as the porn texts themselves – are used to demonstrate the promotion of body-punishing sex (see also Tyler and Paasonen, this volume). The slide show considers the ways in which pornography sexualizes

women and girls in all kinds of roles and settings and identifies the racism in much contemporary pornography.

4 Sheila Jeffreys identified the need for a new language to talk about sexual experience of this kind in 1990. Jeffreys' concern was to accurately describe the emotional dissonance some women and children experience during rape when their physical response is one that, in other circumstances, would be understood and experienced as arousal (e.g. orgasm). The term 'dysrotic' may have been coined in response to this, but we have been unable to trace and so credit its first use.

5 Such as Adult DVD Talk <www.adultdvdtalk.com>: see Whisnant (this volume).

6 Max Hardcore is a US 'gonzo' director convicted of obscenity charges in 2008. (His films are still widely available.)

7 24 September 2007: <http://www.howardstern.com/rundown.hs?d=119060 6400> (accessed 27 June 2009).

8 Adult Expo is the trade show of the primarily US porn industry, held annually in Las Vegas. See Jensen (this volume).

9 <www.zootoday.com> accessed 18 March 2009. These images are no longer available, as the site is regularly updated with new photographs of young women for readers to rate.

10 *Suicide Girls* is a porn site which presents itself as 'a community that celebrates alternative beauty and alternative culture from all over the world': <http://suicidegirls.com/> (accessed 27 June 2009).

11 Jenna Jameson has been described as the world's first true 'porn star' and has achieved a degree of crossover success with a best-selling autobiography (Jameson and Strauss 2004) and exposure on television and throughout pop culture.

12 The slide show, in its original form, includes a slide identifying terms for women in pornography, drawn from the porn industry's own marketing of its product.

13 See also Boyle (this volume, Chapter 9).

14 See < http:www.object.org.uk>, <http://www.womenssupporproject.co.uk> and <http://www.thefrontpagecampaign.co.uk> (all accessed 27 June 2009).

15 See <http://www.calledtolove.org> (accessed 29 September 2009).

16 See Jones and Carlin, and McGlynn (this volume).

17 Nina Hartley is a porn performer and producer who has been working in porn for more than twenty-five years. Interview conducted at Adult Expo, 11 January 2008.

18 See Flood (this volume) for a review of the existing literature on men's consumption of pornography.

19 Jensen writes, 'The search for causation demands "science," while a concern for pornography's role in rape leaves us more open to listening to stories. Because science has no way to answer the question, predictably the search for causation and the use of science leads most everyone to conclude that we just don't know enough to say for sure. But a shift in emphasis and method offers a way to state not The Truth (or conclude that we don't yet know The Truth), but a way to tell true stories and begin to make trustworthy moral and political decisions' (1998b: 101).

20 Details about forthcoming training and events in the US can be found on the Stop Porn Culture web site (as above). For UK events and activism refer to the organizations listed in note 14.

Chapter 2

Methodological considerations in mapping pornography content

Ana J. Bridges

The content of pornography has been of interest not only to media scholars within the humanities (where close textual analysis has become the favoured method in recent years)[1] but also to psychologists and sociologists. Implicit in the debate among social scientists about pornographic content is an assumption that both pornography's production and consumption can be harmful (Boyle 2000) and that mapping the pornographic text is critical to the understanding of how pornography stems from and propagates sexism and violence against women. This chapter will briefly outline the research supporting this assumption before moving on to consider content analysis as a method for mapping pornographic media content, reviewing a number of recent studies in the field, including original research by this author and her colleagues (Wosnitzer and Bridges 2007).

Media studies scholars have described that people are impacted by the content of the media they consume. Albert Bandura, a psychologist, discovered that children learn behaviours by observing models, which he called Social Learning Theory (Bandura *et al.* 1961; Bandura 1986). Even more important, people learned to imitate the behaviours of a videotaped model when the model's behaviours led to rewards or positive outcomes and learned to avoid engaging in behaviours which led to punishments or negative outcomes. These discoveries seem intuitive now but, at the time, the field of psychology was dominated by behavioural theories that assumed learning must take place via direct experience rather than learning by proxy (Bandura 2004). As refinements to the social learning model have been made, we now know that the degree to which the observer identifies with the model, or sees the model to be 'like me', also affects the extent to which observed behaviours will be imitated (Schunk 1987).

The application of social learning theory to pornography viewing focuses on how sexually explicit media model sexual behaviour for viewers. Specifically, pornography can teach viewers about how to behave sexually with another, how to sexually please a partner and what to expect when becoming sexually intimate. It is no wonder, then, that pornographic media are so popular among adolescents (Carroll *et al.* 2008). Presumably, many of these consumers have had limited sexual experiences of their own when they first seek information about sex from pornography. For example, a 2009 study of 100 college-age men and women in the US demonstrated that youth first see pornographic depictions around age fourteen, while average age at first sexual intercourse is sixteen.[2] Less than 10 per cent of these study participants reported first pornography exposure that occurred *after* sexual intercourse.[3] Pornography thus serves as a teacher – a way to instruct youth about appropriate and expected behaviours in sexual situations. Studies of adolescents confirm that a sizeable number see pornography as an important source of sexual education (Borzekowski and Rickert 2001) and, indeed, the porn industry has a vested interest in presenting itself as a sex educator. As such, it seems critical to ask: what are youth learning about what constitutes sexual behaviour?

Content analyses involve a systematic exploration of behaviours, verbal utterances, or themes that are contained within a specified media unit. For example, researchers have examined the content of jokes told on late-night television shows such as *David Letterman,* the content of violence in children's cartoon television shows and the content of sexual messages contained in teenage girls' magazines (Carpenter 1998; Niven *et al.* 2003; Wilson *et al.* 2002). Within the domain of pornography, most content analyses ask one of three questions:

1 What are the sexual behaviours in pornography?
2 How much violence/aggression is contained within pornographic materials?
3 To what extent does pornography dehumanize or objectify persons, particularly women?

These questions all reflect a specific theoretical perspective on pornography: namely, that pornographic media can be harmful both in their production and consumption (Boyle 2000). Because there has been such a focus on the negative effects of violent and degrading pornography, numerous content analyses have attempted to document changes in violence and degradation over time (Bogaert and Turkovich 1993; Malamuth and Spinner 1980; Scott and Cuvelier 1987, 1993).

Specifically, following the Meese Commission on Pornography in 1986, the veracity of the statement that pornography usually contained violence and therefore was a growing public health concern became the focus of much content analysis (e.g. Scott and Cuvelier 1987, 1993). As a whole, findings from these studies suggest that violence in popular pornography is rare and decreasing over time. However, there are numerous methodological and theoretical problems with studies that have arrived at these conclusions. These problems, and recommendations for future content-analytic efforts, are the focus of this chapter.

The pornography genre and aggression

Media can be divided into genres. When movie renters go to the video store, their search for entertainment is facilitated by the organization of the videos on offer into genres. For those in the mood for a light and fun evening, heading to the Comedy section is recommended. For mixed-gender adolescent gatherings, perhaps something from the Horror genre will be fun. For a younger audience, the Children and Family movies are of interest, and so forth. Each of these genres has a core structure. While much leeway is permitted and some movies do cross genres, generally speaking movies within the Adventure or Horror or Comedy sections have some similarities in their narratives. Take the Romantic Comedy genre: it relies on a humorous sexual miscommunication between two individuals that ultimately results in their resolution and happily ever after.

The genre is the larger context within which a movie's action takes place, and aggression or violence looks very different in different film genres. In children's cartoons, Wile E. Coyote is burned, thrown from a cliff and run over by trains in his efforts to catch the Road Runner. In a drama, the protagonist may be harmed or killed by an angry ex-lover. In slapstick comedies, people are oftentimes knocked over, poked, dragged or tripped. While each of these behaviours can be considered aggressive, the results or consequences of such acts are largely dictated by genre. While Wile E. Coyote may be shown limping in crutches after a particular fall, a second later he will be back to full health and pursuing the Road Runner. Aggression in dramas may focus largely on the emotional impact or results of aggression. In slapstick comedies, characters rarely show lasting negative effects from being targets of aggression. Not only are character responses to aggressive acts largely dependent on film genre, so too is the anticipated audience response. Children laugh with delight at the antics of Wile E. Coyote, as do adults with much slapstick comedy. In drama, aggression may lead to tears or viewer anxiety and tension, while in horror the intended response is one of recoil.

If we can agree that aggression may be present in diverse film genres but that how it is portrayed and how both characters and audience members respond vary as a function of genre, and if we can agree further that portrayals of both aggressive acts and their consequences are important in discerning the impact of media on viewers (Bandura *et al.* 1961), then it becomes critical to consider how the genre of contemporary, popular pornography portrays aggressive acts and character responses to them.

I argue that the pornographic film genre requires that characters demonstrate *indifference to or erotic pleasure from aggression*. This argument rests on one important assumption: most consumers of pornography state that they are unaroused by violence and aggression (Loftus 2002). In fact, I argue that if pornographic films showed the natural consequences of violence and aggression, these consequences would decrease or eliminate arousal altogether for most pornography consumers, something the producers and marketers of pornography clearly would not want.[4]

Producers and marketers of pornography are in the business of making money. Therefore, it is in their interest to cater to as wide an audience as possible and avoid isolating or offending consumers. However, in recent years the market has exploded with increased content and outlets for sexual media. Furthermore, these media have reduced the distinction between producer and consumer: anyone with a digital camera or a keyboard can produce pornography and the internet permits an immediate and worldwide outlet of distribution. In this changed market place, barriers to industry entry have all but eroded (Barron and Kimmel 2000).

With such a large selection of pornographic materials available, how do individual producers compete for consumers? The answer is: by making their material something of note – something different. Bogaert and Turkovich (1993) noted this as a possible explanation for why *Playboy* centrefolds increased in degrading and objectifying content initially after the introduction of *Hustler* magazine, but then decreased a few years later: they argue that *Playboy* may have decided to differentiate itself by remaining more elite and high-brow rather than attempting to mimic *Hustler's* style. Furthermore, *Hustler* began to obtain success in large part because it offered something to consumers that they were not getting from *Playboy* – a more explicit, hard-core and aggressive sexual experience. The content of internet newsgroup stories was analysed and compared with video and magazines by Barron and Kimmel (2000). Consistent with marketplace arguments, the researchers found that Usenet stories were more violent and degrading than videos or magazines. The authors note that more traditional pornographic producers may not be free to change content as quickly and must maintain standards set in part by advertisers and theatres or stores. If they make content that is too extreme or controversial, then they risk losing investors and alienating consumers. However, if they are to remain competitive, they must evolve and present novel material.

Not only will pornographic material become more explicit over time as the market place expands and production costs diminish barriers to marketplace entry, so too will consumers demand increasingly novel material. It is well known in the field of psychology that images or events initially evoking strong emotional responses, such as gory or fearful pictures, lose their shock value over time and with repeated exposure (Marks and Dar 2000). This process is called *habituation*. Even from shortly after birth, human beings quickly learn to direct attention to what is novel or new and stop paying attention to what is old and predictable (Colombo and Mitchell 2009). This occurs even with pleasurable stimuli (Leventhal *et al.* 2007).

In short, we become bored quickly. Scholars have argued that people habituate to sexual material too, so that what was previously arousing becomes less so. Studies of men viewing sexually explicit movies have demonstrated that habituation occurs over time such that sexual arousal (as measured by penile tumescence) decreases with repeated viewing of the same film (Koukounas and Over 2001). Therefore, the pornography consumer searches for ever novel material to recreate the same arousal or excitement that was initially experienced. Some have compared this process to the tolerance that a drug addict may develop – requiring increasing quantities or more potent drugs in order to obtain the same high (Grunder 2000; Schneider and Irons 1996).[5] This novelty can come in a variety of forms, including unusual sexual acts, increasingly violent or aggressive behaviour, a focus on particular fetishes or characters, seemingly taboo subjects such as incest, or body shapes and sizes. In 2009 my research lab obtained evidence supporting the increasing appetites for more violent and degrading pornographic media in more habitual users: college students (both men and women) who reported more frequent pornography use were also more likely to report being aroused by violent and degrading pornographic videos compared with less frequent consumers.[6]

The reason that it is important to lay out this argument is to better critique the methodological approaches taken in content analyses of pornographic media. If, as I have argued, popular pornography generally avoids showing negative consequences of aggression (as these would interfere with consumers' sexual arousal), but if, simultaneously, consumers require increasingly unusual or extreme content to continue purchasing such media, then the natural result will be an increase in unusual and emotionally arousing content in popular pornography, including violent or aggressive content, but *without negative consequences*. Therefore, attempts to map the pornographic text must divorce aggression from negative consequences (including that the recipient of aggression attempts to avoid being harmed) to be true to the genre.

Another point to consider when mapping the pornographic text is that consumers of popular pornography are predominantly male (Cooper *et al.* 2002; Stack *et al.* 2004).[7] It is logical to assume, then, that popular pornography attempts to maximize *men's* sexual arousal. Koukounas and Over (2001) found that men who viewed sexually explicit films from a *participant* perspective (that is, films in which they were picturing themselves as the protagonists or as 'in the scene') had increased sexual arousal compared with men who viewed the same films from an *observer* perspective.

For men to enter into the fantasy world portrayed in pornography from the participant perspective, the best strategy is to make male actors as anonymous and unobtrusive as possible. In this way, few cues will remind men that it is not *they* who are the sexual performers, desired by the women in pornography. Even before pornographic films were widely disseminated, an analysis of explicit books found:

> The world of pornography is a male's world. Compared to females, little attention is given to the physical characteristics of the male. Physical characteristics of the female are described in minute detail, down to the last dimple. For more than one-fourth of the male characters, however, nothing is said about their physical features with the exception of almost universal reference to the large size of their genitals.
>
> (Smith 1976: 21)[8]

Film directors can augment viewers' sense of being an active participant in the sexual action to maximize men's sexual arousal in a similar fashion. In heterosexual pornography, this may mean that the camera lingers on women's bodies more than men's. It also may mean that film shots will minimize men's roles while maximizing those of women. For example, fewer male speaking parts, fewer cues about men's social status or occupation and increased focus on women's responses may serve to increase male viewer's sense that they *are* the protagonist: that they have entered into the fantasy world created by pornography.

This point-of-view filming means two things: first, that social modelling conditions are optimized because men are more likely to identify with actors, since there will be little information stating that this actor is 'not like me' (Bandura 1986). Second, studies of point-of-view camera angles have determined that when a camera is focused on a particular person, that person is seen as more responsible for a behaviour than when the camera takes a more neutral view or focuses on someone else (Lassiter and Irvine 1986). While this research is in the field of police interrogations to determine suspect guilt, the same might hold for pornographic films. That is, because cameras tend to focus on women's faces, bodies and behaviours, women may be seen as more *responsible* for what happens to them (including being targets of aggression).

This brief discussion gives some indication as to why social scientists have been interested in the content of pornography. But the researchers' ideological position further shapes the research in ways I will now discuss.

Methodological choices in mapping the pornographic text

An analysis of pornographic content must consider numerous methodological choices, as each of these greatly impacts results (Cowan 2002). Cowan cautions that researchers are operating under theoretical models that should be articulated, as these can bias every step of the content analysis. To the extent that researchers are clear about their theoretical model, readers can determine whether or not they find the results to be useful and valid.

First, researchers conducting content analyses must determine what they are intending to study. In the case of mapping pornographic texts, researchers have focused on areas as diverse as the nature of sexual behaviour in pornographic media (Wosnitzer and Bridges 2007), how violence in popular pornographic magazines has changed over time (Malamuth and Spinner 1980), racism in popular pornography (Cowan and Campbell 1994), objectification of women in pornographic films (McKee 2005b) and *Playboy* centrefolds (Bogaert and Turkovich 1993) or comparing the content of porn films directed by women and men (Sun *et al.* 2008). Diversity can also be seen in attempts to map a range of pornographic media, from comics (Palmer 1979), cartoons (Matacin and Burger 1987) and books (Whissell 1998) to magazines (Scott and Cuvelier 1987), movies (Cowan and Campbell 1994; McKee 2005b) and the internet (Barron and Kimmel 2000; Gossett and Byrne 2002; Mehta and Plaza 1997).

Next, researchers decide what they are going to code. The decision by McKee (2005b) to code aggression as occurring only when the target clearly exhibited some effort to avoid the aggressive act versus Prince's (1990) to code any verbal or physically aggressive act regardless of how playful or well received it was by the actor illustrates the importance of this methodological choice. Not surprisingly, McKee obtained much lower estimates of aggression than Prince.

Following the development of a coding scheme, researchers must decide how to sample the content of interest. This is not a simple decision and depends on numerous variables, such as (1) how diverse the media are with respect to the content in question; (2) the sorts of research questions being investigated; (3) local laws that govern the availability and types of materials that can be purchased; and (4) the time period to which the content should generalize (Manganello et al. 2008). At times, the population sample is small enough that all instances can be coded – Bogaert et al. (1993) examined every *Playboy* centrefold from the first issue to the time of their study. Most often, the population to which the researcher hopes to generalize is too large to analyse each instance. In such cases, researchers need to be careful about how they select the sample and use random sampling to the extent possible.

Most content analyses have not utilized true random sampling. For example, Barron and Kimmel (2000) content-analysed videos rented from five different stores in a suburban township of New York. Similarly, Palys (1986) content analysed videos rented from stores in four communities in Vancouver, Canada. Duncan (1991) selected fifty video-cassettes from one local video store (presumably in southern Illinois, where the researcher was located).

The problem with these sampling methods, as Cowan and others note (Cowan 2002; Yang and Linz 1990), is that video selection can be systematically biased in unpredictable ways. For example, the most popular videos may have been rented already and thus not available for content analysis. Perhaps the most popular videos were also systematically different from those that were present in the store (more *or* less violent or aggressive). Local laws regulating the availability and display of pornographic materials may result in systematic differences among samples. McKee (2005b) notes that the results of his content analysis of best-selling films available for rental in Australia were impacted by the country's legal prohibition against pornographic films that contain violence and aggression. Local laws are created and modified over time, also contributing to potential limits to generalizability of content analytic findings. Finally, Palys (1986) noted that managers at video rental stores have varying degrees of autonomy when deciding what videos to provide to the public. Scandal, protests, and negative media attention led to some video store managers opting to stock only mild and relatively non-controversial sexually explicit video titles. Obviously, such decisions impact on key findings in content analyses of violent and aggressive pornography.

Cowan (2002) recommends that researchers use catalogues of videos whenever possible in order to best randomly sample the population of interest. Some researchers (e.g. Sun et al. 2008) have opted to examine 'best-selling' and 'best-renting' lists and to select randomly from these lists. These are preferred procedures that largely eliminate systematic bias. Nevertheless, the limitations of local laws and norms remain. Given these described limitations, it seems prudent to consider any content analysis as a snapshot in time and place.

Inter-rater reliability is affected by the coding scheme. When coding categories are larger, versus more specific, reliability increases (Cowan 2002). However, oftentimes content analytic researchers are interested in nuanced questions that large categories might obscure. For example, rather than asking whether violence occurred at any point in the scene, a researcher may be more interested in what types of violent behaviours occurred, how many times they occurred, how severe they were and characteristics of the perpetrator(s) and target(s). Adequate inter-rater reliability is more difficult to obtain with very specific categorization schemes. Therefore, researchers often must strike a balance between a coding scheme that provides rich information with one that is broad enough to yield good agreement between coders.

Studies have also differed in how much training coders receive and how disagreements between coders are resolved. At the most basic end, one person may code all of the content and therefore inter-rater reliability cannot be established (e.g. Palmer 1979). This is problematic for the interpretation of content-analytic results, particularly when subjective judgement is part of the coding scheme, as the coder's biases will not be made apparent. When two or more coders are used, coders may receive little more than a set of written instructions indicating how to code material. For example, Scott and Cuvelier (1987, 1993) used such a minimal training method: they provided coders with a set of instructions and asked them to indicate which of a set of pictorial representations were 'violent'. (Violence was not further defined for coders.) Not surprisingly, inter-rater reliability estimates were low for both studies. On the other hand, multiple coders may receive extensive hands-on training and practice in coding before research begins (e.g. Barron and Kimmel 2000:163; McKee 2005b). For example, McKee (2005b) met with coders for several sessions in which they discussed the coding scheme and practised coding as a group. He also provided coders with images as a visual reference for some subjective codes, such as the size of particular body parts.[9] To the extent that content-analytic studies require some degree of subjective judgement, it is preferable to provide more extensive training and practice to coders as well as sample items or pictures. One unfortunate limitation in reviewing the body of research on content analyses of pornography is that some studies do not report any information on inter-rater reliability, despite indicating that the study employed multiple coders (e.g. Monk-Turner and Purcell 1999).

Of the methodological considerations described above, the largest focus in the following discussion of key findings from content analyses will be on how aggression and violence were defined and coded. Because many researchers provide details on what behaviours were considered for coding, and because much of what has been coded in pornography is from film scenes, their results can be compared with a content-analytic study I and my colleagues conducted in 2007. In short, by reanalysing current results within the context of past studies, a better and more comparable estimate of changes in violent and degrading content can be documented.

Defining key terms in prior content analyses

Attempts to document violent behaviours in pornographic media have used varied definitions of violence. One potential limitation in coding for violence is that many definitions require some degree of judgement. For example, Yang and Linz (1990) coded violence as behaviour occurring when a person intentionally imposes or attempts to impose 'hurt, abuse, or force'. They further differentiated between violent behaviour that occurred in the context of sexual behaviour (such as sexual activity with deception, coercion, or threatened or actual aggression) and that which occurred outside of sexual activity. However, what specifically constitutes hurt, abuse and force is not clarified. In another content analysis, coders were simply instructed to code pictures for the presence of violence, defined as rape, sadomasochism or exploitative/coercive sexual relations (Scott and Cuvelier 1987). Details for how to recognize coercion or rape were not provided, requiring coders to determine for themselves whether a picture was violent or not. Indeed, such subjective judgement, common across many content-analytic studies, highlights the importance of establishing adequate inter-rater reliability before beginning full coding.

Some researchers have opted to code only acts of physical aggression, while others have coded both verbal and physical aggression. However, most studies do not provide sufficient information regarding what specific behaviours are considered verbal aggression. For example, is calling someone a 'slut' an act of verbal aggression? With rare exception (e.g. Monk-Turner and Purcell 1999), such distinctions are unclear.

Some researchers are clear that aggression can be coded when it is self-directed, such as when a person slaps themselves (Palys 1986; Sun et al. 2008). However, most research studies do not explicitly state that aggression could be self-directed and results are not presented in such a way, leaving the reader to wonder if those acts were counted or excluded. Similarly, researchers differ in how they handle more ambiguous instances of aggression. For example, Scott and Cuvelier (1993), in their analysis of violence in *Hustler* cartoons and pictures, specifically instructed coders *not* to code instances in which the cartoons or pictures were ambiguous. A preferred approach is to employ additional coders or to meet as a research team to discuss the problematic or ambiguous picture and arrive at a consensus regarding its final coding (Primack et al. 2008).

Regardless, some common behaviours that are coded within pornographic films include slapping, hitting, spanking, hair pulling, unnecessary roughness in an otherwise 'normal' activity,[10] bondage, actual or threats of weapon use and mutilation or murder (Cowan *et al.* 1988; Monk-Turner and Purcell 1999; Sun *et al.* 2008; Yang and Linz 1990).

Another key term – degradation – has proved equally slippery. Feminist theorists have argued that pornography is degrading to women when it demonstrates power imbalances or active subordination of one gender over another (Dworkin and MacKinnon 1988; Steinem 1980). Others have suggested that portrayals of women as oversexed, always ready for men and orgasmically pleased at whatever touch they may receive, constitute degradation towards women (Donnerstein *et al.* 1987). Content-analytic studies therefore have attempted to code behaviours that are considered potentially degrading or dehumanizing to both men and women. For example, Palys (1986) coded sexual interactions as being either egalitarian or unidirectional (with one person dominating and the other being dominated). Bogaert *et al.* (1993) coded photographs for dehumanizing elements, defined as reduced eye clarity, low facial clarity and body turned away from the camera. Cowan and Dunn (1994) found that perceptions of degradation were more closely associated with active subordination and blatant disrespect of women, particularly when women were treated as sexual objects. The authors conclude that active subordination and objectification, more than portrayals of women as oversexed, are responsible for perceptions of degradation in pornographic films. Importantly, none of the categories employed by Cowan and Dunn focused exclusively on aggression or violence. Given these findings, it may be wise for future content-analytic efforts to code for subordination and objectification.

In addition to specific acts of violence and degradation, some researchers have focused on the specific sexual behaviours which are part of pornographic texts and considered whether they might be understood as degrading or physically harming the performers. Frequently there are attempts to code for things like anal penetration, vaginal penetration, fellatio and ejaculation (Cowan and Dunn 1994; Palys 1986; Sun *et al.* 2008; Winick 1985; Yang and Linz 1990). While some studies have focused on sexual behaviour exclusively (Winick 1985), most have analysed sexual behaviour in the context of other variables, such as character gender or race (Cowan and Dunn 1994) and frequency of aggression (Palys 1986). Some researchers have explored how specific sexual behaviours may be indicative of aggression or objectification. For example, Cowan and Dunn coded for penis worship, which they defined as 'sexual activity that revolves around worship of the penis. The ejaculation (semen) is especially central to the woman's satisfaction' (1994: 13).[11] Penis worship was found to be significantly associated with perceptions of degradation in pornographic film clips. Similarly, Sun and colleagues (2008) coded a sequence of sexual acts they describe as 'ass to mouth' (ATM) in which the male actor first inserts his penis into a woman's anus and then, immediately upon withdrawal, inserts his penis into either her or another person's mouth. As Dines (2006) argues, this unhygienic and degrading practice does not enhance the actor's physical pleasure. Wosnitzer and Bridges (2007) found that the presence of ATM in a pornographic scene was strongly associated with the presence of physical aggression.

Results of prior content analyses

Estimates of violence and aggression in content analyses vary tremendously. This is not surprising, given the dramatic differences in definitions of violence and aggression. On the low side, McKee (2005b) estimates that fewer than 2 per cent of scenes in popular pornographic videos available in Australia contain violence. However, recall that McKee required the recipient of aggression to be motivated to avoid harm – in other words, the violence had to be non-consensual. Furthermore, McKee notes that Australia has made it illegal to purchase pornographic videos that display violence – therefore, his estimate that 2 per cent of popular pornographic video scenes contain violence is really an estimate of the proportion of pornographic video scenes *that are considered to be non-violent* that nevertheless contain violence. When a similar definition was used by Cowan and colleagues (1988) analysing videos rented from seven family video stores in California, 23 per cent of explicit pornographic film scenes and 73 per cent of pornographic movies contained physical aggression. As such, McKee's figure is influenced both by a definition of aggression that requires motivation to avoid harm on the intended target's part *and* a specific locale that bans violent pornography.

On the high end, Wosnitzer and Bridges (2007) estimate that 88 per cent of scenes in popular pornographic videos available for rental in the US demonstrate some form of verbal or physical aggression. However, their content analysis was very inclusive and liberal in their definitions of violence and aggression. For example, they coded for additional aggressive acts, such as gagging, and verbal insults, such as name calling. Furthermore, they did not require the target of aggression to appear motivated to avoid the harm. Most other analyses demonstrate estimates in the 5–40 per cent range for the proportion of sexually explicit scenes that contain physical aggression. The number of full-length pornographic movies that contain at least one physically aggressive scene is much higher, in the 60–80 per cent range (Barron and Kimmel 2000; Cowan *et al.* 1988; Malamuth and Spinner 1980; Yang and Linz 1990).

Interestingly, the overtly aggressive content of pornographic media, in which targets of aggression attempt to escape from or react negatively to a perpetrator's actions, appears to have peaked during the 1970s and early 1980s (McKee 2005b; Scott and Cuvelier 1987). Since then, fewer professional films and magazines have demonstrated high rates of violence and aggression, or have simply levelled off. While some scholars argue that actual violence is decreasing since that time such that today's popular pornography is less problematic than before (e.g. McKee *et al.* 2008), other explanations may account for these results. For example, Barron and Kimmel (2000) found that sexually violent content was more common in internet pornographic stories (42 per cent) than in magazines (25 per cent) and videos (27 per cent). Gossett and Byrne (2002) completed a content analysis of internet rape sites and found that many produced disturbing and aggressive images of sexual assault: most did not include a disclaimer that the assaults portrayed in the website content were staged and 13 per cent specifically advertised their images as being real. Another possibility is that violence rates are actually increasing even in pornographic magazines and videos, but such violence is being portrayed in more playful and erotic ways. While estimates of rates of aggression and degradation in pornographic media differ, what appears to be a consistent and robust finding is that the targets of most aggressive acts are women (Cowan and Campbell 1994; Prince 1990; Sun *et al.* 2008).

In order to overcome numerous methodological and ideological weaknesses we perceived in prior efforts, my colleagues and I conducted a content analysis of best-selling, best-renting pornographic videos available by catalogue in the US (Wosnitzer and Bridges 2007). In order to improve on previous sampling techniques, we compiled lists of the top thirty best-selling and best-renting videos published monthly by *Adult Video News* from December 2004 to June 2005 (*Adult Video News* 2005). After deleting duplications, our final list of popular films consisted of 275 titles. Fifty titles were randomly selected from this list to comprise the sample, yielding a total of 304 scenes.

We sought to examine both scene-level variables (e.g. percentage of scenes that contained aggression) and aggressive-behaviour-specific variables (e.g. when an aggressive act was perpetrated, what were the characteristics of the perpetrator, target and target response?). At the scene level, variables coded included characteristics of the principal actors, sexual behaviours and the presence of both verbal and physical aggression. We were particularly interested in sexual behaviours that have been implicated in degradation of women, such as penis worship and ass-to-mouth.

In coding aggression, we chose to employ the 'gold standard' in the field of Communications: the method employed in the National Television Violence Study (1998). This method included coding information about who was the perpetrator of the aggressive act, who was the target and what specific aggressive act was observed. In defining aggression, we chose to use definitions most consistent with those employed in prior content analyses. Specifically, we sought to identify (1) observable behaviours; that (2) were purposeful (to avoid coding accidental acts of harm); and that (3) could be directed either at oneself or another. Notably absent in our definition was the target response to aggression: this was coded separately. As such, consensual acts of aggression were still counted.

The specific behaviours we coded under aggression were of two sub-types: physical and verbal. Employing definitions similar to those by Barron and Kimmel (2000), Cowan and colleagues (1988) and Palys (1986), we coded for (a) pushing/shoving; (b) biting; (c) pinching; (d) pulling hair; (e) spanking; (f) open-hand slapping; (g) gagging (when an object or body part, e.g. penis, hand, or sex toy, is inserted into a character's mouth, visibly obstructing breathing); (h) choking (when one character visibly places his/her hands around another character's throat with applied pressure); (i) threatening with weapon; (j) kicking; (k) closed-fist punching; (l) bondage/confining; (m) using weapons; and

(n) torturing, mutilating or attempting murder. Verbally aggressive acts were (a) name calling/insulting and (b) threatening physical harm.

Target responses to the aggressive act were coded as either (a) responded with pleasure; (b) responded neutrally; or (c) responded with displeasure. In order to obtain adequate inter-rater reliability, we had to collapse responses (a) and (b) into one category. However, this did permit us to explore how often aggression was presented as consensual versus non-consensual.

Coders were three women of diverse ages, ethnicities and educational backgrounds. One limitation to our content analysis was that we did not employ coders of both genders: although the coding scheme was developed and refined by a male member of the research team, the bulk of the coding for this analysis was completed by the three female research assistants. Training occurred over multiple sessions and included refinement to coding categories and independent practice followed by group discussions until category consensus was achieved.

Our results suggested that physical and verbal aggression are the norm rather than the exception in popular pornographic films. Physical aggression occurred in 88 per cent ($n = 268$) of scenes. Verbal aggression was relatively less common and present in 48 per cent ($n = 146$) of scenes. By far the most common verbally aggressive act was name calling (e.g. 'bitch', 'slut'). Spanking (36 per cent of physically aggressive acts), gagging (28 per cent) and open-hand slapping (15 per cent) were the most frequently observed physically aggressive acts.

Across all acts of aggression – both physical and verbal – 94 per cent were directed towards women. Men were the perpetrators of aggression more than twice as often as women, committing 70 per cent of the aggressive acts recorded. Even when women were perpetrators, their targets were frequently other women. When aggressed against, 95 per cent of targets responded with either expressions of pleasure (encouragement, sexual moans, and so forth) or neutrally (e.g. no change in facial expression or interruption of actions). While both men and women responded to aggression with behaviours indicating consent on most occasions, men were four times more likely to show displeasure when aggressed against compared with women. Specifically, 16 per cent of aggressive acts targeted towards men were portrayed as non-consensual, versus only 4 per cent of aggressive acts targeted towards women.

Considering the two sexual behaviours that were specifically identified as degrading towards women, we found both to be present in approximately half of coded scenes. Male character ejaculation almost always occurred outside of the female character's vagina, most frequently in her mouth. Forty-one per cent of scenes included ass-to-mouth.

In order to determine the effect of definitions of violence and aggression on content analysis results, I reanalysed data from Wosnitzer and Bridges (2007) to match the definitions offered by McKee (2005b) and others who focus on the role of consent in determining aggression. To do so, all verbal and physically aggressive acts *where the target demonstrated some sort of displeasure* or otherwise notably attempted to avoid harm were coded. Results indicated that 12.2 per cent of scenes were coded as non-consensually aggressive. Two things are important to note from this finding. First, the result remains in excess of the aggression found in McKee's study (although this may also be due to the differences in location: recall that in McKee's study, violent pornographic films cannot be distributed legally). Second, the resulting estimate of violence is substantially smaller than that contained in the parent study.

Data from the Wosnitzer and Bridges (2007) study were also reanalysed to provide comparable results to those obtained by Barron and Kimmel (2000). As can be seen in Table 2.1, using the same behavioural codes and categories, there was a notable increase in many aggressive behaviours in the decade between studies. While the more extreme forms of violent behaviours, such as punching, weapons use, or shoving, did not change, the later content analysis demonstrated an increase in more mild and playful sorts of aggressive acts, including pinching, hair pulling and biting, and spanking or slapping. In short, reanalyses confirm that mild forms of aggression are increasing in popular pornographic films, while at the same time these mild forms of aggression are being met with pleasure or, at minimum, in a neutral fashion.

What are the effects of showing sexual violence without negative consequences? Apart from maintaining arousal, it is possible that such depictions result in beliefs that people like to be slapped or insulted during sex; that double penetrations and gagging are erotic, and that treating a partner as a sexual object is arousing. Because pornography is a major source of sexual education for youth and so many consumers are adolescents and emerging adults, the potential problem with demonstrating a sexual world as one in which people insult one another, tug each other's hair, slap each other's bottoms or faces and gag each other with sexual organs is one that may result in greater intimacy difficulties for these youth. Even more troubling, youth may expect that these behaviours *should*

Table 2.1 Comparison of Barron and Kimmel (2000) with Wosnitzer and Bridges (2007) (%)

Category	Barron and Kimmel	Wosnitzer and Bridges
Pushing/shoving	3.8	6.4
Pinching	3.8	11.9
Hair pulling/biting	8.0	36.6
Threatening with a weapon	0.8	0.0
Slapping/spanking	9.3	77.0
Choking	0.8	26.2
Punching/kicking	0.8	0.6
Confining/bondage	2.7	7.6
Using a weapon	1.6	1.5
Torturing/mutilating	0.3	0.0
Attempting/completing murder	0.0	0.0

feel erotic and arousing and, if they hurt, may choose to ignore that or avoid saying something to a partner, for fear of being seen as prudish or inexperienced.

What should be done? Increasing media literacy is important (as Flood also argues, this volume). Questioning the reality of the world portrayed in pornography, and, specifically, of a world that is devoid of interpersonal intimacy and whose apparently realistic images are crafted to help make money for the producers, seems critical. Avoiding a discussion of the topic is nearly impossible: adolescents have greater access to sexual imagery than any adult can imagine. Even those not specifically seeking such imagery will come across pornography-like images in social networking sites, e-mail spam and cellular texts. A survey of a nationally representative sample of US youth revealed that 42 per cent of ten to seventeen-year-olds had been exposed to internet pornography in the past year; two-thirds of these youth reported being involuntarily exposed (Wolak *et al.* 2007).

Continued content-analytic efforts should be as detailed as possible in coding violent and degrading content, including potentially degrading sexual content. The ability to aggregate categories after study completion suggests that the greater the level of coding detail, the more researchers will be able to provide results that can be compared to prior studies. More universal or generally accepted definitions of violence, aggression and degradation will help track trends and changes over time, too. Regardless, researchers should be clear about how they constructed categories for analysis. For example, although many studies have coded for verbal aggression, their descriptions have been so sparse as to not permit me to compare our content analysis results with those of prior studies, leaving us with the question of whether verbal aggression is also increasing in popular pornographic videos. Finally, comparable sampling standards would permit continued generalizability and comparisons between studies and across time.

Notes

1 On porn studies' textual turn see Boyle (2006).
2 Unpublished research by Ana Bridges, Kaitlin Thulin, Tara McGahan and Corinne Anton. For further information contact Ana Bridges.
3 See also Flood (this volume), Centers for Disease Control and Prevention (2009) and Sabina *et al.* (2008).
4 However, see Whisnant (this volume) for a discussion of how the contemporary industry grooms male consumers to accept more extreme material.
5 Habituation is not limited to recreational consumers of pornography. Researchers also experience a reduction in strong emotions after repeated exposure, to the point where one noted that she became bored with pornographic images while performing a content analysis and that 'the only types of scenes that elicited my interest were those in which the sexual behavior was more atypical or extreme' (Cowan 2002: 362). See also Jensen and Boyle (Chapter 7 and Epilogue, this volume) for a discussion of the impacts of pornography research on researchers.
6 Unpublished research by Ana Bridges, David Estudiante, Tara McGahan and Arthur Andrews III. For further information contact Ana Bridges.

7 While notable efforts are directed to producing pornographic media that appeal to female consumers, these efforts have generally fallen flat (Dominus 2004).

8 A similar emphasis on men's genitalia remains in current popular pornography (McKee *et al.* 2008).

9 Despite the use of pictures, many of these categories did not achieve sufficient inter-rater reliability to permit analyses of content (McKee 2005b).

10 What is considered 'normal' in pornographic films is certainly open to debate. This definition of unnecessary roughness in an otherwise normal activity was provided by Barron and Kimmel (2000).

11 See Moore and Weissbein (this volume) for a fuller discussion of this point.

Chapter 3

'Now, that's pornography!'

Violence and domination in *Adult Video News*

Meagan Tyler

> As usual, the pornographer himself is more honest and astute about pornography than are the cultural experts engaged in defending it.
>
> (Kappeler 1986: 61).

This quotation from Susanne Kappeler highlights a disjunction between a certain kind of academic critique of pornography and what pornographers themselves have to say about their product. In this chapter I will demonstrate the enduring relevance of Kappeler's observation, using a content analysis of pornographers' own descriptions of their product as a way of understanding the marketability of violence in contemporary pornography.

There has been, and continues to be, significant debate within academic circles about the content of mainstream pornography. The content of pornography has been of interest to feminist scholars and activists for decades (e.g. Cornell 2000; Dines 1998; Dworkin 1981, 1994; Itzin 1992; MacKinnon 1993; Millet 1971; Russell 1993, 1998) but it has also more recently become a popular subject of analysis within film and cultural studies (Attwood 2002). The domination and dehumanization of women as well as the depiction, and/or actual inflicting of, violence against women remain particularly contentious within the field of pornography research.

While many feminists have argued that pornography often contains violence against women (e.g. MacKinnon 1993; Russell 1993, 1998) and that it may be inherently degrading (Dines *et al.* 1998), many pro-porn writers have suggested that these claims are, at best, exaggerated (Assiter and Carol 1993a; Kipnis 1996; Klein 2006; Loftus 2002; McElroy 1995; McKee 2005b; McKee *et al.* 2008; Rubin 1993; Strossen 1995). Some advocates have based criticisms on their own anecdotal experiences (Assiter and Carol 1993a), while others have undertaken content analyses (McKee 2005b; McKee *et al.* 2008), or questioned consumers about their interpretations (Loftus 2002). In these approaches, pornography is largely taken out of its context as an industry. There is little or no discussion about how those within the industry, producers in particular, perceive the issues of violence and domination. An analysis of *Adult Video News* (*AVN*), the leading US pornography industry magazine, also known as the US 'porn industry bible'

(McElroy 1995: 171), offers an opportunity for such discussion. As the following analysis will demonstrate, the content within *AVN* tends to directly oppose current academic analyses which characterize mainstream pornography as non-violent or less violent than in previous decades.

Violence and sadomasochism in mainstream pornography

A number of scholars have downplayed the prevalence and extremity of violence in mainstream pornography over the last two decades (Assiter and Carol 1993a; Kipnis 1996; Klein 2006; Loftus 2002; McElroy 1995; McKee 2005b; Rubin 1993; Strossen 1995). One of the most recent examples of this can be found in *The Porn Report* (McKee *et al.* 2008). McKee and colleagues claim that only 2 per cent of the scenes in mainstream video pornography available in Australia contain violence against women (McKee *et al.* 2008: 53). In *The Porn Report*, it is suggested that the content of current pornography has changed substantially from the 'bad old days' of the 1970s, when the feminist critique of pornography was at its peak, to a modern era of diverse pornography that liberates rather than oppresses women. Rather than a change in pornographic content, however, the central change seems to have been definitional, as Bridges (this volume) also demonstrates.

The opportunities for coding acts as violent in *The Porn Report* were severely limited by the use of Robert Baron's definition of violence as '[a]ny form of behaviour directed toward the goal of harm; or injuring another living being who is motivated to avoid such treatment' (quoted in McKee *et al.* 2008: 52). This definition, as McKee notes, rules out coding acts of bondage, discipline and sadomasochism (BDSM) as violent because they 'include no intent to harm and no motivation to avoid such treatment' (McKee 2005b: 282). In *The Porn Report*, this approach is justified as 'common sense' for, the authors argue, if someone enjoys a violent act then it is clearly no longer violent. In sum: 'If they [the actors] seemed to be enjoying it, it didn't count as violence' (McKee *et al.* 2008: 53).

Such reasoning, however, is severely flawed, particularly in regard to an analysis of pornography. On a conceptual level, it makes little sense to claim that BDSM practices contain no 'intent to harm'. While BDSM advocates may assert that the ultimate aim of their practices is to promote sexual arousal or orgasm, this does not rule out the immediate intent to harm. Even if the harm creates sexual arousal, and is claimed to be 'consensual', it does not suddenly become un-harm (Green 2001). On a more practical level, coding an act as violent *only* if the person *appears* motivated to avoid the violent act/harm, renders the violence in the vast majority of pornography invisible (see Bridges, this volume). McKee *et al.* (2008: 52) state that it seemed like common sense to not code as violent acts where participants were shown 'enjoying themselves' or if they 'requested the behaviour'. The fundamental problem here is that women in pornography are frequently shown enjoying their own abuse, humiliation and degradation

(Dworkin 1994; Jensen 2007a). Best-selling titles such as *Jenna Loves Pain* make this problem abundantly clear. As Andrea Dworkin (1994: 152) has argued, '[p]ornography says that women *want* to be hurt, forced and abused … that women say No but mean Yes – Yes to violence, Yes to pain' (emphasis original). It is therefore seriously misleading to avoid coding such acts as violent.

The Porn Report is not alone, however, in its claims about the non-violent nature of current mainstream pornography. In *Pornocopia*, journalist Laurence O'Toole asserts that there is no violence in mainstream US pornography and that 'one reason you don't find violence in porn is because it's illegal' (1998: 46). Even sociologist Simon Hardy, who is relatively sympathetic to feminist analyses of pornography, writes:

> In pursuit of this argument [that pornography objectifies women] anti-porn feminists have often overstated the degree of violence to be found. It is important to remember that, as a market commodity, pornography cannot afford to be too extreme or controversial.
>
> (Hardy 1998: 63)

Indeed, Hardy is correct in so much as pornography has to be broadly popular to make a significant profit. However, this is a fundamental misunderstanding of the current mainstream US-based pornography market. 'Extreme' pornography is often what appears on best-seller lists (Amis 2001; Anderson 2003; Hentai 2001; Whisnant, this volume). Moreover, while scholars like McKee and Hardy continue to deny, or at least downplay the existence of, violence, dehumanization and domination in mainstream pornography, those within the industry itself are open about the existence of these themes. As the following analysis of *AVN* will demonstrate, the extent to which the *AVN* editors acknowledge the use of violent themes, and indeed often highlight them as a particularly marketable aspect of pornography, suggests that those within the industry assume that violent pornography is certainly something that consumers will buy.

Consumption and production

Another trend in much current academic work on pornography is a focus on the consumption and potential interpretations of pornography by consumers (Attwood 2002). There are a number of studies by academics and journalists, for example, which have considered the content and consumption of various (often obscure) pornographies (e.g. Lehman 2006b; Williams 2004b) and have aimed to interrogate what consumers say about their own pornography use (Kingi *et al.* 2004; McKee 2005a; McKee *et al.* 2008; Paul 2005). Indeed, the emphasis on consumption in pornography research is not only limited to the recent cultural studies turn. There has been a significant concentration of work on the consumption of pornography and the role of consumers in older approaches, both those which have sought to defend pornography and those which have sought to critique it. This is perhaps most obvious in the well publicized laboratory-style experiments which attempted to measure men's reactions to pornography and their subsequent inclination to endorse violence against women (e.g. Malamuth and Ceniti 1986; Malamuth and Donnerstein 1984). The centrality of consumption in all these approaches is problematic not only because it frequently divorces interpretations of pornography from their social context but also because an almost exclusive focus on consumption overlooks the importance of the production process and the role of the pornography industry.

This is not to say that there is no value in analysing pornography consumption. A number of feminists have sought to understand the harm that may result from the consumption of pornography and its effects on societal attitudes towards women (e.g. Itzin 1992; MacKinnon and Dworkin 1997; MacKinnon 1993; Russell, 1993, 1998) but this focus has often come at the cost of analysing the production side of pornography. Ignoring production processes and focusing only on potential interpretations serves to separate pornography from its context. As Gail Dines and Simon Hardy have separately argued, the persistent focus on consumer interpretation has resulted in much work presenting pornography as though it is created in a social and political vacuum (Dines 1998), almost 'by accident' (Hardy 1998).

Hardy argues that in order to understand the 'text' of pornography, the intentions of the producer must be taken into account: 'whatever the function of pornography actually is, we must assume that it is performed by design and not by accident, so that we are concerned here with the purposes and intentions of the producer' (Hardy 1998: 47). Dines argues for the importance of placing pornography within the context of the pornography industry itself:

> Pornography is often mistakenly referred to as 'fantasy', as if the images just appeared from nowhere and are produced in the private head of the consumer. Missing from this position is an analysis of the actual workings of the industry located in the concrete world of capitalism. Because methods of financing will ultimately affect the nature of the content of pornography, it is a mistake to assume that analysis of the text can take place divorced from analysis of the economic realities of pornography production.
>
> (Dines 1998: 62)

As these critiques stress, there is significant need for research on pornography production, both understanding the intentions of producers and contextualizing pornography as a product produced by a multi-billion-dollar industry. This chapter will therefore focus on the content of recently produced, commercially available video pornography and the ways in which this pornography is understood *within the pornography industry*, in particular, the way in which content is represented by producers and marketed to distributors through *AVN*. To date, these areas have received scant attention, and it is hoped that further research into such aspects of the industry will provide a more thorough understanding of pornography which is grounded in the social and economic contexts in which it is actually produced.

Analysing content in *AVN*

One way of putting the economic and social context of production back into pornography research is to consider pornography from within the context of the industry itself (Jensen 2007a). To this end, a content analysis of AVN was undertaken in 2006, with a particular focus on the 'Editor's Choice' reviews from all 2005 editions of *AVN*. An interpretive content analysis was chosen in order to allow for flexibility and also to avoid the problems of decontexualization often associated with more traditional quantitative content analyses involving pornography.[1]

AVN is the US pornography industry's main trade publication. While the print version is released monthly and is generally several hundred pages in length, my own data collection was conducted via the now defunct *AVN* archives, which housed only original content (that is, articles and reviews with no advertising).[2] *AVN* covers a range of issues which are of concern to those within the pornography industry including legal threats to production and latest trends as well as interviews with performers, directors and producers. It is marketed predominantly to pornography distributors and vendors and is shipped, at request, free for a year to any video store in the US. The Editor's Choice section is particularly important, as each month's reviews of the latest pornography releases carry significant weight within the industry. These are generally reviews of mainstream (i.e. not categorized by *AVN* as fetish, fringe or sadomasochism) titles that the editors believe will be easily marketable and highly profitable for production companies and vendors. At the end of most Editor's Choice reviews there is a section which includes marketing and retailing advice to vendors and in some there is also the suggestion of nominations for one or more *AVN* awards.[3] The Editor's Choice reviews offer useful insights into the production side of the pornography industry, particularly with regard to the rise of extreme and violent pornography.

In order to consider the extent to which violence was mentioned in the Editor's Choice section, one year's worth of reviews was singled out for content analysis. As the *AVN* archives were removed from public access in mid-2006 the last remaining complete calendar year of reviews was chosen, in total, amounting to 103 reviews over twelve issues (January–December 2005). The text from each review was then searched electronically for key words which could be defined as describing violent acts. The definition of violent acts was drawn from Yang and Linz:

> Violence was defined as occurring whenever a person intentionally imposes or attempts to impose hurt, abuse, or force upon another person. Such behaviour might include slapping, hitting, spanking, pushing, pulling hair or

clothes, striking with fist or kicking, severe beating or fighting, using a weapon or threatening with one, confinement, bondage, kidnapping, torture, dismemberment, mutilation, attempted or actual suicide, and attempted or actual murder.

(Yang and Linz 1990: 33)[4]

The coding of specific terms for violent acts was drawn from both Yang and Linz (1990) and Barron and Kimmel (2000); acts of sadomasochism were coded as violent for reasons explained previously. Rather than simply counting the terms as they appeared in an electronic search, each term was analysed in context before it was included as describing a violent act in order to avoid incorrect coding.[5] The reviews were also read in their entirety to ensure that violent acts which were missed due to slight differences in wording or spelling errors could be included.

It is important to note that this analysis is not intended to support the idea that there is a clearly discernible difference between violent and non-violent pornography. Rather, the aim of this research was to examine the ways in which violent content is discussed and understood within the pornography industry. The focus was not simply on 'specialist' genres but instead on those that the industry itself recognizes to be its most mainstream and profitable. The fact that descriptions of violent acts do appear frequently in *AVN* is important information in an environment where mainstream, violent pornography is often considered to be almost non-existent.

AVN and the rise of extreme pornography

There have been no comprehensive academic studies of *AVN* to date, but the publication is sometimes briefly mentioned in works dealing with pornography (e.g. Dines *et al.* 1998: 60; Jensen 2007a: 56; McElroy 1995: 171; Ross 2007: 39). There is also a passing reference to an informal analysis of *AVN* in *The Porn Report*:

> During our three years of formal, funded research, we subscribed to *Adult Video News* (*AVN*), the US trade journal for the porn industry. In her survey of all three years' worth of *AVN*s Kath was struck by the images and language used to market porn to US buyers. Although an actual sexual fetish for humiliation is rare, even in the BDSM scene, a substantial amount of porn was marketed as if audiences and producers alike believe that sex is inherently degrading and that female porn performers should be humiliated for being sexual.
>
> (McKee *et al.* 2008: 171)

As will be discussed further on, the language used to market pornography in *AVN* is indeed striking. It is rather a leap of logic, however, to claim, as McKee *et al.* do, that the descriptions found in *AVN* emanate only from the assumption that women should be humiliated for being sexual. They dismiss the possibility that the sexual humiliation of women is something which may hold erotic value for male pornography consumers even when, as they point out, distributors regularly emphasize the humiliation of women as a useful selling feature. To suggest that this humiliation stems only from women being 'sexual' ignores the extreme and violent nature of much of the mainstream pornography discussed in *AVN*.

Unlike various academic defences of mainstream pornography discussed above, within the pornography industry itself, there is open acknowledgement that the acts required are becoming more extreme and are increasingly pushing the physical and emotional limits of the women who perform them (Anderson 2003; Ehrlich 2002; Ramone and Kernes 2003). In August 2002, for example, *AVN* ran a cover story on the '25 events that shaped the first 25 years of video porn', one of which was the 'Mid-1990s – Porn turns extra hard':

> It wasn't until the mid-to-late '90s that porn took a turn for the extreme ... There was the requisite 'spit and gape' maneuver, where a guy would stretch his partner's asshole as wide as it would go, and then hock up a good-sized loog into it. Anal and d.p. became a requirement; soon it became the 'airtight' trick (a cock in every hole), the ultimate-in-homoerotic-denial position (double anal), mega-gangbangs, choke-fucking, peeing, bukkake ... even vomit for a brief unsavory period. We can only wonder what'll hit next.
>
> (Ehrlich 2002)

The trend continued, and 'harder' pornography became the norm. In 2003, *AVN* ran a cover story entitled 'Harder, faster: can porn get any nastier?' The author, *AVN* editor Acme Anderson, noted:

> There's no question there's been a turn for the harder in the XXX in recent years. In the mid-1990s, double penetration seemed to be the bar for nasty. Then came the massive gangbangs, such as the Houston 620 in 1999, bukkake vids (also 1999) and today ... throat fucking, ass to mouth, double-vaginal and double-anal penetration is [*sic*] not uncommon.
>
> (Anderson 2003)

The variety of acts described in these *AVN* excerpts likely require some further explanation. Double penetration, or 'DP', as it is commonly labelled in the industry, refers to a woman being anally and vaginally penetrated simultaneously. Bukkake refers to the practice of multiple men (sometimes numbering in excess of 100) ejaculating on a woman's face, and has been described by forensic psychologist and hate crimes expert Karen Franklin as 'symbolic group rape' (2004: 29). Acts are classified as 'ass to mouth', or 'ATM' in porn industry language, when 'a man removes his penis from a woman's anus and, without cleaning it, places it in her mouth, or the mouth of another woman'

(Jensen 2007a: 59). ATM is recognised even within the industry as unhygienic and potentially dangerous (Jensen 2007a). Lastly, the Houston 620, to which Anderson refers, was the filming of a 'porn star' – known as Houston – being penetrated vaginally and anally in excess of 600 times in one day by hundreds of different men. Some days later she described the pain of the process, mentioning having to ice her swollen genitals because it felt as though she was 'on fire': 'I literally started crying and I needed off. I mean, I *hurt*. And I was exhausted' (Bisch 1999, emphasis original).

As Robert Jensen (2007a) explains, these new and extreme sex acts, which are rapidly defining current pornography, are at the very least taking a physical toll on women's bodies. There is also some concern being expressed within the industry about the physical consequences of more extreme acts (e.g. Anderson 2003; Ramone and Kernes 2003). Pornography director and performer Francesca Lé, speaking in 2003, states, 'I think it [porn] has gone to its limit legally and maybe physically. I don't know how much more a person can take' (Anderson 2003). Also in 2003, *AVN* printed a round-table discussion between eight high-profile pornography directors which appeared to confirm both the trend toward extreme pornography and the concern within the industry about its limits. One serious issue of contention between the eight directors was whether or not the push for more extreme pornography, particularly violent pornography, was a positive or negative shift. A significant point of agreement, however, was that pornography the directors themselves labelled as 'sexually violent' and 'abusive' is becoming both more common and more popular with consumers (Ramone and Kernes 2003).

Editor's Choice reviews and the eroticizing of violence against women

The content of the Editor's Choice reviews in *AVN* also suggests that extreme and violent pornography is permeating the industry and becoming increasingly mainstream. In 2005, *AVN* printed 103 reviews of new release pornography titles. The full text of ninety-eight of these reviews was still available on line through the *AVN* archives during the data collection process in 2006. The majority of pornography which was selected for the 2005 Editor's Choice reviews was labelled by *AVN* as either wall-to-wall (thirty-one of ninety-eight) or gonzo pornography (twenty-eight of ninety-eight). In many commentaries these two types of pornography are collapsed into one, but *AVN* offers a minor distinction: wall-to-wall videos are '[a]ll sex productions without plot structures. A series of sex scenes that may or may not include a connecting device' (quoted in Jensen 2007a: 56). Gonzo is slightly different and is defined as '[p]orno *verité* or reality-based porn, in which performers acknowledge the presence of the camera, frequently addressing viewers directly through it' (*ibid.*).

It is predominantly though the gonzo style that hard-core pornography and the sex acts within it have become more extreme. Gonzo pornography is now one of the most common forms of pornography available on video and DVD. This trend reflects the overall shift in the industry away from film and plot-based productions to the 'reality' genres, which tend to return greater profits (lower production costs) and trial more extreme sex acts (Amis 2001; Jensen 2007a). Both the gonzo and wall-to-wall genres of pornography are now considered thoroughly mainstream. In contrast to the fifty-eight reviews of gonzo and wall-to-wall titles, only seven of the ninety-eight Editor's Choice reviews were of 'specialty' titles, the category which contains fetish and fringe productions.

The Editor's Choice section of *AVN* contains reviews of latest-release pornography which is deemed by the editors to be 'good porn'. As the following excerpts show, what tends to define 'good porn' for the editors is commercial potential for vendors and the potential sexual arousal of consumers. The reviews are primarily focused on describing scenes from each new release with specific details regarding the sex acts found to be the most arousing by the reviewer. There is also marketing advice provided at the end of each review. This generally suggests how many copies a vendor should purchase, what location within a store a vendor should stock a particular title and what type of consumer it is likely to appeal to. The consumer is almost always assumed to be male and the reviewers make numerous references to 'solo strokers'.

There are several occasions, however, when a title is singled out as being a good 'couples' release. These titles are considered softer and in some cases almost boring. Jarred Rutter describes *The Secrets of the Kama Sutra*, for example, as 'wall to wallpaper' but, despite this, recommends it to vendors as likely to sell well amongst 'beginners, couples, women' (Rutter 2005a). These are generally the only titles lauded for high production values and, very occasionally, story lines. Such reviews are almost as rare in *AVN* as reviews of 'speciality' releases. Only nine of the ninety-eight reviews are listed as being potentially suitable for couples.

Overall, within the ninety-eight available *AVN* Editor's Choice reviews, covering everything from fetish to couples releases, there are forty-four clear descriptions of violent acts such as slapping, hitting or choking (see Table 3.1). These descriptions occur in twenty-four separate reviews. This equates to approximately a quarter of all the 2005 reviews containing descriptions of at least one violent act, a figure much more in line with the findings of content analyses from Barron and Kimmel (2000), Monk-Turner and Purcell (1999) and Yang and Linz (1990) than with McKee (2005b). Indeed, such a high figure suggests that, within the industry, violence in pornography is understood as systemic rather than isolated.

In some of the Editor's Choice reviews reference is made to a violent act simply in passing. In the January 2005 review of *Ass Quake*, for example, there is passing mention of 'spitting and tit and face slapping' (Rutter 2005b) as though they hold no specific importance. Similarly in the March review of *The Story of J* there is a brief reference to 'gentle knife play' (Anderson 2005), with no further comment. At other times, however, the violent or extreme nature of the sex is highlighted. In *Tales from the Crack*, for example, editor Mike Ramone notes that the wall-to-wall release is 'rougher and harder than the vast majority of the

Table 3.1 Violent and sexually violent acts in *AVN* reviews

Categories of violent acts[a]	No. of descriptions in AVN reviews
Verbal aggression	3
Slapping	9
Hitting	1
Spanking	2
Pushing/Shoving	0
Pulling hair or clothes	0
Biting	0
Pinching	0
Choking	3
Striking with a fist/Closed-fist punch	1
Kicking	0
Severe beating or fighting	5
Using a weapon	1
Threatening with a weapon	0
Confinement	2
Bondage	7
Kidnapping	2
Torture	0
Dismemberment	0
Mutilation	1
Attempted or actual murder	0
Being rough in other ways	2
Mud wrestling	0
Sadomasochism	5

Note: [a]Adapted from Yang and Linz (1990) and Barron and Kimmel (2000).

competition', and recommends that vendors 'stock deep', as 'there's no way this can't be a monster mover' (Ramone 2005c). Also in January 2005, the gonzo production *Spent* was reviewed as a 'solid, oh-so-satisfying sex release', including a scene where 'Asian goddess Katsumi (wearing a hot little kimono ensemble) is bent like a lithe little fuck doll over her friend's knee. Her teeny tiny ass gets smacked crimson with his belt' (Katz 2005). Racism and misogyny intertwine here, and as is frequently the case in pornography, an Asian woman is fetishized as passive and compliant (Dines *et al.* 1998; Jensen 2007a).

What is most striking, however, is that extreme, violent or degrading acts are often singled out by the *AVN* editors specifically for their potential to sexually arouse. The suggestion is repeatedly made that the more extreme the sex acts the better the pornography. In the May review of *Neo-pornographia*, for example, Mark Kernes writes:

> Finally, Julie Night gets anal-ized [*sic*] by dildos, buttplugs and three guys, with more d.p. and double anal – and in the finale, Nicki spoons cum from Julie's ass to her mouth! Now, that's pornography!
>
> (Kernes 2005)

Here, the reviewer could not be more explicit in his claim that, at its best (i.e. most profitable), contemporary pornography is physically damaging for female performers and built on their degradation. Similarly, in the November issue, Peter Warren deemed *Squealer* 'a masterpiece', highlighting that it was 'unrelentingly filthy, full of dirt-streaked bodies, d.p.s [*sic*], double anal, slapping, tying, gagging, spitting, asphyxiation, you name it' (Warren 2005). These acts of violence are not considered by the editors to be barriers to the enjoyment of consuming pornography but rather an integral part of it. As Kernes appreciatively notes, 'Now, that's pornography!'

Of the twenty-four reviews which mention violent acts, the endorsement of such acts as sexually arousing is most obvious in the December review of *Service Animals 21*. *Service Animals 21* is a gonzo production directed by Joey Silvera, who also appears on camera in a number of scenes. In the review, *AVN* editor Jared Rutter writes glowingly of Silvera's work:

> Silvera builds his intros patiently, and they burst aflame with often explosive eroticism. Here, three (at least) sequences are classic. In the first scene, Sandra Romain locks Karina Kay in a closet in order to 'break her down'. It's an experiment in sexual control and perseverance. Sandra and two guys in leather work the younger girl over with lotsa [*sic*] choking, but it's Sandra who does the d.p. and double anal.
>
> (Rutter 2005c)

In one of the most obvious endorsements of violence against women in the reviews, a scene with lots of choking is described here not only as classic but containing 'explosive eroticism'. In one of the other 'classic' scenes Rutter describes, it is the eroticizing of child sexual abuse which is cause for heightened sexual arousal:

> Kara, just 18, from Ohio, is a blue-eyed teen angel who seems to have been born with a fully developed talent for tease. Joey feeds her ice-cream and fondles her small breasts. Trent Tesoro fucks her, but she returns the next day to blow Silvera, old enough to be her grandfather. The scene teeters on the cusp of the forbidden but doesn't quite fall. Guaranteed stroke fodder.
>
> (Rutter 2005c)

Presumably Rutter describes this scene as almost 'forbidden' in reference to the representation of either paedophilia or incest ('old enough to be her grandfather') eroticizing both hierarchy and abuse. Instead of being a problem, Rutter suggests, this creates greater arousal ('guaranteed stroke fodder'). The review ends with the following retail advice: 'This super-hot series is not a hard sell.' Rutter's advice is supported by the *AVN* most-rented and best-seller lists, in which the *Service Animals* titles frequently appear (Ramone 2005a, 2005b).

As with *Service Animals 21*, many of the *AVN* reviews include marketing notes or retail advice about the commercial value of a particular title. Of the ninety-eight reviews considered here, only one contained retailing advice which suggested the title would not have wide consumer appeal. The specialty production *Go Fuck Yerself 3* was given the cautious marketing tag 'Stock carefully' and offers some insight into what is deemed to be pushing the boundaries of legal US-made pornography. Marc Star's review of *Go Fuck Yerself 3* begins with an overview:

> Take equal parts female masturbation and equal parts angry biker beatdown [*sic*] and the result is the next generation of Extreme originality. Five girls willingly subject themselves to the bald, tattooed Coffee Ron's merciless beatings – while masturbating. These aren't titillating floggings. When Ron whacks these girls, they jump.
>
> (Star 2005)

Star also notes that the women who are beaten cry, 'squirm, jump and howl in pain'. The box cover shows a woman strung up as a human punching bag and 'Coffee Ron' posed next to her wearing boxing gloves. This appears to be an example of how extreme the violence has become in pornography at the margins of the legal industry. While the advice to retailers may be 'Stock carefully', this is not illegal or underground pornography, but rather legal pornography created by a production company which, in 2003, was said to have turned a profit of almost US$50 million (Huffstutter 2003). Given the enthusiastic embrace of other forms of violence against women in the reviews discussed above, it seems likely that it is the women's *response* rather than the specific acts depicted which leads to the caution to retailers. Had the women seemed to enjoy the abuse, it is likely it would have been an easier sell (Bridges, this volume).

There are also 'non-violent' instances where women's submission, degradation or the extremity of a sex act is emphasized by the reviewers as being arousing. These are examples that did not come up in the coded word search as violent, but force is still a theme. Even in seemingly routine sex acts women are described as being 'savagely pounded' (Ramone 2005d) and 'brutally subjugated' (Rutter 2005d). In contrast, at times it is the extremity or degradation of an unusual act that is singled out as a title's main value. The review of gonzo release *Mouth 2 Mouth*, for example, encourages vendors to 'stock deep' and highlights 'vile' sex acts as the title's attraction. The review begins, 'Is there a viler visual act in all of jizzdom than long range, high dive pop-swapping? Doubtful. Which is why *Mouth 2 Mouth* is such satisfyingly base wank fodder' (Ramone 2005e, emphasis mine). Indeed, the link here is clear, it is the fact that the reviewer finds the sex to be 'vile' that makes it sexually arousing.

An analysis based on accounts from *AVN* therefore suggests that there is acknowledgement within the industry that the current content and practices of mainstream pornography involve significant incidence of violence against women. Indeed, the content of *AVN* suggests that commercial pornography is becoming more violent and more extreme and this seriously undermines many current academic approaches to pornography which have sought to show its potential for sexually liberating women. Furthermore, it is often pornography which contains explicit violence against women which is promoted by the *AVN* editors as likely to create greater sexual arousal, thereby heightening appeal to male consumers and increasing vendor profits. Given the significant disparity between intra-industry dialogue about, and academic characterizations of, the current content of mainstream pornography, it would seem that the production side of the pornography industry will continue to be fertile ground for research in years to come. This is especially relevant in regard to feminist debates, as the commentary from the *AVN* editors, rather ironically, tends to lend support to the traditionally radical feminist claims that mainstream pornography is violent, male-dominant and dehumanizing to women.

Notes

1 For a discussion of the problems of contextualization in quantitative content analyses see Dines *et al.* (1998) and Bridges (this volume).
2 A digital version identical to the print copy is also now available on line but the
  old archives on which my research was based contained all issues between February
  1998 to May 2006. These were available at: <http://www.adultvideonews.com/
  archives/index.html> but are no longer on line.
3 The annual *AVN* awards are the pornography industry's supposed equivalent to
  Hollywood's Oscars. Production companies and individual performers vie for the
  awards as a way of increasing sales. *AVN* awards for particular titles are often used
  as marketing tools by distributors, and winning an individual award affords a porn
  performer a better chance of negotiating a higher pay rate in future films (Ross
  2007: 16). As yet another indicator of how mainstream pornography has become,
  it is worth noting that the *AVN* Awards are shown on the non-specialist cable
  television channel Showtime in the US.
4 Examples of *sexually violent* behaviour were similar: 'The violent component
  might include slapping, hitting, spanking, pulling hair, being rough in other ways,
  sexual harassment, bondage and confinement, coercion with weapons, mud wrestling, sadomasochism, and sexual mutilation and murder immediately preceding,
  during, or after sex' (Yang and Linz 1990: 33). Yang and Linz did not use a lack
  of visible consent as a requirement for coding acts as violent.
5 For example, there are several occasions where the editors mention a title 'pushing
  the limits' or 'kicking off' – the terms 'pushing' and 'kicking' are used but these
  are clearly not descriptions of violent acts occurring in the pornography and
  therefore were excluded from the count.

Chapter 4

Repetition and hyperbole

The gendered choreographies of heteroporn

Susanna Paasonen

Pornography is generic and predictable even in comparison with other popular genres. Familiar (stock) characters, phrases, scenarios, acts, expressions, shots and framings are repeated from one set of images or videos to another, from commercial to amateur productions and numerous things in between. All this tends to involve a low degree of surprise. To the degree that repetition, predictability and hyperbole can indeed be considered as generic features of pornography, their role begs for closer consideration that goes beyond stating the obvious – namely that such characteristics do exist.

This chapter draws on a content analysis of a sample of 366 porn spam e-mail messages in an attempt to chart some of the key generic features of commercial heteroporn and its gendered underpinnings, as made accessible through this particular set of material. The chapter both investigates the specific modality of pornography and argues for the need to resist literal readings of its meaning. In the first part, I address the sample of porn spam e-mail in order to map out some of the main generic features and dynamics of commercial pornography. The second part takes a broader look at online pornography and the ways in which the generic features and dynamics of porn (as mapped out in the first part) are played out in the case of viral videos displaying extreme porn, as well as what kinds of challenges are involved in making sense of such videos. All in all, the chapter suggests that feminist analyses should push beyond readings of pornography that are either literal (as in reading relations of control displayed in pornography as exemplary of social power relations, one-to-one) or symbolic (as in interpreting pornography as symptomatic of an ideology).

Pornography relies on clear divisions based on identity categories such as age, class, gender, ethnicity and 'race', and these categories are often tied to (explicit, exaggerated) hierarchies and relations of control. Rather than starting with a conflation of the notion of control with that of power, the chapter investigates the meanings of reiteration and recognizability within and for pornography. This analysis paves way to a discussion of the changing roles of pornography in the media landscape, namely its mainstreaming (Attwood 2009a). Little doubt exists as to the development of digital media technologies – cameras and image manipulation software, networked communications and online platforms of all kinds – having, together with changes in media regulation and media economy, facilitated transformations in the cultural position, and perhaps even the status, of both soft-core and hard-core pornographies (see Paasonen *et al.* 2007a). In terms of such mainstreaming, it is important to enquire as to which *kinds of* pornographic texts or examples can gain broader fame or circulation across the media, as well as how the discussions concerning them work to frame pornography and its social implications. All in all, this chapter involves an attempt to articulate spaces for feminist critique sensitive to contexts and differences within the genre, its producers, consumers and platforms of distribution.

Mapping the pornographic

My studies of online pornography began in 2002, when I began archiving unsolicited porn spam e-mail sent to my university account. This provided me with a solution to one of the fundamental challenges involved in studies of pornography, namely sampling. It is, after all, not too uncommon that people choose particular kinds of examples for study in order to justify specific premises concerning the meanings, forms or implications of things pornographic. At the same time, the internet facilitates access to a seemingly endless range of pornographic sub-genres, niches and aesthetics that facilitate drastically different analytical investigations into, and interpretations of, the genre and its meanings.

Rather than seeking out any particular kinds of porn for analysis, my rather pragmatic solution was to focus on the porn spam adverts sent to my in-box via massive spam e-mail address databases. Whilst this was not going to be a sample representative of the range and diversity of online pornography (to the degree that such sampling would be possible in the first place), it did present me with one view into everyday, unsolicited encounters with online pornography. The spam adverts are exemplary of rather mainstream commercial pornography, yet the sample also involves examples that are more marginal in nature, such as fetishism, urophilia and bestiality. As spam the sample may be bulky, yet it also illustrates something of the contingency of the 'mainstream' and the ways in which niche pornographies tend to become appropriated into its palette of choice.

For seventeen months in 2002–04 I archived well over 1,000 messages. After deleting messages with faulty image files and discarding duplicates, I was left with 366 messages making use of HTML (hypertext markup language) that makes it possible to adjust the background colour, layout and text type, so that messages resemble the graphic interfaces of the worldwide web. In fact, the spam adverts tend to be virtually identical in content to the 'free tour' sections of the sites they promote. I have since explored the material using a range of methods varying from content analysis to close reading, as well as studies of representation and affect (e.g. Paasonen 2006, 2007a, b, 2010).

The type of analysis addressed in this chapter is mainly the initial one that I carried out, namely content analysis. While applying this strategy of reading in

2004, I coded the sample according to its visual and textual elements, as well as the forms of address involved in the e-mails themselves. The coding involved sub-genre, performers (i.e. gender, ethnicity, approximate age, mode of dress or degree of undress, hair style), acts performed, terminology used (for women, men, genitalia, sexual acts or the action offered in general), as well as the ways in which the sender and the recipient of the message were marked (i.e. how the sender was identified, whether the greetings or invitations involved were of a general or personal nature, how gender was marked, etc.). Within the different categories, further differences emerged: penetrative sex, for example, could be vaginal, anal, double, involving objects, fingering, fisting or masturbation, while money shots (ejaculations) could be directed at a female partner's face, mouth, breasts or elsewhere on the body.

The most popular act depicted in the messages is oral sex, appearing in 59 per cent of the spam adverts (217 out of 366). In contrast, vaginal intercourse is featured in 39 per cent, money shots in 22 per cent and anal sex in 16 per cent of the messages. In terms of all the acts depicted in the messages, oral sex was featured 502 times, encompassing 29 per cent of all the sexual acts. Penetrative vaginal sex (14 per cent) is the second most common act depicted in the messages, followed by money shots (12 per cent), girl-on-girl acts (9 per cent), variations of foreplay (8 per cent), group sex (8 per cent) and anal sex (7 per cent). After these come female masturbation (3 per cent), vaginal insertion with objects (3 per cent) and fetishes (3 per cent). Bestiality, bondage, fingering and fisting all amount to 1 per cent whereas double penetration encompasses less than 1 per cent of all sexual acts depicted.

Within the oral sex category, the overwhelming majority of the acts depicted (78 per cent) involve a female performer giving oral sex to a male partner. In 11 per cent both parties are female, in 6 per cent the active partner is male, in 2 per cent women are performing with animals, 1 per cent depict bisexual acts with several male performers and 2 per cent involve transgender acts in various combinations. As such, oral sex performed by a female on a male is by far the most widely repeated sexual act. These oral sex depictions are often complemented by money shots (207 instances in total), of which the majority are targeted at a female face (93), mouth (73) and breasts (21). According to Linda Williams's (1989: 93–5) now classic study of film pornography, money shots were established in the 1970s as compulsory and highly visible signs of sexual climax that both verify male sexual pleasure and culminate the sexual act. Ejaculation is present in my material also as evidence of female orgasm: female ejaculations are depicted in 6 per cent of all money shots.

Of all performers featured in the messages, 72 per cent are female: slim (98 per cent of all female performers), young (92 per cent), white (66 per cent) and with long (84 per cent) and blonde (48 per cent) hair. Of the male figures, 65 per cent are present only as penises while the rest of the male body has been framed out. This convention follows the general tendency of heterosexual pornography to focus on female bodies (face included) as its central spectacle while considerably less attention is paid to male ones. Consequently, women are also described with a wider range of adjectives and nouns than men. Most popular terms are girl (31 per cent of all terms used for describing female performers), slut (22 per cent), babe (10 per cent) and lesbian (7 per cent); others include woman, chick, bitch, whore, virgin, lady, honey and dame. Popular adjectives to describe female performers include hot (33 per cent of female performers), teen (22 per cent), sexy (9 per cent), young (9 per cent), nasty (4 per cent), sweet (3 per cent) and innocent (3 per cent), as well as hungry, starved, dirty, nympho and naughty. Women are described with nouns in 410 accounts, whereas there are only 49 descriptions of men. Men are also depicted with a considerably more narrow and homosocial terminology as guys (64 per cent of male performers), men (10 per cent), studs (8 per cent), mates (6 per cent), buddies (4 per cent), dudes (4 per cent) and brothers (2 per cent). As a rule, they are not defined with adjectives other than 'horny' except for when describing their penises. The homosocial tone is also echoed in the forms of address: in all instances where the implied recipient of the message is gendered, s/he is gendered male.

Hard and soft, dominant and submissive, active and passive are familiar binary opposites used to schematize masculinity and femininity. Such opposites are in active use in e-mail porn spam and its displays of heterosex as choreography made of clear-cut differences. This is perhaps most evident in my material in depictions of genitalia, on both a visual and a textual level. The most popular terms for male genitalia include big (45 per cent of all adjectives used for describing male genitalia), monster (17 per cent), huge (12 per cent), over 12 in. (9 per cent), fat or thick (8 per cent), massive (4 per cent), as well as gigantic, long, hard, enormous, abnormal, colossal, amazing and large. These are juxtaposed with diminutive terminology for female genitalia as tight (73 per cent of all descriptions of female genitalia), tiny (11 per cent), little (8 per cent) and small (8 per cent). Meanwhile, female breasts are big (96 per cent of all descriptions of breasts) or huge (4 per cent). Such hyperbolic juxtaposition leads to a specific vocabulary used for penetrative sex acts: in addition to the general terminology of fucking (43 per cent), banging (12 per cent), sucking (11 per cent) or blowing (8 per cent), these are a myriad of terms describing the interfacing of the colossal and the miniscule, such as stretch, stuff, nail, punish, give hard, pound, gag, torture, screw, rip, split open, exploit, choke, dilate, ream, bash, break, hump, devour, ravage, violate, squeeze and slam.

Heterosexual structuralism

Several issues surface from this vocabulary. It reads as a textbook example of morphology of the body that displays 'the opposite sexes' as mutually opposing yet interconnected by heterosexual desire (Butler 1993: 90–1). Faithful to the logic of such 'heterosexual structuralism', pornography zooms in on body parts marked as primary signifiers of gender difference, such as genitalia, breasts, buttocks, long hair or red-painted lips. As Annette Kuhn (1994: 34–7) has pointed out, in pornography gender differences are defined as primarily sexual, and they culminate in the presentation of genitalia. At the same time, however, the terminology of porn spam e-mail stretches the very morphology to its extremes. Rather than suggesting that the two genders complement each other all the way to their interconnecting genitalia (Richardson 1996: 7), their genital interactions are framed as markedly fractious, laborious and potentially violent – and especially so to the female partners in question. It is indeed rather difficult to miss the ways in which the bodies 'split open', 'tortured' or 'ravaged' are overwhelmingly marked as female. At the same time, the markers of gender difference are heightened and exaggerated to the degree that heterosexual coitus becomes a near impossible play of colossal penises and the tiniest of vaginas. The spam material offers abundant examples of a compulsive and hyperbolic reiteration of gender categories that, following a deconstructive strategy of reading, seem to suggest their own artificiality whilst, at the same time, pointing to the marketability of sex as something that pushes the boundaries of female embodiment (also Tyler, this volume). In hard-core, embodied differences are displayed as unequivocal and overtly pronounced. Content analysis of this material helps to make evident something of its modality, namely the hyperbolic, excessive and even spectacular display of gender as a binary structure of embodiments, desires, characteristics and positions.

To the degree that the messages feature the highlights of the sites advertised, such hyperbole is connected with titillation and potential arousal – the more elaborate the marks of gender, the more drastic the embodied differences displayed and the more blunt the language (as with 'starving nymphos' or 'cumguzzling sluts') the more hard-core the representation appears to be. It is also noteworthy, and striking, that the male and female performers are given dissimilar characters and diverging positions, particularly on the level of the language used: women may be sluts and bitches while the men are simply guys. With the important exception of oral sex, female partners are marked as the ones whose bodies various things are done to. This not only suggests but emphasizes the primacy of heterosexual male initiative, desire and domination in such scenarios. Browsing through video listings on sites such as RedTube makes the same convention evident: for example, in group sex videos with two women and one man, the man is being 'made happy' whereas in videos with two men and one woman, the woman is being 'used' or is 'getting it'.

The aim of my analysis is not to 'reveal' the heterosexual structuralism involved in all of this (cf. Sedgwick 2003: 130–5), since it hardly necessitates much revealing after three decades of feminist analyses of pornography. Rather, my interests lie in the characteristics of pornography as a popular genre: its overall modality and the modes of interpretation connected to it. Embodied differences are not only made explicit but are also excessive in the spam material: the size of genitalia and the intensities of arousal, desire and pleasure know no bounds; the women are hot and starving, the men perpetually horny. In addition, identity categories such as class, ethnicity, nationality or 'race' are continually and endlessly accentuated and dramatized, as are the acts of transgressing their boundaries ('interracial porn' remaining the most elaborate of sub-genres in this respect). Such differences are often tied to relations of power and control in which social categories and hierarchies become sexualized. Women may be marked as working-class and as lacking in respectability by default (cf. Skeggs 1997) whereas black men may be framed as ghetto inhabitants on the prowl for 'white meat' (Paasonen 2006, 2007b). All in all, it seems unnecessary to look for subtexts of any kind, as the identity categories, social relations and desires spelled out tend to be done so in capital letters.

I am hardly the first to note that pornographic choreographies (particularly of such a mainstream kind) are largely repetitive – after all, the repetition of characters, positions and acts is at the heart of popular genres in general. What I do want to argue is that critical feminist analyses of pornography would benefit from considering relations of control as tied to categories of identity, and not only literally as expressions or symbols of social relations of power (and as abuse thereof). In many instances porn imageries can and should be read as sexist, racist and classist. It remains crucial that feminist research insists on creating analytical spaces for addressing such conventions and their multiple underpinnings – along with the political issues involved in porn production and distribution, ranging from the positions of women within the porn industry to its principles of profit generation. My argument is that the analysis should not be limited to considerations of representational conventions *per se*: recognizing pornographic images as being stereotypical, for example, requires little analytical effort since types and stock characters of all kinds are fairly much the stuff that porn is made of. Pushing a bit further, one might ask whether there could be more to these choreographies in terms of the overall modality of porn that should be accounted for.

Tracing the modalities of (online) pornography

First, and obviously, pornography – in a range of media – is not primarily occupied with narrative (character development or motivation) as much as it is with sexual scenarios and the anatomical aspects of its performers. While fantastic in its display of desire, stamina and gratification, porn also lays claim to a certain kind of realism in its minute attention to detail (also Hardy 2009). Second, and in connection with the previous point, in porn, embodied differences, but also desires and pleasures as conveyed through bodies, are rendered instantly recognizable – and hence accessible to the viewer as something to relate to. Third, this involves both repetition (for in order for things to be recognizable, they need to be familiar to a degree) and exaggeration (meaning that there is little room for ambivalence). All these aspects are quite evident in the e-mail spam material addressed above.

Through minute realism combined with hyperbolic depiction, porn tries to mediate the sensory and to find points of resonance with its viewers. At the same time, its scenarios are much more fantastic and elaborate than those routinely exercised (at least by most) in extra-pornographic everyday practices. Highly stylized and standardized, porn contrasts fantasy scenes with actual bodies. (Patton 1991: 378–9.) This results in highly carnal and visceral relations between pornography and its consumers. Film scholar Linda Williams (1991) has famously categorized pornography, melodrama and horror as body genres that aim to move their viewers in bodily ways, and the quality of such genre films is evaluated through their sensory and sensuous effects. In pornography, bodies move and move the bodies of the people watching it. This motion may involve sexual arousal, but equally such sensations as puzzlement, amusement, embarrassment, anxiety, boredom, disgust or any combination of these (Paasonen 2010).

For some decades now, intellectuals have celebrated pornography as subversive in the sense of overturning bourgeois moral conventions and sexual norms (Ross 1989). This really is not my argument. What I am suggesting is that, in porn, irreverence to social codes regulating appropriate behaviour is rather programmatic and that the attraction of porn stems from its ability to disturb such codes. In other words, the incorrect becomes somewhat dogmatic. Not only does porn require disapproval in order to maintain any of its status as forbidden fruit amidst its ubiquitous everyday presence, but the attraction of the genre relies largely on evoking contradictory affective reactions. The genre operates in the register of gut reactions, aiming to get under one's skin in one sense or another. Following this principle, unsolicited porn spam e-mail makes use of explicit images and hyperbolic captions in an attempt to get the recipients' attention and, by *moving* them, arouse their curiosity and interest to the point of visiting the sites advertised.

Considering the excessive and abundant displays of things sexual within pornography as symbols of social relations or ideologies makes it more difficult to explore the ways in which they may become reworked through acts of repetition. The relations between teacher and student, seducer and the virgin, or even master and slave, are seldom ambiguous and are also open to change: people of different genders, ages, classes and ethnicities can, and do, take up different roles and positions. Furthermore, these roles are recurrently framed explicitly as ones of contract: types, scenarios and roles are played into with some degree of reflexivity, and they come as if in inverted commas. Consider, for example, stock characters such as the 'cheerleader', 'mature housewife', 'hitchhiker', 'pool guy', 'pizza delivery boy' or 'girl next door' of US porn. To the degree that such findings can be generalised on the basis of the spam e-mail material considered here, the *modality* of pornography involves hyperbole and stylization. Displays of embodied differences or relations of control in porn spam e-mail follow the fault lines of social hierarchies but often as spectacular, hyperbolic variations. Hyperbole both grounds these depictions in social hierarchies *and* creates a sense of detachment, a kind of fantastic 'as if' that literal readings fail to grasp. Porn is a fantasy about social relations turned quintessentially and even exclusively sexual.

Within the sexual, again, all kinds of exchanges may take place, even if the most commonly circulated scenarios do point to a rather narrow and predictable set of positions.

However, given the popularity of the 'reality' genre since the early 2000s, as well as the 'new rise' of amateur porn on line (the first being the short-lived wave of amateur video porn in the 1980s), a slightly more nuanced view of realism, repetition and reiteration is called for. Video publishing platforms such as Red-Tube, YouPorn and PornoTube are rife with not only clips harvested from professionally produced productions but also amateur videos operating in the modality of realism and authenticity: seemingly endless arrays of bodies repeat familiar acts, scenarios, poses and sounds in short videos involving little narrative. The videos balance home video realism in the sense that overtly fantastic *mise-en-scène* is rarely seen (unless the video is 'ripped off' from a commercial production), yet their sheer abundance and availability create a sense of excess.

Zabet Patterson (2004) has associated the attraction of online porn with its promises of immediate gratification and perpetual novelty: there is assumedly always something new, something different, something arousing that one just needs to find. At the same time, finding examples of exciting, arousing and innovative pornography remains more challenging a task, given the degree to which link sites, portals or randomly accessed mundane pornography such as spam e-mail highlight rather standard variations of pornographic imagery. The perpetual movement towards something new in searching for online porn is continuous and no closure can be provided by any individual image, text or video (also Lillie 2002; Coopersmith 2006; Hardy 2009). At the same time, the question is one of variations on a theme, since pornographic images, texts and videos inevitably look much like those seen before and those that will be seen soon after. This is another take on the reiteration of the codes and conventions of porn. Imageries, scenarios and acts may be repetitive, yet their repetitions are not altogether void of difference or alteration (since no two repetitions are ever exactly the same).

With online platforms, the genre of pornography has been divided into more niches and sub-categories than ever before. In her analysis of the rhetoric of freedom and choice related to online porn, Wendy Chun (2006) shows that porn sites offering endless sub-categories and special preferences simultaneously form new micro-markets and increase the visibility of fetishes and kinks that were previously deemed subcultural or highly marginal (e.g. Dahlquist and Vigilant 2004). Porn distributed in newsgroups and bulletin board systems (BBS) was difficult to index, whereas portals, metasites and search engines have helped to identify and differentiate a far broader range of categories for users to choose from. This also implies the expansion, diversification and increased visibility of different porn choreographies. Nevertheless, plenty remains the same, as is evident in the focus on (mainly young and conventionally gendered) female bodies or the perennial appeal of oral sex and cum shots in the porn spam e-mail material surveyed here.

The extreme as mainstream?

The centrality of hyperbole in pornographic depiction, together with the fragmentation of the mass market of porn, has also added to the visibility of the more extreme imageries (bukkake-style cumshot galleries, 'brutal' oral sex, girls eating faeces or being urinated upon) that are made accessible as parts of heteroporn sites. Something of this is also evident in my material, which features adverts for sites likes *Piss Place, Taboo Insertions, Spunk Farm* and *Bukkake Barn*. In many instances, extreme pornography in general works on hierarchical gender relations, with ritualistic determination reminiscent of Pier-Paolo Passolini's *Salò* (1975), yet without a social framework or commentary. Lauren Langman (2004) has named such extreme and often aggressively sexist sub-genres as 'grotesque degradation', which he sees as symptomatic of late modern capitalism and masculinity, both in crisis. Parallel to such symbolic and symptomatic readings of extreme pornography, one would do well to contextualize it within the framework of the attention economy of online pornography. As porn sites are trying to attract customers, they aim to grab users 'by their eyeballs' by showing them images amazing in their novelty, eccentricity or extremity in order to mark themselves apart from that which is already familiar (Dery 2007; see also Whisnant, this volume). Since the use of online porn involves a considerable amount of searching and clicking from one link and site to another, extreme imageries may be a means to make users stop at, stay at, return to and explore a site. The bizarre catches the eye, attracts attention and perhaps even renders the visitor a paying user (see Johnson, this volume).

Addressing the popularity of extreme gonzo hard-core pornography on DVD, Stephen Maddison (2009) argues that pornography has become increasingly hard-core and focused on depictions of female abuse and degradation that have become mainstreamed in the process. It is indeed true that some conventions previously deemed extreme, such as ass-to-mouth (ATM) shots, have become more common in the course of the 2000s (see Bridges, in this volume). According to Maddison, the polarized nature of the porn debates (as either for or against, with the battle lines drawn in the US porn and culture wars of the 1980s and 1990s) has been efficient in blocking feminist critiques of pornography even in cases where the pornographies in question would seem to call out for such investigations. While I agree with this concern – for a great deal remains to be said of the sexualized gender dynamics of heterosexual hard-core and the hierarchies constructed within them – I am less sure as to what degree the popularity of a series of DVD titles from the early 2000s, such as that studied by Maddison, can be generalized as characteristic of the genre and its recent developments. As I argue elsewhere, studies of pornography should be more self-reflexive in terms of sampling, methods of interpretation, and practices of generalization than they tend to be (Paasonen forthcoming, also Jones and Mowlabocus 2009). Considerations of one set of films say little of others. The situation becomes even more complex as the analysis is broadened across the boundaries of specific media technologies, publishing practices and platforms, or patterns of porn consumption. It may also be that as the consumption of online pornography, generally watched as clips rather than feature-length films, has increased in popularity, the porn industry has responded with DVD titles offering something else – such as *Forced Entry*, the serial killer porn film addressed by Maddison.

While Maddison sees pornography as growing more misogynistic in its mainstream variations, Mariah (alias Maria Kekkonen), a female adult film performer and producer with a decade-long career who I talked to in 2005, argued that the general trend is towards fetishes. According to her, the limits of hard-core have been reached and consumers are now exploring a more diverse range of depictions. Whatever the case may be, it seems that online distribution has caused the mainstreaming of *all* kinds of pornographies. Conflating their meanings, again, comes with some ethical risks, given that they may share precious little in terms of production systems, performers, economic principles, aesthetics, technical platforms or politics, not to mention crucial regional or national differences. I argue for the centrality of defining pornography as a plural category and accounting for its different instances without suggesting that one's findings be categorical in the sense of being able to speak of the genre as a whole: generalizations such as those made in this chapter are tentative, based on a specific set of examples, and sensitive to the fact that numerous counter-examples are easily identified in the field of the pornographic. This makes critiques of pornography stronger and better grounded while allowing for the existence of diverse practices that beg for a different kind of analysis.

Fascination and disgust

The increased visibility of the bizarre also broadens the boundaries of the pornographic in terms of consumption, exchange and discussion. This is the case with viral videos such as the infamous '2 girls 1 cup' or 'Eel soup'. The first of these videos, featuring two women, a cup and one minute of coprophilic play, became famous in 2007 as exemplary of Brazilian fetish porn. The second one, involving two Japanese women and numerous eels, gained similar fame, albeit of more modest kind, three years earlier. Such online videos, certainly exemplary of 'grabbing users by their eyeballs', are circulated in social networks as something amazing in their extremity. Here pornographic images become exemplary of the more generally affective, disturbing or confusing, as is evident in the numerous 'reaction videos' of viewers to watching '2 girls 1 cup' for the first time published on platforms such as YouTube. In these reaction videos, people express disgust, hide their faces, turn away from the screen, whimper in disbelief, make comments, even gag and hold their noses, as if escaping the scent of excrement displayed on the screen. Reaction videos are exchanged, new people are invited to make theirs, and affective reactions related to the original viral video become social and to a degree shared.

Rather than interpreting such videos as symptomatic of an ideology or the status of late capitalism, it is possible – and perhaps also more fruitful – to consider their social functions within the framework of the internet as a social medium that is fundamentally affective. In fact, '2 girls 1 cup' can be seen to exemplify affective stickiness, as theorized by Sara Ahmed (2004). As both the one-minute-long video and reaction videos commenting on it are circulated and commented upon their affective intensity (or value) continues to increase, hence attracting new people to join in the affective loop. The video can be categorized as pornographic (or, more specifically, as exemplary of the kinky, the paraphilic, coprophilic or extreme), yet its social life transgresses the boundaries and platforms of the genre. With online distribution, pornography is no longer at the margins of the media landscape, as its phenomena are widely discussed, watched, investigated and commented upon.

In terms of affective stickiness, it is important to note how such viral videos are explicitly connected to articulations of disgust. In both '2 girls 1 cup' and 'Eel soup', female bodies marked as ethnically other become the sites of the extreme, the disturbing and the disgusting. Ahmed (2004: 89) points out how lower regions of the body are associated with 'the "waste" that is literally expelled from the body'. Furthermore,

> The spatial distinction of 'above' from 'below' functions metaphorically to separate one body from another, as well as to differentiate between higher and lower bodies ... As a result, disgust at 'that which is below' functions to maintain the power relations between above and below, *through which 'aboveness' and 'belowness' become properties of particular bodies, objects and spaces.*
>
> (Ahmed 2004: 89, emphasis original.)

As Ian Miller (1997) argues, disgust is a means of separating the lower from the higher and the self from the other – of marking both the boundaries of the culture and those of the self. Wallowing in the disgusting, the female performers in the viral videos become firmly representative of 'belowness'. In a particular affective dynamic, not only the videos or the extreme acts they depict but also their female performers become figures of the disgusting. Karen Boyle argues similarly in her discussion of 'docuporn' that extreme and excessive acts and scenarios addressed in them are constructed as the excesses of women's sexuality: 'they seem be constructed not for the purposes of arousal but of disgust as women are reduced to lengthy checklists of increasingly extreme acts that they will or will not do or have done to them' (Boyle 2008: 45). Once the female performers become the locus of the disgusting and the excessive, it may become easier to ask 'How can they do that?' rather than to enquire after the conditions of labour and production that have led to the acts being performed and recorded in the first place. As affect sticks to the viral videos, it also sticks to the female bodies presented in them.

The visibility and 'popularity' (as calculated in downloads, if not in terms of fandom) of such viral videos works to support views of the internet as not only *the* site of pornography, but as the site of generally disturbing specimens of the genre. This connection has been posed as common knowledge in US television comedy and its references to the 'out there' aspects of online porn. The *Chappelle Show* sketch 'If the internet was a real place' (2006) featured 'goat play', while *South Park* went a step further in the episode 'Over logging' (2008) with references to 'Japanese girls exchanging bodily fluids' and 'Brazilian fart fetish porn' – hence reiterating the connections of ethnic otherness, extremity and disgust exhibited in the viral videos.

All in all, the most extreme of viral porn videos are the ones that gain broader fame through their social circulation. Such selective attention may then resonate with broader moral panics concerning the internet and the accessibility of pornography it has facilitated. It also supports arguments on hard-core becoming forever 'harder' (in the sense of violence, sexism or other forms of oppression). My concern is that such a focus may block from view the diversity of different kinds of pornographies accessible online, from amateur productions and their recent success to alternative, queer and experimental pornographies pushing the boundaries of the genre. Similarly, there is the risk that the e-mail porn spam material I have examined orients attention towards the bulky and the generic at the expense of other options, hence limiting my considerations of the genre at large. Nevertheless, the very 'everydayness' of this material demands critical attention and studies focusing only on the fringes of pornography's own mainstream would be equally distorting. Again, context is all.

Whilst the range of things pornographic is more diverse than ever before, the examples that gain fame, or infamy, are likely to support understandings of pornography as sexist and disgusting. This focus also finds support in the traditions of anti-pornography feminism (which has been occasionally accused of selecting the more disturbing examples of violent pornography as representative of the genre) and partly also in mainstream media's semi-sensationalist coverage of pornography (Jones and Carlin, this volume) and its cultures of production. All this works to support commonsensical understandings concerning pornography and its social meanings at the very moment when these are in critical need of rethinking and redefinition. If pornography is indeed both contingent as a point of reference and internally split, such transformations necessitate feminist analyses that do not confine themselves to predetermined and categorical positions of for or against (as anti-pornography versus anti-antipornography or pro-sex stances). While arguing for the need of contextual analysis is hardly innovative in cultural studies, insisting on it remains pivotal, if feminist critiques are to remain rigorous, as well as credible.

Conclusion

When beginning my investigations into porn spam e-mail, I initially found the literal strategy of reading rather appealing – after all, the material was rife with binary articulations of gender, forms of male homosocial address and recurring instances of 'putting women in their place'. It was no coincidence, then, that the examples I picked for closer consideration, such as 'Suck me bitch' or 'Captain Stabbin', worked for an elaboration of these points (Paasonen 2006). Whilst this interpretation is justified, at closer inspection I also found it partial in the sense that content analysis is efficient in hiding from view the 'odd moments' and those examples that do not quite fit in. My other analyses of the material have not been concerned with readings that would be somehow more 'positive' in the sense of wanting to depict pornography in any particular light. Rather, I have attempted to investigate how pornographic imageries work on their viewers through affect as a particular dynamic of experience and interpretation (Paasonen 2007a, 2010). As theorists of affect have pointed out, images and texts affect certain experiences (Armstrong 2000) and 'configure our ability to respond to, and to do things with, them' (Abel 2007: xiii). Pornographic images and texts possess power to move their viewers and readers. Such affective force, again, cannot be accounted for in content analysis or other forms of reading that assume the interpreter to be the one able to master the material and its meanings. As a body genre, pornography involves an exceptionally carnal modality, a motion of bodies both on and off screen, and it seems that much remains to be said of the gut reactions involved in experiencing it, which may – at times – have little to do with sexual arousal. All in all, my methodological quest has made evident the need to further theorize pornography as a popular genre in terms of its modality, intensity and mediation.

In *principle*, excess, hyperbole and repetition – which I have all identified as characteristic of hard-core pornography – are volatile in terms of social hierarchies and relations of power. Rather than supporting or reiterating rather fatigued social hierarchies and logics of difference, as is often the case, these can go virtually any which way. Pornography can just as well ridicule or exaggerate relations of power to the level of the absurd as support or justify them. There is no unity of intention within the genre, nor is there any among its consumers. If pornography involves fantasies of social relations turned primarily (and, occasionally, exclusively) sexual, as suggested above, it is fair to grant these fantasies some range and variation. Understanding the particular modalities of pornography as a popular genre is essential if we are to come up with nuanced and rigorous analyses of online porn in its mainstream variants beyond the analytically constraining dichotomies that have tended to dominate porn debates since the anglophone sex wars of the 1980s.

Taken seriously, the modalities, volatilities and ambiguities of pornography enable investigations into the power of porn, namely the power of pornographic images and texts to move their viewers and readers. Pornography is not merely about sexual arousal but rather affective responses that range from curiosity and interest to shame and disgust – as well as numerous things in between. The mediated, yet explicitly and elaborately fleshy, presence of the performers is a crucial part of this affective dynamic. The performing bodies function as evidence of the realness of that which has taken place and recorded in detail, and they are the anchors to which articulations of disgust, dirt and nastiness stick. In instances such as '2 girls 1 cup' or 'Eel soup', the extremity of the acts performed leads to ethical questions concerning conditions of production and performance, as well as of the potential pleasures involved in consuming such imageries (be these through reactions of disgust, distanced laughter or curiosity). The movement and translation taking place between the carnally performed, the mediated and the sensed bring forth questions concerning affect as particular kinds of dynamic encounters and exchanges which cannot be confined to the semantic or the semiotic. And this is where some of the really interesting questions begin.

Chapter 5

Cocktail parties

Fetishizing semen in pornography beyond bukkake

Lisa Jean Moore and Juliana Weissbein

Fountains of glory, billboards of fear

A walking tour of the architectural heart of Brooklyn, bounded by Grand Army Plaza, the Brooklyn Museum and Prospect Park, reveals an urban landscape flanked by fountains. In the centre of Grand Army Plaza, the Bailey Fountain presents statues of the water god Neptune together with nude figures representing Wisdom and Felicity, poised under torrents of water bathing them in a continuous and forceful spray. Down the street, the Brooklyn Museum's fountain is banked by stadium seating for an audience to watch syncopated jets of water emerge from the concrete. The forty-eight holes in the sidewalk pump out streams of varying velocity and volume sometimes in a rhythm interspersed with random blasts. One could sit for hours and watch the Museum's fountain as it spurts and splashes, often animated by joyous children dancing in front on hot days. (At the third point in our triangle, Prospect Park's 'Vale of Cashmere', water no longer sprays over the lost fountains that have become overgrown with brush; but, as one of the most celebrated cruising areas in Brooklyn, their representation has been replaced by less mediated activities.)

Fountains are not unique to Brooklyn. Consider how spurting fluids grace many public buildings, parks and town squares across the globe. Although many may not admit a correspondence between these commonplace public celebrations of spurting water and the money shot, that moment in a pornographic film when a penis ejaculates, we believe there is traffic between the everyday celebration of ejaculation in the urban landscape and in pornography. Displays of surging fluids please spectators. Indeed, the term 'bukkake', a popular genre of pornography that valorizes ejaculation in particular ways, is translated from Japanese as 'splash'.

It is not exclusively fountains that revel in the ejaculatory moment. Firework spectatorship, glossy champagne advertisements, images of volcano eruptions, ocean spray, the pilgrimage to Ol' Faithful and fantastical musings about the Fountain of Youth are but a few examples of ejaculatory representation and worship. Depictions of ejaculate, both literal and symbolic, are possibly even more prevalent than phallic images. Perhaps, we are socialized in our semi-conscious to experience ejaculate and admire it – the bursts, thrusts, mini-explosions and spurts. All these homages go beyond the phallic and celebrate the production of fluid, the springing forth of juice.

At the same time, during our walk through Brooklyn's neighbourhoods, we see messages on billboards, buses and jumbo-trons about pregnancy prevention, HIV medication and condoms. These messages convey a sense of semen as filthy, dirty, infectiously diseased and dangerously fertile: something to avoid. This language of fear and protection imagines the borders of the flesh as vulnerable to penetration by the pathogen – the sperm cell. The body must be fortified to avoid the sperm cell, or modified in order to combat the effects of its penetration.

So how can we explain the inconsistencies in the messages we see during our urban jaunt? We participate in celebrating the ejaculate and yet are bombarded with warnings to fear it. And what do we do to these contradictory messages as they resurface in our creative and erotic expressions? In what ways does the erotic representation of ejaculate follow from these seminal expressions of pleasure and danger? Semen within these everyday pornographic renderings becomes simultaneously celebrated, feared, fetishized and revered. In sum, its representations are erotically vital. The constant juxtaposition of the culturally produced *thirst* for semen and the *fear* of its capabilities is precisely what gives representations of semen their power. This anxious tension creates a super-erotically charged substance.

These commonplace examples set the stage for our examination into one example of everyday pornography. We wish to take this observation of the mundane production of meanings about semen and ejaculate and examine the ways in which it is co-constitutive with do-it-yourself pornography broadcast on the internet. In what follows, we posit that semen, its ejaculation and materiality, is invested with social meanings that have the ability to signify ownership over property, corporeal or otherwise, satisfy a female (and in some cases male) thirst or hunger for male body fluid, or humiliate the other or, less frequently, the self. Representations of semen moving through space – how it travels, who it touches, where it lands – provide (for men) a positive inversion of the real materiality of semen's position as a feared and dangerous substance, but do so often at the expense of women. This stylization is meaningful and powerful because it constructs a narrative of men's semen as able to produce certain feelings and values about objects and people. The male gaze is constantly reinforced through the ejaculating of a masculine glaze, a glaze that coats the other or the self with a glossy, slippery substance that modifies social relations.[1] Semen is depicted as a mechanism of marking territory and claiming ownership.

Where sperm is king

Men have created monsters. Up to 50 million swimming monsters are released each time they ejaculate. Since its first 'discovery' in the seventeenth century by Leeuwenhoek, semen was highly regarded and awe-inducing. During these glory days, semen was the exclusive maker of life, a sign of strength and source of energy; it was reproduced over and over every day, an endless supply attesting to male dominance (Moore 2007). And this narrative of fascination and valorization is evident in the scripts from both pornography and everyday locker room talk; men and boys have bragged about their ability to ejaculate, and, frankly, we have listened. But similar to the meanings of the substance itself, the scripts have changed. No longer the conquering hero, since the 1980s semen has been categorized as diseased, evil and toxic. Semen, the substance and its definition, is no longer under men's control, if it was ever. It leaks and can be used against men as evidence of malfeasance.

Communications scholar Cindy Patton (1988) argues that the cum shot is so prevalent in pornography because it demonstrates that the sex that is occurring is purely recreational. Seminal display also reinforces the realness of the sexual acts: 'In traditional male porn the visually spectacular male cum shot is the inevitable consequence of male sexual arousal' (Patton 1988: 74). Since heterosexual pornography is centred on the man, the act is over when the man ejaculates (Jensen 2007a) without concern to the woman's pleasure. Or perhaps this ejaculation is meant to represent women's pleasure?

The role of spectatorship is also crucial for any examination of pornography. Men watch porn as a means to watch one another (Strager 2003: 55): pornography is rife with homoerotic overtones and possibilities. Indeed, pornography scholar Stephen Strager (2003: 56) argues, 'the audience must see the money shot, must see the penis in action, which transforms a shared, internal, concealed, heterosexual act into a solitary, external, visible, homoerotic one'. Most consumers of pornography are men. Therefore, the male gaze is inescapable. The male gaze can identify with the penis in the film because in all likelihood he has been, or will be, masturbating as well. The female on the screen is merely a mediator: necessary, but disposable and replaceable.

How might we understand the pornographic fetishization of semen and stylization of certain seminal displays throughout history? Literary critic Murat Aydemir (2007) explores a transhistorical sampling of images of bukkake, the sexual act where one or more men excessively ejaculate onto a woman's face or body. The woman is often not actively involved in the sexual act but is just a site to be marked (leaving the ejaculator unmarked). The focal point of this fetish is the ejaculate (its quantity and quality). Ejaculation makes the pleasure temporal and real, it is a significant discharge. Similarly, Moore (2007: 72) writes, 'The physical presence of the ejaculate, the seminal fluid, is a material reality that confirms men's pleasure ... [t]he framing of the money shot is perhaps the most sincere devotion to and idolization of semen that I've encountered.' She states that since ejaculate is now monstrous and diseased, images of women fetishizing and adoring ejaculate truly entice male desire. Their male ego is boosted by women not being bothered by their toxicity.

Ian Cook's (2006) examination of web-based pornography explores how heterosexual masculinity is defined as emotional detachment and extreme competitiveness and is constructed and maintained through relationships with other men. He ultimately posits that web porn pressures men to be hyper-masculine because the intimacy within this arena is non-existent. Within pornography, individuality and sexual objectification of women are constructed and maintained through relationships with other men whereby male individuality is conceptualized not only as different from, but better than, female. The male player, since he is aware and fearful of the stigma of the omnipresent homoeroticism and male gaze in ostensibly heterosexual contexts, becomes a competitive and anxious hunter: 'The money shot can be interpreted in a variety of ways ... It may show a female body marked by a successful hunter, or repeated ejaculation is read as visual proof of her objectification' (Cook 2006: 53).

These scholars' contributions have guided our own work. We have expanded their arguments by testing their applicability for an understanding of everyday do-it-yourself video pornography and phone sex calls in ways we will now explain.

The data and the approach

Our methodology combines grounded-theory techniques[2] with textual analysis as a way to explain and interpret spermatic representations. Similar to other qualitative research, textual analysis can be exploratory and descriptive, enabling limited insight into why significant relationships or trends occur. The aim is not to standardize facts into scientific units, but rather appreciate and play with the range of variation of a particular phenomenon. Although, as we will argue, the range of variation in these particular representations is fairly limited, there are 'outliers', representations that do not fall neatly into the most common themes but aid in our understanding of them.

In what follows, we draw on data from three popular adult online communities. First, we surfed *Adult Video News* (AVN) – the online trade magazine of the US porn industry (discussed in more detail by Tyler, this volume) – in order to see how ejaculate was categorized in the context of contemporary commercial pornography, building on previous work in this field (e.g. Moore 2007; Williams 1991). With *AVN* as our baseline, we then analysed a variety of do-it-yourself (DIY) amateur heterosexual arenas in which ejaculate was of utmost concern. We screened over 100 videos on X-Tube.com and noted themes surrounding ejaculate. Finally, we analysed the adult phone fantasy web site Niteflirt.com from an operator's standpoint by noting constants in communication. One author worked as an operator, registered with a Niteflirt account and did participant observation from 30 May 2008 to 9 October 2008. Field notes were taken on all calls, then coded and analysed by both researchers.[3] Based on a character sketch of the operators available on the site, callers would express interest and place calls. Callers also used instant messaging and e-mail to correspond but there are no real differences in type of content in these modes of correspondence. We analysed all data and did *not* select for specific ejaculate based calls. Significantly, ejaculate was *always* the focus of correspondence through Niteflirt.

Our monitoring of *AVN* (from 2006 to 2009) allowed us to establish that a category or sub-genre of seminal celebration exists within commercial heterosexual pornography. *AVN* provides critical editorial reviews of professionally produced adult movies and web sites with a unique rating system that classifies the type of acts depicted in the pornographic movies they review and 'cum shots' are listed as a discrete (and extensive) category. The ratings are derived from a cross-section of US video stores, adult stores and online studios, but the site does not have any places to read viewers' responses. Of our three sites, this is the furthest removed from actual consumption but presents a snapshot of how central cum is to contemporary commercial pornography. Within the master category of 'cum shots' there are further subcategories: 'body' (492 movies), 'bukkake' (245 movies), 'cream pies' (873 movies), 'cum swapping' (133 movies) and 'facials' (1,447 movies).[4] Films featured under these categories include *Semen Demons, Desperately Seeking Semen, The Cum Cocktail, We Swallow, Sperm Overdose, Sperm Burpers, A Splash of Sperm* and *Feeding Frenzy*. In the reviewers' descriptions of these, videos and the images on the dust jackets women appear to be semen-starved and competitive about their desire for ingesting the semen as they rush to get to the ejaculating penis, the full shot glass, or residual ejaculate on a sheet. *AVN* informed our data gathering from X-Tube and Niteflirt by suggesting categories and themes of representation for analysis: is the representation of ejaculate in contemporary commercial porn reproduced in more amateur and participatory modes? This was one of the questions we set out to answer.

The first of the modes to be examined is user-generated video content. In order to collect DIY pornography, we reviewed over 100 amateur videos uploaded to X-Tube. We selected these videos at random from the newest or top-viewed videos listed during our period of study (November 2008–January 2009). This interactive web site (similar to YouTube) is a forum in which users can create accounts and view, upload, rank and comment upon user-uploaded adult videos. There is a portion of the site that is available free to registered users, while other video clips can be viewed for a fee. We focused exclusively on the user-generated free content and registered as a man seeking heterosexual content. We focused our inquiry on images of ejaculate and examined how it was displayed and discussed, using search terms 'cum', 'self-swallow', 'facial', 'semen' and 'sperm' in order to pinpoint user-generated descriptors for relevant content.

It is important to note that although we examined explicitly labelled heterosexual pornography, this by no means limits the displays to those representing male bodies engaged with female bodies. Despite searching for heterosexual content from a male point of view, we still generated videos of men masturbating or videos with no female bodies present. We observed where seminal ejaculate occurred, how often, on whose bodies and how it was described or discussed: from this, themes of 'marking' and 'consuming' (discussed in detail later in this chapter) emerged as particularly significant.

We also gathered data from Niteflirt.com, an entertainment web site where customers can create personal accounts and correspond with phone operators through e-mail, phone and instant messaging. To participate in the exchange, the customer browses advertisements and then calls, or arranges for a call, through other virtual media. The paid calls (charged at a per-minute rate) can last anywhere from a single minute to multiple hours, during which time customers perform role-plays and act out fantasies with an operator. Although phone calls leave everything up to interpretation and manipulation, the 'truth' of the caller's report (e.g. of ejaculation or self-swallowing) was less important for our purposes than the fact that the callers wanted us to believe that certain actions were taking place. In other words, whether reality or fantasy, their descriptions of ejaculate are understood to be key to the experience of the call. From May 2008 to April 2009 we engaged with 481 unique male customers (493 interactions)[5] to observe their role-plays involving ejaculate. Analysis targeted the language, affect and management of seminal ejaculate. In this way, we were able to bring together the data from the DIY pornography with a sub-sample of men as a means of interpreting and exploring our nascent theories of ejaculate. Through the Niteflirt research, an additional theme – of self-swallowing – emerged, which we discuss in more detail shortly.

The money shot *redux*

The first point to note about the 100 amateur videos (of between thirty seconds and three minutes in length) from X-Tube is that, mirroring contemporary commercial porn, all involve unprotected sex, whether that sex is masturbatory, penetrative (penis/vagina, penis/anus, penis/mouth intercourse) and/or facial (whereby a penis ejaculates on to a woman's face or back or chest). A majority of the videos feature Caucasian-appearing able-bodied slim people who are normatively gendered. Female bodies are generally shown in their entirety, whereas male bodies are most often disembodied, with a voice, a penis and ejaculate standing in as representations for the entire male body.[6] A frequent pop-up interactive ad also emphasizes a curiously disembodied ejaculation: your cursor turns into a clip art of an ejaculating penis and you can roll over a dancing female and ejaculate on her when you click while waiting for your content to load.

The most prominent type of video on X-Tube within our inclusion criteria was of disembodied males masturbating to ejaculation on to a still photo of a female. Of our 100 videos, fifteen feature this practice. The women in these photographs, often difficult to see, are described variously as ex-girlfriends or ex-wives, famous models or actresses. Ejaculating on to photos of a specific woman allows the man to claim her as his property. He is the one choosing to mark her, thus he has a right to her. And women's relative invisibility as X-Tube users reinforces this sense of dominance and ownership. It is very uncommon for (supposed) women to post comments; it is not a women-friendly site, and once a woman logs on she is swamped with men trying to chat. The dominance theme was also present in Niteflirt phone interactions whereby there was a clear relationship between financial spending and seminal spending. The closer the operator and callers became, and the more money the caller contributed to the relationship, the more he expressed feelings of ownership towards her.

Indeed, on Niteflirt, sperm, semen and ejaculate were the main focus of calls. Whether the customer was spending money (ejaculating cash) into the operators' bank account, or narrating his imagined ejaculation of semen in/on to her physical form, the moment of release was the focal point. A majority of caller fantasies were explicitly about ejaculation, and fantasies ended immediately after the subject ejaculated with no attention paid to the operator's completion. While we obviously cannot say with any certainty whether callers actually ejaculated, the emphasis on the caller's pleasure in the narration of the fantasy scenario is nonetheless interesting and, again, chimes with conventions established in commercial pornography. The caller would tell the operator where, how and why he intended to come before he (apparently) did so. Submissive men often enjoyed financial domination (a fetish in which an operator would 'wallet rape' a customer and demand he pay high sums of money before he could be granted the privilege of ejaculating). Dominant men often referred to the operator as a cumslut and demanded she take his semen where he desired. The way in which the ejaculate was treated ultimately defined the fetish.

Marking, consuming and self-swallowing

Having established the centrality of the 'money shot' in these more participatory modes of contemporary pornography, we now turn our attention to the common narratives in which scenes that feature seminal ejaculate are embedded. To be clear, there are multiple versions of these types of videos and calls, and although the bodies and settings may slightly change, the mechanism, stylization and placement of ejaculation are similar. In this section we explore three themes – admiration and ownership, consumption by others, and consumption by the self.

The first theme we interpreted, 'marking', features ejaculation as an admirable act of marking objects, representations or bodies. For the most part this is a form of taking ownership or claiming property. However, a great deal of attention is also paid to the qualities of the 'load' in the ways the videos are entitled, narrated or commented upon. The size of the load or the velocity of the ejaculate is visually emphasized through slow-motion video, close-ups and replays. Men also use a variety of words and phrases familiar from other pornographic genres to describe their own semen in both videos and phone sex sessions: jizz, cum, breed juice, explosion, facial, ropes, streams, thick hot cum juice, cum shot, creamy cum, medicine, load, cum load, cream pie, high-pressure squirter, protein lunch, wad of juice, feeding and cummy.

Take for example, these poster-titled video clips (and our descriptions of the video action they contain):

- *Cummin on kaci-love pics.* This video features a disembodied uncircumcized white penis ejaculating on two pictures of a young Caucasian girl holding her large naked breasts. He ejaculates two streams of ejaculate on to each photo and then closes in on the cum before the video abruptly ends.[7]

- *Me fuckin' her doggy before I cum on her ass.* A heterosexual white couple are having sex in the doggy-style position. The male is holding the video camera and filming a close-up of the penetration. She is hardly making any noise. He pulls out right as he is about to ejaculate and shoots four streams of ejaculate on to her back. He quickly turns the camera to his face and laughs. She moans as if upset and says, 'What are you doing, babe?'[8]
- *Cum in a plastic box.* A video featuring a disembodied Caucasian male ejaculating (a lot) into a clear Tupperware container. After he ejaculates he shows the viewer how much he came and shakes the ejaculate around the container.[9]

Woman's pleasure and agency are not the focal point of these videos: rather, she is absent or, when depicted, is only in a one-dimensional photograph or secondary role. She is essentially a surface or receptacle to be marked. While these videos do come up in heterosexual searches, they do not depict traditionally heterosexual sex between men and women, nor do they necessarily follow filmic heterosexual porn conventions: there are few penetration shots and there is little build-up to the 'money shot'. Moreover, women's on-screen appreciation of the ejaculate is not essential here: it appears the only reason these are worth filming and posting is due to the quality, quantity and direction of the ejaculate itself.

'Marking' is also in evidence in the men's comments during phone sex calls on Niteflirt. Men describe their ejaculate in detail – its quantity, consistency and taste – but, more significantly for our purposes, it is the destination of their cum which is key to these narratives. For example, in an e-mail, Ellis[10] details how he would like his subsequent call to the operator to unfold:

> [I want] to finish off with a forced huge messy facial cumshot being firmly held in place not able to squirm away and looking very humiliated knowing you are about to get your cute innocent picture perfect face, with the makeup you spent 40 minutes putting on and making just perfect, ruined by massive cumloads. (if possible, tell it like youd get a one-man drowning, describing how each huge ropes of cum hit your face. Do a few cum-rope descriptions … the really thick and sticky kinda cum, you know, the kind that just stays where you shoot it.) Maybe even a 'after' description of what you look like.
>
> (E-mail correspondence, 28 June 2008)

Or take these two examples from instant messaging exchanges:

> Yes, slap you face with my cock, leave you marked and wet. Do you like how I make you feel sticky and degraded?
>
> (Bendingman via instant messaging, 16 January 2009)

> [I will be] using you like the little cheap cumslut we both know you love to be … just as you feel my cock thicken and grow, knowing im about to cum down your throat, i pull out and jerk myself off all over your face and

tongue, painting you, marking you ... claiming you ... then i gather my load with my finger and let you suck and lick it off, feeling daddys cum sliding down your throat and into your tummy, thick, salty, warm.

(Crazywildcat via instant messaging, 20 February 2009)

The operator is never *asked* what she thinks of ejaculate: rather she is scripted within the fantasy. The caller wants to hear her acknowledge his power, to describe how his semen 'marks', 'claims', 'humiliates' and 'degrades' her. For Ellis and Crazywildcat, the power differential is further eroticized by descriptions which infantilize the operator: she is an 'innocent', he is 'daddy'.

The second theme, 'consumption', is anticipated in Crazywildcat's description of his cum sliding down the operator's throat and his emphasis on its consistency and taste. He is hardly unique in this: both in the X-Tube videos and in the Niteflirt calls, men express an almost insatiable desire for female partners to consume ejaculate in multiple forms. This consumption often occurs through a facial whereby a man, or multiple men, ejaculates on to a woman's face and she then licks it off or uses her fingers to get it into her mouth. Our first examples are again taken from X-Tube:

- *Cum complilation. Girls suckin, blowin, eating cum, getting facials & jerking off.* This video features about fifteen shots of all Caucasian younger females receiving facials. Each clip is about ten seconds long. This video seemed quite popular with users, as it received 10,000 views in two minutes.[11]
- *All Facials, Vol 1, Narrative Of Soul Against Soul. An older Facial Comp I made. ENJOY!* A compilation of four amateur clips of younger Caucasian women receiving facials. The women swallow, squint at and rub the ejaculate on their cheeks. There is punk rock music in the background. The females are embodied while the males are disembodied.[12]

During phone sex sessions, men described choreographing their ejaculation in order to present their cum for the operator's consumption: to be drunk from shot glasses, sucked off teaspoons, licked from dog bowls, slurped off her body, wiped into her mouth from her face, and taken from inside her body to be licked off her fingers. Common nicknames the men gave the operator included Cum Slut, Jizz Junkie, Cum Guzzler and Cummy in my Tummy. These monikers are also found in X-Tube videos when audio is present. To the extent that they echo the hyberbolic language of mainstream porn (where, as noted in our discussion of *AVN*, women's uncontrollable thirst for semen is a recurring theme), these examples demonstrate the relatively limited scripts men are working with. As Dines argues (Chapter 1, this volume), this reflects the extent to which pornography is scripting these men's fantasies such that masturbation is almost unimaginable outside of pornographic scenarios.

This consumption is often narrated by men through encouraging women to get it all in their mouth, or drink the fluid as if it is precious, delicious and satisfying. As argued elsewhere (Moore 2007), this practice appears to be deeply pleasing to male partners, as it affirms that their semen, contrary to claims about its toxicity, is tasty, desirable and enjoyable. There is slippage between this fantasy pornographic life and certain mainstream representations. Take, for example, an advertisement for Imedeen (a skin-whitening tablet) where a beautiful woman, suggestively positioned on satin sheets, is flanked by the tag line 'My secret to beautiful skin? I swallow.'[13] Women are constructed as willing consumers and, indeed, this consumption is framed as being for their own good, making them more desirable to the hegemonic male gaze. Similar to the marking in DIY pornography, advertisements that suggest women must maintain beauty also degrade and mark women as flawed (something the product can 'cure'). In the Imedeen ad, women are marked so deeply by male desire that they begin to take pleasure in marking themselves, literally consuming, products to make them more 'beautiful', 'docile' and obedient.

Scenarios in which men describe swallowing their own ejaculate may seem to trouble the more straightforward reading of pornographic ejaculations as an expression of men's power over women. Significantly, this was the least common representation in our study and, indeed, at the time of our research it did not appear to be a significant theme in commercial heterosexual pornography, although, perhaps unsurprisingly, specialist sites devoted to the practice can be found.[14] This practice was shown or described in three of the X-Tube videos[15] but was more common in the Niteflirt calls, particularly among men who liked to be dominated. Since we posit that semen is ultimately toxic, self-swallowing is used as a measurement of self-humiliation, a means for a man to control his own sexuality. Whoever is ingesting the semen (or being ejaculated on) is disciplined by it.

During phone sex sessions, self-swallowing involved the man describing how he put his body into awkward positions, so his penis was aimed directly at his mouth, then ejaculating into himself. Men also described scooping it up with their hands to put into their mouths or ejaculating into a shot glass or cup in order to drink their fluid. In the pornography we analysed, very few men voluntarily ingest their own fluids. Unsurprisingly, then, in setting up the phone session, men indicated that they wanted to be coerced or forced into drinking their own cum and subsequently went to great lengths to demonstrate that they did not enjoy this humiliating activity. Ironically, this is the moment when the actual man on the other end of the phone appears to be able to ejaculate, signalling the end of the call. Although the fate of the callers' actual ejaculate remains unnarrated, their projections of its quantity, quality and direction are – in true pornographic fashion – essential to the fantasy.

Conclusion

Returning to the opening walk in the heart of Brooklyn, we notice that the urban landscape is also dotted with public drinking fountains, delivering a steady stream of water to a user through a spout attachment. Although the water fountain was probably not conceived as a public thirst-quenching ejaculating machine, we are struck by the similarities between their everyday use and representations from our pornographic sample. The cultural consciousness is mediated by the interplay of the urban spaces, media images and interactive experiences.

Through our interpretation of semen in these field sites, we posit that, although powerful, everyday pornography and everyday ejaculate are part of a larger cultural moment where men's relationship to their own bodies has shifted away from the realm of the rational, solitary, intact, knower to a more leaky, fleshy, unpredictable and more complicated masculinity. The fragility of masculinity in a post-feminist, HIV/AIDS culture has radically transformed men's traditional power as well as their own conceptualizations of semen. Men, if they ever were, are not in exclusive control of their destinies. Moreover, in everyday interactions those who have produced ejaculate cannot always predict where it will appear and to what end. But in the fantasy world of DIY pornography and phone sex work men have great control over their seminal discharge. They wrest control from the uncertainty. They can put it where they want it and when they want it there. It is striking that while in DIY pornography we can see evidence of ejaculate and in phone sex we can only imagine it, men narrate the seminal exchange in remarkably similar ways and in ways which echo commercial pornographic representations.

Importantly, though, once it is released, seminal ejaculate continues to do things such as produce stigma, claim ownership, humiliate subjects or satisfy a desire – sometimes in line with the producer's wishes and sometimes beyond his control. The social landscape of messages of desire and revulsion add to the mix and create a world of multiple iterations of men processing semen in amateur DIY pornography and phone sex. The most common iteration, the use of semen to mark objects and body parts (primarily of women), is perhaps the most obvious expression of self-control whereby ejaculate and male desire work in concert. Ready, aim, fire.

Forcing others to consume semen is in line with disciplining women to want to please men, in spite of a continuous stream of negative ideas about the ejaculate. As the fantasy goes, women either want to please men or are so overcome by desire to consume that they throw caution to the winds. Beyond this, male ejaculate is a precious resource, a fuel, a craving, that women go wild for. Men again are in control and able to direct videos or phone sex calls in order to guide consumption. The widely discussed but less often represented act of self-consumption does not fundamentally disturb this reading: there is an act of release in the humiliation of self-swallowing, as well as a potential relationship to self-worship, that requires further analysis.

Images of seminal ejaculate proliferate in fountains, champagne explosions, fireworks, water fountains, DIY pornography and phone sex. Despite these omnipresent images surrounding our lives, we must also navigate the erotic with the lethal as we are reminded through ubiquitous messages that the fluid is toxic. We argue that these simultaneous messages create a unique sexual tension between men and their own ejaculate. This bifurcated sexual tension would not be possible without the everyday messages we are given about ejaculate and its potential.

Acknowledgements

We wish to thank Karen Boyle, Mary Koust, Lara Rodriguez, Sian Killingsworth, Jason Pine, Monica Casper and Paisley Currah for their invaluable comments, which strengthened this chapter.

Notes

1 We are indebted to Lara Rodriguez for this observation.
2 Grounded theory is a deductive process whereby analysts incorporate as many data as possible in order for the formative theories to be used as deductive tools. This tool, the grounded theory, ultimately aims to incorporate the range of human experiences in its articulation and execution.
3 The men did not know they were participating in this research and the researcher's interaction with the men was, in other respects, consistent with those of other operators. Whilst there are ethical implications of deception in research (Babbie 2009) we felt this approach to be justified because of the difficulty of accessing this material any other way: as well as the potential disruption to the caller–operator interaction, the fact that the callers were paying by the minute meant that any discussion of the research would have taken place at their expense. Individual men are not identified here, there is no audio-recording of the call or identifying information which could trace individual callers, and the field notes taken during the research will be destroyed on the completion of the project.
4 Material gathered 7 May 2007. The categories can be defined as follows: body – any video that features human bodies; bukkake – multiple men ejaculate simultaneously, or one after another, on to an awaiting female body; cream pies – the focal point is ejaculate seeping out of, or filling up, a vagina; cum swapping: ejaculate is passed from one body to the other, mainly by kissing a partner(s) with semen already in one's mouth; facials – men ejaculate semen onto a woman's face.
5 The callers were twenty- to seventy-four-year-old men who rarely specified their race/ethnicity. A majority of the callers did self-identify as heterosexually married. The financial exchange on Niteflirt does not appear to interrupt the flow of the fantasy. Even as calls were interrupted to add more funds, conversations were treated as if uninterrupted. Despite becoming personal with the operator, most callers never questioned the financial aspect of the relationship. Payment was never denied or withheld. The notion of fantasy, while vital for the process to occur, was never spoken of.
6 See Bridges (this volume) for a discussion of commercial pornographic films in which the male performer is a similarly disembodied presence.
7 <http://www.X-Tube.com/play_re.php?v=RFvPFDz611-&cl=eSCQr6wrvJ-> (accessed 17 December 2008).
8 <http://www.X-Tube.com/play_re.php?v=AFxsecv108-&cl=mFBV4Sip69-> (accessed 17 December 2008).
9 <http://www.X-Tube.com/play_re.php?v=Gpu1H2h409-&cl=hzmSBZic2r-> (accessed 17 December 2008).
10 All names have been changed. The spelling and grammar in these quotations are as in the original.

11 <http://www.X-Tube.com/play_re.php?v=zb4uP_S224_&cl=syZ3S_S224_> (accessed 21 December 2008).
12 <http://www.X-Tube.com/play_re.php?v=2fuIY_S524_&cl=z0KZD_S524_> (accessed 23 December 2008).
13 The advert can be seen at: <http://www.feministing.com/archives/014034.html> (accessed 9 November 2009).
14 For example <http://www.idrinkmyself.com/> describes 'a brotherhood of men who share the common bond of self-swallowing' with a collection of poetry and short stories about the experiences of self-swallowing. See also, <http://www.mymasturbation.com/male/swallowing.htm>; <http://ehealthforum.com/health/topic33720.html>; <http://ask.metafilter.com/38376/Do-straight-guys-ever-eat-their-own-come-after-masturbating> (all accessed 2 January 2009).
15 The videos featuring this practice are: *Selfsuck and cum in mouth. Simple self suck on a couch with cum finish* (<http://www.X-Tube.com/play_re.php?v=2ed4Y-J713-&cl=YdFny-J713- >); *Cumming in my mouth again part 5. Love the taste* (<.http://www.X-Tube.com/play_re.php?v=gUbMTfx310_&cl=n00BzjpIJr_>); and *Spitting Myself, Original. Original clip of spitting my own CUM. I like the slurping sounds!!!* (<http://www.X-Tube.com/play_re.php?v=nMNNp-S622-&cl=ttTxV-S622- >) (all accessed 31 December 2008).

Chapter 6

Virtually commercial sex

Sarah Neely

This chapter considers how pornography and other forms of commercial sex function within the immersive 3-D virtual world of Second Life. Set against an historical account of the porn industry in relation to technological change, the analysis seeks to distinguish the virtual world from other forms of online porn. Particular attention will be given to the way in which boundaries of production and consumption in Second Life are blurred, thinking through modes of participation and identity.

Sex and technology

Developments in technology are continually led by the sex industry. As Laurence O'Toole argued in 1998:

> The porn industry continues to be a key driver behind advances in internet technology. Recently pornsters have pioneered deluxe online shopping mall designs, secure payments systems and video streamlining, as well, of course, as inspiring the design and manufacture of an ever-increasing array of filtration software.
>
> (O'Toole 1998: 369)

DVD technologies have also been argued to have served the demands of the porn consumer because of the way in which viewers can skip over superfluous narrative to key sex scenes. But perhaps the most notorious and often cited example of the pornography industry's influence on mainstream commerce is Sony's ill-fated decision to exclude pornography from its Betamax titles and the resulting popularity of VHS, which did allow the release of pornographic films. More recently, Blu-ray and HD-DVD became locked in a similar battle. Because Blu-ray initially made the decision not to enable the distribution of pornography, it was thought that Blu-ray would be the next Betamax; the decision was subsequently reversed and now both formats allow pornographic content. In addition, technologies such as video-streaming, interactivity and mobile phone technologies are all also argued to have developed largely as platforms for the distribution of pornography. Interactive television services – such as those enabling viewers of sports programmes to select specific camera angles – are similarly representative of the fruits of the labour of research directed by the porn industry (Coopersmith 2006).

As Brian McNair (1996) points out, such developments not only make material easier to obtain but also allow a more private consumption of pornographic media. Further, McNair claims, these technological developments have 'democraticized' porn production, as 'Many people use video cameras to make pornographic recording of their own sexual behaviour, for their own private use' (1996: 116). However, the number of 'leaked' celebrity sex tapes, supposedly created for private consumption but later distributed without the consent of the participant, serves as one high-profile example of how the 'democratization' of technology does not always deliver what it promises: inequalities persist, and being a participant in the production does not always guarantee participation in the distribution or consumption. Nevertheless, the rise of amateur porn sites and the subsequent decline in porn industry profits demonstrate a shift from traditional commercial structures. Porn sites like RedTube or YouPorn – modelled on YouTube, allowing users to post clips from existing pornographic films or their own amateur films[1] – offer what is essentially free pornography and have been blamed by the porn industry for the decline in DVD sales and the subscription pornography sites run by them (Fritz 2009). While some of the traditional producers of pornography have attempted to emulate the popular amateur style, others have sought to further differentiate their product either by adopting higher production values, more in line with mainstream Hollywood, or, alternatively, by becoming more extreme in their offerings, as Whisnant and Bridges argue in this volume.

As well as presenting new platforms for delivering commercial pornography and facilitating the amateur porn boom, technological developments have also created opportunities for new forms of sexual interactions. Before 3-D virtual worlds, cybersex was largely text-based. In the 1970s, the chat-room format of MUDS (multi-user domains) provided users with a way of interacting through text. There was no visual component; whatever was experienced was limited to what participants wrote. Later, in the 1990s, MMORPGs (massively multi-player online role-playing games) allowed a visual element, but the interaction was still limited to textual exchange (Gillis 2004). Today's visual depictions of sex in 3-D virtual worlds may also have antecedents in early video game technology. While some games were more explicitly built around sexual activities, for others the sexual content was something hidden that had to be hacked into, as was rumoured to be the case with *Tomb Raider* (where one could apparently hack into the game to get rid of Lara Croft's clothes). From the textual to the visual, technological developments over the years have aimed to simulate a 'real' sexual experience, not only in terms of the increased verisimilitude of representation but also in relation to the simulation (and stimulation) of sensation. Teledildonics, or cyberdildonics, is the classic example here, using haptic interfaces which, when attached to the body, recreate the tactile sensations of physical sex. Other researchers have suggested the possibility of eventually linking a computer direct to a user's brain, a vision explored by Kathryn Bigelow in her film *Strange Days* (1994).

The technological advancements in cybersex have been described by some as potentially revolutionary to the sex industry, promising – as they do – to eliminate the risk of disease or actual bodily harm to performers. For consumers, virtual worlds also offer the possibilities of interactions which, in the real world, may be illegal or stigmatized, as well as risky. For example, prostitution in virtual worlds is considered unproblematic in legal terms, essentially viewed as no more than chat. However, for my purposes here, the most significant impact of these developments has been their discursive framing and, specifically, the continual conflation of *sex* and the sex *industry* that occurs.[2] The driver behind the development of the sexual possibilities of technology has been the sex industry and, as I will argue in this chapter using the virtual world of Second Life as a case study, this has particular implications for the kinds of sex that have been imagined and enabled within these spaces.

Introducing Second Life

Second Life is a virtual world which is free to join for anyone over eighteen, enabling users – or 'residents', as they are termed in Second Life – to interact with others within the virtual community. It was created by Linden Labs, a San Francisco-based company, in 2003. When it was first launched, the virtual world contained 500 residents: today its population runs into the millions. Although some claims have reported over 15 million residents, many of the 'residents' may represent users with multiple accounts or people who logged on to see what the virtual world was like but never returned; still, the population rise of Second Life is undeniable. In fact, the number of residents logged in to Second Life at any given time is likely to equal that of a decent-size city. For instance, at the time of writing, Friday 30 October 2009 at 2.40 p.m., there were 51,164 residents logged in.

Popular activities in Second Life include visiting spectacular virtual locations usually based on the real world – such as Hollywood or Neo Kowloon City, designed after the famous district of Hong Kong. There are also communities based around fantasy role-playing games. Although generally avatars are modelled after humans, there is also a thriving community of what are termed 'Furries', people who prefer to model their avatars after a variety of animals. You can go shopping, buy land, build the house of your dreams, meet your friends at a club, take in a music gig or have a hot-air balloon ride – just to give a few examples of the ways in which Second Life activities mirror those of the real world. Of course, it is not only individuals who have a presence in Second Life: organizations and corporations do too. From universities who view the virtual world as a valuable 'shop window' for dispersing information to potential students, to charities like the Rape Crisis Centres who have utilized the virtual world as a safe space to generate debate and discussion, there is an assumption that Second Life reaches, and allows for engagement with, audiences who might not be so effectively addressed through more conventional forms of advertising and/or service delivery. Big-name corporations have also tapped in to the opportunities provided by Second Life. A whole range of companies maintain a presence there, from Toyota, American Apparel, Disney and Sky News to Apple, IBM and even the publisher of this book, Routledge. It is hardly surprising, then, that the porn industry has recognized the virtual world's commercial potential. For instance, Playboy produce a Second Life magazine featuring provocative images of avatars. They have invested in virtual property, building a Playboy island featuring a club and a place to buy Playboy merchandise. And, although now closed, Jenna Jameson also owned property for commercial use in Second Life.

While Second Life's tag line is 'Your world. Your imagination', like the real world it is still organized around capitalist interests. There are a number of Second Life entrepreneurs who make a real living trading in virtual dollars – or what's called the Linden dollar in Second Life.[3] On 16 April 2009, Linden Labs reported that despite the real-world economic crisis (which, unusually, has had a fairly dramatic impact on the business of pornography) the virtual world continues to experience significant growth, its economy reaching over US$120 million in the first quarter of 2009 (Linden 2009). Battles over commodities – in Second Life as in other virtual worlds – have led to real-world disputes. Linden Lab's ban on billboards intentionally placed by residents to obstruct prized views or generally pollute the landscape in order to drive down the price of prized real estate is just one example of the seriousness with which the virtual economy is dealt with.

Yet, the greatest industry that has built up in Second Life is the sex industry and, as I will now discuss, the fusion of sex and commerce in Second Life is particularly marked.

Sex in Second Life

New residents to Second Life quickly learn that, in-world, sex is not a birthright. To have sex in Second Life you must first buy your genitalia (all avatars are born essentially sexless in this sense), find a place to have sex (either a house you have bought or a hotel or some other space that is approved for sexual activity) and purchase sex positions – all of which will have been created and sold by fellow residents. In Second Life, then, all sex is commercial, but this commercial imperative is – perhaps unsurprisingly – rebranded in ways that resonate with wider discourses around internet identity-play and creativity.

The appearance of avatars is carefully constructed: from what an avatar wears to the texture of their hair or skin, or even their genitalia. All is alterable, and although the virtual world holds the promise of creating a unique and individual identity by allowing residents to change appearance using various settings and commands, for the most part significant appearance-altering objects, such as genitalia, are bought and sold. Detachable genitals have their uses, mechanically and aesthetically. Some would say they serve an aesthetic function and are just one further way of refining your avatar's appearance. But, of course, the main reason you buy your avatar a penis or vagina in Second Life is so that your avatar can have sex with other avatars. Some residents create 'skyboxes' or rooms located high in the sky, out of sight of the passing traffic at ground level, as locations for sex. Otherwise, sexual activities can potentially be seen by anyone who happens to pass by. There are few truly private spaces in Second Life and, as such, sex is typically potentially public, a form of representation as well as an in-world activity.

The potential for sex in virtual worlds has been promised as offering a safe ('public' but potentially anonymous) place for participants to explore their sexuality. Philip Rosedale, founder and CEO of Linden Lab, suggests:

> In a lot of ways, the presence of sex as an aspect of creative expression and playful behavior in a place like this is healthy, because it indicates we're doing something right. The presence of sex is also a sign that people are engaging with the community and with each other, and connecting with each other as human beings.
>
> (Rosedale, in Wagner 2007)

This idea of creative expression is mentioned a lot by the very people who seem to be getting the greatest commercial gains out of the virtual world.

Kevin Alderman, whose avatar is Stroker Serpentine, was the first resident to create and sell realistic genitalia in Second Life. He also sold his Amsterdam sim,[4] the first adult-oriented region in Second Life, on eBay for US$50,000.[5] Alderman claims to make a six-figure sum through his activities in Second Life and employs six people full-time. He owns a successful business selling a range of sex-related products, but his most lucrative and successful product range has been his SexGen beds, which sell for US$40–$50. Once an avatar has purchased their genitalia, and found someone who will have sex with them, they can purchase one of the beds for their home. When the object is clicked on, you are presented with a menu of sex moves. Alderman designed the moves himself, using a $25,000 motion capture suit, the kind of suit you would use for creating gestures and movements for characters in animation films.

In Alderman's description of his activities in Second Life, he is quick to emphasize the creative role that he plays:

> I get so involved in the character that Stroker really is more me than he is a character. But let's see. Stroker is a pervert at large. Erotic facilitator. Pornographic mogul. I like to think of myself in terms of being an adult friend finder, operating in an immersive environment where I can use my creative talents to bring people together. Stroker is a character I developed three

years ago within Second Life, and I started out with small events with like-minded individuals who also enjoyed the aspects of avie [avatar] erotica.

(Alderman in Lynn 2007)

The description provided by Alderman emphasizes his role as a 'player' in the 'game', his strong identification with his avatar and his creative engagement with the virtual world, while foregrounding the importance of connecting with the community. Although Alderman refers to himself as a pornographic mogul, this is humorously lumped in with a definition of his avatar as a pervert at large. Commercial endeavours are discussed but only in terms of how they articulate an authentic identity ('Stroker really is more me ... '). Although Alderman's invest-ment in Second Life clearly increased over the years – he gave up his plumbing business to pursue commercial enterprise in Second Life full-time – he still fore-grounds his commitment to his avatar, and to Second Life, as more of a hobby than a job.

In Stebbins' typology of the amateur and professional, an amateur is defined as a non-professional whose engagement with the activity is a hobby, conducted within leisure time, and is intended for private consumption. The professional on the other hand, is trained, engages seriously with the activity as work conducted within working hours, with an emphasis on public consumption (Stebbins 1992). This conflation of amateur and professional roles mirrors the ways in which the virtual world renders sex and commercial sex indistinguishable.

Much writing on virtual worlds celebrates their utopian possibilities. Citing Castronova's (2005) description of synthetic worlds that can be 'anything we want [them] to be', Hilde Corneliussen (2008: 68) argues that the environments can be the perfect cultural playground for perceptions of gender in our modern world. But how much is it about embodiment and exploring identity through a free construction of outward appearance and how much is it about controlling a sexualized virtual body? In the popular online role-playing game *Age of Conan*, anger erupted when a virus plagued a number of large-breasted avatars, shrinking their cup size considerably. What became apparent from the incident was that most of the players behind the large-breasted female avatars, and those most outraged by the sudden reduction, were men (Anon. 2008a). Alderman hints at a similar dynamic in Second Life in his description of its potential to explore identity without limitation:

It's interesting how much freedom you get in that you don't have any inhi-bitions to restrain you. If you want to be a Gorean and prostitute yourself to a master or become their personal sex slave, then go for it. If you want to be an escort in Amsterdam, or a domme, go for it. So many freedoms – things you couldn't normally do in real life or that you would love to do – the fantasy aspect is limitless.

(Alderman, in Lynn 2007)

Alderman's thoughts here reflect the general enthusiasm of residents who see freedom of expression opened up by the ease with which physical appearance can be altered and roles taken up or discarded. Or, recalling Sherry Turkle's work on identity and the internet, the online spaces becomes 'laboratories for the construction of identity' (1995: 184). But these freedoms are clearly not limitless. It is not down to each participant's imagination but, instead, to the imagination of the creators of the virtual world and those – like Alderman – who have developed and commercialized the possibilities for sexual engagement within it. It is striking that in the above quotation Alderman's 'fantasies' are so tied to *commercial* sex and, specifically, to assuming a feminized position within the commercial sexual exchange (or, more accurately, a male fantasy of that position). Of the many potential freedoms, he seems fixated on the 'freedom' to prostitute oneself, something that, apparently, only inhibition prevents 'you' from doing in real life.

However, Second Life does have real-life consequences, something Alderman himself has been driven to acknowledge in his court case for intellectual property theft when another avatar was found to be selling counterfeit copies of the SexGen bed. The court case took place in the real world and illustrates some pertinent points relating to the real-life relevance of virtual worlds: in the end they couldn't prove who the real person was behind the avatar, although they traced the account to a nineteen-year-old Texan who denied it (Leominster 2008). The theft of Alderman's sex-related merchandise has continued, and Alderman sued Linden Labs for its failure to protect his virtual property (Modine 2009; Kravets 2009).

Clearly, then, Second Life is not just a game, a fantasy space or utopian online community, but is a commercial enterprise in which goods of real-life value – many of which are directly linked with the pornography and sex industries – are exchanged. Although sex forms a large part of the activity within Second Life, there is no mention of the sexual activities or pornographic content available in the extensive official guide to Second Life (Rymaszewski *et al.* 2008). For all their claims about sex and creative expression in other contexts, Linden Labs clearly recognize that the promotion of in-world sex would, at some level, compromise the company's public image, a further reminder – if one were needed – that Second Life also has to function in the real world. Despite Linden Labs' apparent coyness on this point, the inherent commercialization of sex in-world raises important questions about the position of commercial sex activities within it. If, as I have suggested, all sex is already commercial in Second Life, what does this mean for the in-world activities (like prostitution and pornography) which, in real life, function within commercial sex industries?

Pornography and prostitution in Second Life

Second Life offers the full range of pornographic commercial goods. In addition to pornographic magazines, participants can subscribe to adult television channels to watch in their Second Life homes, or they can go to cinemas to watch a full range of adult films, including retro porn classics, hard-core and amateur films, as well as those using Second Life avatars. The standard viewing perspective is not wholly from the point of view of the avatar, although such a perspective can be activated using the 'mouselook' mode. Instead, the avatar is typically viewed within the context of the surrounding environment. In a virtual theatre (cinema), residents may choose to zoom in on the material presented on the screen or to keep the wider context of the theatre and its visitors within view. In this respect, the theatre provides a further platform for meeting prospective sexual partners. Some theatre seats also come equipped with in-built masturbation scripts.

This theatrical pornographic experience in-world contrasts with the real world, where people are forgoing public consumption of pornography in favour of a more private one. Yet the framing of the fantasy world acts as a distancing device between the real-world participant and the pornographic text. In reality, many of the films shown within the virtual world are streamed from existing pornographic web sites. But the virtual world transforms someone watching a porn film on their computer into someone's avatar watching a porn film in a virtual theatre, with other participants – the layering of virtual experiences detracting from the real activity.

Prostitution is also a lucrative business within the virtual world, and, indeed, many of the designated 'sex' areas simulate the seedy, undesirable areas associated with real inner-city crime and commercial sex. One of the most notorious areas of Second Life, involving extreme acts of sexual violence, is called Hard Core Alley. Other areas exist offering simulated rape experiences and there is even a Sex Trafficking community in existence. Sex workers earn US$10–$30 for a couple of hours. But, as one report highlights:

> It's not something that a brand-new character would be able to pull off, though; an expensive wardrobe of realistic avatar clothing, skins and anima-tions is an asset, as are gender verification and a location in which to practise. The industry supporting the sale of these items, and arranging escort encounters, seems more profitable than actual on-the-street work.
>
> (Lees 2006)

An overwhelming number of participants visit prostitutes in the virtual world. The statistics are considerably higher than ones usually quoted in the real world. As Alderman explains:

> Probably 60 percent of the women and men that come in-world at least try escorting or use the service because it's the jumping off point, where you can explore your sexuality anonymously. You can see what it is that Second Life has to offer in terms of avie erotica.
>
> (Alderman, in Lynn 2007)

Even if Alderman's figures are inflated (he has a commercial interest in nor-malizing this, after all), it is striking how easily sexuality becomes inextricably associated with commercial sex in the virtual context. While soliciting sex in real life may be illegal or considered morally or politically problematic, for the people behind the avatars (depending on where they are really located in the world) visiting a prostitute in a virtual world translates to a legitimate exploration of an authentic sexual identity.

Writing on sex workers in Second Life, journalists are quick to emphasize the high number of men working as female prostitutes, as if signalling a democratization of a labour force historically comprised of women (Ruberg 2007). Yet, sexualized representations in Second Life, from fashion to sexual positions to pornographic material, generally fall in line with the real world's gender/sex binaries. Women's clothing is often represented by the hyper-feminine, with only a slim offering of styles, ranging from beauty-queen ball gowns to dominatrix gear. Fairly stereotyped and generally unimaginative, shops are more like the real world (and often more stereotyped) than any sort of utopian fantasy, with aisles of clothing for women overwhelming the miniscule sections housing plain trousers and shirts for men. Similarly, sex in Second Life mirrors that seen in mainstream pornography depicting the objectification of one dominant group over another, the kind of representation anti-pornography feminists like Dworkin, MacKinnon, Dines and Jensen constantly oppose (Dworkin 1981, 1997; Dworkin and MacKinnon 1988; MacKinnon 1987; Dines *et al.* 1998; Jensen 2007a). In fact, one Second Life activist who has developed a version of the anti-pornography slide show (discussed in Chapter 2, this volume) for awareness-raising purposes in Second Life explained in an interview that all of the themes found in the real-world slide show are present in Second Life, but often in 'more extreme' forms. Although the interviewee was enthusiastic about the potential of the virtual world as a creative space, she also explained that what she was most struck by was the misogyny.[6]

While Linden Lab's tag line 'Your world. Your imagination' plays on the promise of freedom to explore identities outside constraints of the corporeal world, the reality of virtual worlds is that, for the most part, they tend to adhere fairly rigidly to the norms and conventions of the real world. Virtual worlds may seem to possess a destabilizing potential akin to Judith Butler's development of the ideas around 'genderfuck' (1990), but the promise of performances of gender in the virtual world that are not linked to biological sex is rarely a reality; instead, the virtual usually merely reproduces what lies in the frame of the heterosexual matrix.

Many of the sexual gestures for sale in Second Life mimic the content of hardcore porn, focus on sexual difference and include sex-related physical violence. General acts of violence place women, or avatars posing as women, in a position of vulnerability and submission, where women are punished and generally degraded. For instance, one animation entitled 'Slapable Cum Face' includes ten slap levels, three pain sounds, three cum levels and red cheeks, presumably allowing a more realistic representation of violence. Although the use of violent animations is presumably with the avatar's consent, some residents have reported abusive treatment from more experienced residents who choose to exploit new residents' lack of knowledge and experience with the virtual environment (Linden 2007).

Yet in many respects it seems inconsequential whether or not the person behind the female avatar being physically abused is a man or a woman, just as it doesn't really matter if the female stripper working in Second Life is a man or a woman. The fantasy of the gender roles of dominance and submission, and the acting out of sexual violence along the lines of gender, remain the same. The identities in Second Life are temporary but the engagement with sexual inequalities is the same no matter which role you are playing in the game. A player's embodiment as a sex worker in Second Life only seems to further pornography's narrative of dominance and submission. If a large proportion of pornographic content is about serving up sexually submissive images of women for the sexual pleasure of men, what better way of ensuring the centrality of the male consumer within this transaction than allowing him to serve as the director of the fantasy – choosing the appearance and body type, actions and gestures, of the fantasy's key performer?

As I have already established, prostitution within Second Life is always also a form of pornography, a representation to be viewed not only by participants but also, potentially, by other residents. As such, Second Life prostitution/pornography can be usefully contextualized in relation to other forms of avatar and anime pornography popular outside of virtual worlds as well as within them. Whereas the body types represented in 'real life' pornography are limited by what is possible under the plastic surgeon's knife, in avatar (avie)/anime porn (including in Second Life) such physical restrictions do not apply: you can create an avie porn star to fit your own unique preferences. Here the blurring of fantasy with real world proves problematic, however. In many instances, avie/anime porn is available on free sites and remains largely uncensored, its content seen as relatively harmless even when the actions represented would be illegal if enacted by real people. For example, one infamous interactive internet game, entitled *Drug Rape Girl*,[7] features an anime of a child, stripped, gagged, bound and seated over a toilet with her legs forced apart. You cannot make out any facial features and a ransom note hangs around her neck. A message above explains the object of the game 'Dirty girl tied up and ready to get raped' – the object is to insert a number of objects into the victim's vagina until she is visibly sexually pleasured. Another, perhaps more infamous, example of sexual violence from interactive gaming is in *Grand Theft Auto 4*, where players can have sex with a prostitute, then kill her.

While some users may feel more comfortable with virtual porn stars and cyberpornography, the scenarios played out are never divorced from their real life significance. It is not just pornographic images depicting graphic violence that are of concern, but the interaction and role playing involved in virtual pornography: the viewer is invited to actively participate in sexual violence. Whilst it would be a jump to claim that a willingness to rape in Second Life (or in a video game) *necessarily* impacts on subsequent real-life behaviour, it is a mistake to think that Second Life is completely divorced from real life. Not all rape within Second Life is role play: there have been instances of rape, and the abuse of one's avatar can cause real-life trauma (Linden 2007). You can now buy genitals that can be used only by unlocking them with a special code that can be activated only by the avatars themselves. The sense of threat (and the need to purchase commodities to offset the threat) is a way of policing the virtual space and closing down possibilities for mobility and freedom within it for those less confident in the technology, echoing feminist arguments about the impact of real-life rape on *all* women.

Whatever persona is adopted, levels of subjectivity are variable. Writing on gaming, Aylish Wood describes the layering of attention divided across the multiplicity of levels evident in the game's architecture (2007: 105–32). Similarly, although the adoption of first-person personas and active participation in events unfolding in virtual worlds clearly differs from traditional cinema spectatorship, a player's experience is never one of complete immersion. Although a first-person point of view may be invoked, players' avatars are most likely to be visible. Furthermore, players' interaction with the on-screen world often involves a layering of attention similar to that which Wood refers to. A variety of tool bars, relating to general navigation, player inventories or general chat, serve as distancing devices, enforcing a player's agency outside of their adopted persona. Ultimately, the player in Second Life operates simultaneously as both the subject and the object.

The existence of rape as role play in Second Life raises further questions not just about viewer engagement but also about Second Life as a representation viewed by others not involved in the activity. (Representations of rape fantasies can look a lot like representations of rape.) The representational status affords Second Life activities protection in some instances (e.g. rape and prostitution in-world are not crimes but, rather, protected speech) (Brenner 2008: 52), but it is not simply the case that 'anything goes', and debates about appropriate behaviour in-world tend to be framed as debates about censorship, fantasy and representation. In 2007, Linden Labs issued a statement on its blog site that it would not tolerate 'broadly offensive content', including 'real-life images, avatar portrayals' of sexual acts 'appearing to involve children or minors' or 'other depictions of sexual violence, including rape' (Linden 2007: 1). There was a good deal of response from Second Life residents, resulting in over fifty printed pages. Responses were both in favour and against the decision (although more against). One resident echoed a number of responses that interpreted Linden Lab's actions as an infringement of their freedom and the utopian possibilities of the virtual world, stating, 'If you truly accepted diversity, then you'd accept all groups equally' (Sekai Axon, in Linden 2007: 2). Furthermore, while many users understood the ban on 'ageplay', concern was expressed over whether sex between the furry community (animal avatars) would be banned as an act of bestiality. The ban on representations of rape was also questioned, due to its popularity in the BDSM community: 'You are making no difference between someone "griefing" someone else by playing a rape scenario out to them against their will and two people playing out a role-playing fantasy on their own land while being spyed [*sic*] on by nosy AR [Abuse Report] hawks' (Linden 2007: 12). Some argued the bans imposed would make it more or less like the real world and would repress the potential for the exploration of fantasy: 'Your list of bannable behavior up there completely trumps any sort of fantasy whatsoever and reduced "acceptable" behavior to that which you would expect to see in public in real life' (Farallon Greyskin, in Linden 2007: 9). Others viewed the proposed bans as exceeding the restrictions of the real world: 'Role playing a rape is now not acceptable in SL, while completely legal in RL' (Maeve Maidstone, in Linden 2007: 17).

Again, it is the virtual qualities of Second Life, and their conflation with the material, that create the greatest point of conflict. As Tom Boellstorff explains 'binarisms like material versus representations ... are reconfigured – not eliminated' within the virtual environment (2008: 164). While many assess the offensiveness of Second Life content through its comparison with what might be seen in films, ratings for films are generally based on the context and not just the sexual acts themselves. On the other hand, if you accept Susan Sontag's argument that 'experiences aren't pornographic, only representations' (1967) where does Second Life fall in relation to this? As the comments from the blog noted above reveal, for many residents Second Life is not just a game but is often seen as an alternative world where the activities and experiences are just as significant, if not more so, as those that take place in the real world. Nevertheless, on a material level, the virtual will always evoke representation. As Waskul *et al.* explain, 'in the social worlds of on-line computer-mediated environments, there are no corporeal bodies. There are only symbolic representations of bodies' (2004: 17).[8]

For such reasons, regulating Second Life is a challenging task. Linden Labs has taken further steps to address the circulation of pornographic content in-world. Following a report to the United States Congress on the availability of explicit online content to minors, Linden Labs has moved to ensure adult content is restricted to certain areas. Eventually all explicit material will be on a separate continent. They are also tightening their registration procedures to ensure minors are not able to sign up for adult accounts. Linden Labs also proposes a rating system akin to film classification guidelines. What is not clear, however, is how content will be assessed. As discussed earlier, ratings for films are often assessed in relation to context, something that would be impossible to measure in Second Life.

Not surprisingly there are emotive responses both for and against the proposals. Although the new regulations may go some way to appeasing those dissatisfied with the pervasiveness and unavoidable nature of explicit content in Second Life, there is also the possibility that moving the activities to one contained area may mean there is more freedom for developing extreme content. While these increased measures have excited anger on the part of residents who believe their personal rights are being infringed, the actions further emphasize the virtual world's existence as a public, regulated, commercial space where, as this chapter has attempted to illustrate, personal expressions of sexuality are almost always expressed through commercial means.

In Second Life all sex is ultimately commercial sex.

Notes

1 See Dines, Whisnant, Thompson and Boyle, in Chapter 1 of this volume, for anecdotal accounts of women's distress at their male partner's pornography use.

2 A typical example is the web site 'Through the Flame', a 'pornography and sex addiction support group' on line at <http://www.throughtheflame.org/> (accessed 16 November 2009).

3 Linden Labs operates the LindeX exchange, the main resource for buying and selling Linden dollars. The exchange rate is roughly 250 Linden dollars to one US dollar.

4 A sim is a simulated space in a virtual world.

5 It was bought by an investment group in the Netherlands for marketing purposes.

6 Interview with a Second Life feminist activist conducted for this article, 25th June 2009. It is a reminder of the potential consequences of speaking out in both real and virtual worlds (see also Chapter 1, this volume) that my interviewee asked not to be identified in this article, either by her real name or avie name. Her insights into Second Life have been extremely valuable in preparing this chapter and I would like to acknowledge her contribution here.

7 Available HTTP: <http://www.funny-games.biz/yumi-rape.html> (accessed 23 November 2009).

8 Second Life's introduction of voice chat capabilities raises issues for further analysis. However, initial reports suggest that the function is generally used as an extended form of communication between people who have some form of real-world connection and that many Second Life residents prefer not to enable voice chat.

Part II

Address, consumption, regulation

Chapter 7

Pornography is what the end of the world looks like

Robert Jensen

To start off my lectures to college audiences about pornography, I often ask students to fill in the blank in the sentence 'Pornography is – ' It's a simple exercise designed to get people to articulate their understanding of the subject and reflect on the role such material plays in their lives. To try to elicit the most honest responses, I jokingly tell them that they can respond the way they would fill in the blank, or with words that others they know might use. That gives them plausible deniability: if people around them cast a negative glance at their answer to the 'Pornography is' question, they can say, 'Well, I certainly wouldn't say that, but my brother/friend/roommate would.'

The responses are predictable: Pornography is 'awesome', 'hot', 'sexy', 'a turn-on'. It's also 'degrading' and 'disgusting' to some. And pornography is 'big business', 'profitable', and 'everywhere'. People recognize that pornography is effective in delivering sexual stimulation to the mostly male viewers, while some people, especially many women, reject the misogyny of the genre. Everyone understands that a lot of money can be made selling pornography, which is part of why there is so much pornography so readily available in so many places.

With those responses out on the table, I give folks my answer. After twenty years of research on the pornography industry, the products it produces and consumers' use of them, I explain that I fill in the sentence this way:

> Pornography is what the end of the world looks like.

By that I don't mean that pornography is going to bring about the end of the world; I don't have apocalyptic delusions. Nor do I mean that, of all the social problems we face, pornography is the most threatening. Instead, I want to suggest that if we have the courage to look honestly at contemporary pornography, we get a glimpse – in a very visceral, powerful fashion – of the consequences of the unjust and oppressive systems in which we live. Pornography is what the end will look like if we don't reverse the pathological course that we are on in patriarchal, white-supremacist, predatory corporate-capitalist societies.

If we look honestly at pornography, what can we see? Imagine a world in which empathy, compassion and solidarity – the things that make decent human society possible – are finally and completely overwhelmed by a self-centred, emotionally detached pleasure-seeking. Imagine those values playing out in a society structured by multiple hierarchies in which a domination/subordination dynamic shapes relationships and interaction. What would the result of those kinds of political and social forces look like? If we have the courage to look, pornography can help us imagine that. Pornography can act as an unsettling mirror, forcing us to look at the consequences of dominance of men, white people and wealthy First World people.

When I make this claim, people are often at first perplexed. After all, pornography is just sex that shows up on a screen. Maybe it's raunchy a lot of the time, and maybe it's mean-spirited sometimes, but it's just sex, and people have always had sex and will keep having sex, so what's the big deal? Isn't it a bit melodramatic to start a lecture that way? Isn't such a claim, as a friend of mine once suggested, 'a little overwrought'?

Actually, I wish he were right; I would find it comforting to be able to write off my conclusion as histrionics or hysteria. I would be overjoyed to find out that my assessment of the pornography industry, the products it produces and the consumers' use of those products was misguided. But, in fact, every year my sense of despair deepens over the direction in which pornography and our pornographic culture are heading. That despair is rooted not in the reality that lots of people can be cruel, or that some number of them knowingly take pleasure in that cruelty; humans have always had to deal with that aspect of our psychology. But what happens when people can no longer see the cruelty, when the pleasure in cruelty has been so normalized that it is rendered invisible to so many? And what happens when, for some considerable part of the male population of our society, that cruelty becomes a routine part of sexuality, defining the most intimate parts of our lives?

In this chapter I want to explore these questions by retracing my steps in those two decades of research, not for the sake of nostalgia or self-indulgence but to help come to terms with that despair. In addition to reporting some of what I have learned, I want to chart what it has felt like. Mapping the emotional landscape of the study of pornography helps illuminate why most of the culture – whether liberal supporters of pornography or its conservative critics – find it so hard to look honestly in the mirror that pornography offers. Such an emotional journey can be difficult, but it can lead us to political insights, through a feminist critique of pornography and the sexual exploitation industries, which can help us not only face that grief but deal realistically with the crises we face.

The images that produce erections: 'disturbing and exciting'

For the first ten years I worked on the issue of pornography the focus of my writing was on the legal and philosophical issues around sexually explicit material. Except for one small study of pornographic novels that contained no pictures, I stayed away from an analysis of the magazines and movies. That decision was rooted in the recognition that, as someone who had been raised in a porno-graphic culture and used pornography as a child and young adult, I needed to make sure that I wasn't studying pornography simply as an excuse to continue watching it, under the guise of 'research'.

Finally, in 1997, as it became clear that the industry was changing and that we needed an up-to-date analysis of images, my friend Gail Dines and I decided to undertake a qualitative content analysis of contemporary video pornography that became the basis for a chapter in a co-authored book (Dines *et al.* 1998). We rented a representative sample of popular pornographic films based on conversa-tions with porn store managers and clerks, and we began evaluating the patterns in representations of gender and race. It became clear quickly that the experience would be very different for me and for Gail. She struggled to cope with watching the woman-hating sexual activity, which so often included what she came to call 'body-punishing' sex in which women were the targets of men's contempt. She would turn to me and ask, 'Why do men like this?' I had the answers that the feminist anti-pornography critique had articulated. Men routinely are socialized in patriarchy to find male dominance and female submission sexy. That's true not just of the 'bad guys' or the sociopaths, but virtually all men. For that claim, I had the evidence of my body. I had an erection. 'These movies are disturbing, and exciting,' I said.

That research project made it clearer than ever to me that a decade of intel-lectual and political work to understand the nature of pornography had not erased three decades of social training to find the material arousing. It reminded me that reading feminist theory and being part of a feminist movement did not elevate me above men's struggles with our sexist training. The patterns in the material were clear: sex in contemporary pornography was relentlessly misogynist and overtly racist. Even though my politics were feminist and anti-racist, my body reacted the way it was trained.[1]

Four years later, this time working by myself in Austin, I undertook a similar study to determine whether the patterns that Gail and I had identified had changed. Once again I gathered up a representative sample of pornography from local pornography outlets and this time sat down alone in a room at my uni-versity for three days of viewing. The basic patterns in the material hadn't chan-ged, nor had my physical reaction; I still was sexually aroused by material that was designed to sexually arouse me.

But something was different this time. I found the work emotionally more draining, perhaps because I was working alone, without a comrade, and perhaps because my understanding of the issue had continued to develop over the years. Whatever the case, at the end of one day's viewing I was driving home when, with no warning and no apparent provocation, I began to sob. The images from the videos I had watched that day flooded over me, especially a young woman in one film who had been kneeling while eight men in turn forced their penises down her throat far enough to make her gag before ejaculating on her face and in her mouth.

'I don't want to live in this world,' I found myself saying to myself.

There was something about those images, in conjunction with my years of study and public presentations about pornography, that pushed me into a deep despair. It's not just that the images were so cruel, but that the cruelty was there to intensify the pleasure for men. The world is full of barbarism, of stories reminding us of what violence and cruelty humans are capable of. But there was something about seeing so clearly that violence and cruelty packaged and sold as entertainment that left me profoundly sad. It's not that I had stumbled on to any insights that were original, but that the viewing had deepened my understanding. When that project was over and the article about that work was written (Jensen 2002), I wasn't sure I would continue to follow the industry or write about the issue. But as the industry changed rapidly with the rise of the internet and the mainstreaming of pornography continued, I decided to repeat the study two years later and wrote another article (Jensen 2004), which I expected to be my last. But about that time I met two documentary film makers who wanted to explore these issues, and so I found myself in Las Vegas.

The industry that produces the images: 'unkind, violent'

I have attended the Adult Entertainment Expo (AEE), the annual gathering of the pornography industry in Las Vegas, three times to interview the people who make and use sexually explicit material.[2] Each year, one of my questions to the producers was why pornography, especially the more extreme gonzo pornography, had become so overtly cruel and degrading to women. Porn director Richard De Monfort explained to me that he saw no reason for pornography to emulate Hollywood in storytelling style, that pornography shouldn't pretend to be something other than raw sex. 'The reason for pornography's existence is to get guys off,' he said. Even men in sexually active relationships with a woman will want to use pornography, because 'men are beasts. We are creatures of lust who never get enough sex.' The kinds of images that the contemporary pornography industry produces to feed the beast didn't bother him, and De Monfort saw no reason to try to change it. 'Nothing human disgusts me – that's a famous quote, and I believe that,' he told me. It is indeed a well known line, but the porn director's incomplete recollection of the statement by the character Hannah Jelkes in Tennessee Williams's play *The Night of the Iguana* reveals much about pornography. The complete line is 'Nothing human disgusts me unless it's unkind, violent' (Williams 1961: 418).

De Monfort is the director of such films as *Vicky Vette's Amateur Ho's*, *Fresh Asses*, *Lip Lock My Cock*, *Little Latina Cum Slaves*, *Asian Sex Objects* and *Black Girls Wanna Cracker?* Based on his comment, I assumed that he did not find these titles unkind or violent. Perhaps that is because so much of contemporary pornography is relentlessly unkind and violent, within a larger society that is relentlessly unkind and violent. When unkindness and violence become routine, they become invisible.

Pornography presents women as objectified female bodies that exist for men's sexual pleasure. Because women in pornography are not subjects but objects, not fully human, kindness toward them is no more required than would be kindness to any other object. If while out for a walk I picked up a stone and threw it down the road, no one would chastise me for being unkind to the stone. So it is in pornography. Violence along a continuum from abusive language to slapping and hair pulling to a brutal body-punishing penetration is the inevitable result of objectifying the women. After many years of work on the subject and those three content-analysis projects, comments like De Monfort's hardly surprised me.

When I attended that first AEE, I knew I could learn a lot from talking to people there, but I didn't think that being there would have much of an effect on me. I was going as part of the group working on a documentary film – *The Price of Pleasure* (Sun and Picker 2008)[3] – and we had an ambitious schedule for interviewing and filming. I thought I would be too busy to be affected emotionally. I went into journalist/researcher mode, as emotionally detached as possible. But it didn't work.

As we roamed the huge Sands Expo and Convention Center, which accommodated about 300 booths and thousands of people a day, rock music pulsated from multiple directions. There were photos of naked women everywhere, video screens running porn loops scattered throughout the hall, display tables of dildos and sex dolls. And around every corner were performers in various states of undress, signing posters and posing for pictures. Flashes popped constantly as fans photographed their favourite stars.

I talked with young men who told me that pornography had taught them a lot about what women really want sexually. I listened to Paul Hesky, chief operating officer of Multimedia Pictures, tell me that he thinks anal sex is popular in pornography because men like to think about fucking their wives and girlfriends in the ass to pay them back for being bitchy. And I interviewed producer/director Jeff Steward, who told me with great pride that his *Gag Factor* series was the first to exclusively feature 'aggressive throat fucking'.

One of the strangest aspects of my trips to AEE was talking to producers and directors who agreed that some of the more extreme gonzo material was pushing the limits but didn't see their own work as problematic. Sal Genoa, a director for the gonzo company Anabolic, described his work as 'really good hardcore sex with artistic flair,' which included double-anal scenes, in which two men penetrate a woman anally at the same time. I asked him about the attraction of double anal. 'It's a limits thing. It's taking that girl to the limits. What's double anal? That's insane – two dicks in the ass,' Genoa said. He went on to explain that he tried to 'get the most you can' from a female performer. He also said that he wanted 'the girl to have the greatest experience ever' in his scenes. He didn't seem to consider that those two objectives might conflict. Pushing a woman into performances that include multiple penetrations that he himself describes as 'insane' provides the 'greatest' experience possible'? How much greater could it get for the women in pornography? Like most of the directors I talked to, he was unsure of what the new trends in gonzo would be. 'Where can it go besides [multiple penetrations]?' Genoa said. 'Every hole is filled.'

Lexington Steele, one of the industry's most successful producer/directors, agreed. 'Gonzo really always pushes the envelope. The thing about it is, there's only but so many holes, only but so many different types of penetration that can be executed upon a woman. So it's really hard to say what's next within gonzo.' Steele had his own standards for what is acceptable sexual activity in pornography. He said he shoots double-penetration scenes, in which two men penetrate a woman vaginally and anally at the same time, but that he doesn't do double anal. That's going too far. 'A lot of gonzo is becoming circus acts,' he said.

So, a double penetration is fine, but a double anal crosses the line. Such are the conversations one has at AEE. It's tempting to say it's like walking around in a parallel universe based on other values, but the values of AEE are, in fact, the values of the dominant culture, albeit taken to the extreme. That's what's so disturbing – one can't simply write it off as a deviant space. In this claim, the pornographers are correct: they are part of the cultural mainstream in the United States.

After the first day of filming for the documentary, I walked out of the convention hall with the director and told him we were going to stop at a bar because I needed a drink. Shortly after we sat down, I started crying, with that same thought in my head. 'I don't want to live in this world,' I found myself saying to my friend.

After the end of a second day, we were back at the same table in the same hotel bar, with the same thought in my head and the same tears. By the end of the third day, I was mostly just numb. For all that I knew about pornography before I arrived at the AEE, there was something unsettling about being surrounded by the industry – the producers, directors, performers, fans and various hangers-on – in a space where their vision of men and women, sex and power, was unchallenged. After returning from the AEE, I started to think that the pornographers have won the battle to define the most intimate spaces in our lives. That thought was disturbing, and not the least bit exciting.

The images: 'If I look at another one of these pictures I will die'

The second year that I attended the Adult Entertainment Expo, to gather more material for a book (Jensen 2007a), I developed a way to cope with the psychic overload; I realized I would really have to work at shutting down emotionally, which I did fairly effectively. At about the same time, a research group with which I was working undertook a large-scale quantitative analysis of the content of pornographic films (Wosnitzer and Bridges 2007) and I decided to do another qualitative study using the same material they were collecting, which would conclude the research for my book.

So, once again, I sat down in a room at my university to watch a representative sample of the most popular pornography. The patterns of misogyny and racism remained the same, only with a noticeable intensification of both. Contemporary industrial pornography's use of sexism and racism to heighten the sexual charge was not new, but the pace of that intensification seemed to have quickened.

Sitting at my computer, I tried to find that position of detachment so that I could finish the project. As in the previous studies, I had fifteen films that I intended to analyse, but by film number 10 I couldn't go on. In conjunction with what my colleagues' quantitative analysis was finding, the patterns were as clear as ever, and I didn't feel the need to continue. But, more important, I didn't think I could continue and stay emotionally whole. Though it sounds hyperbolic, I remember telling a friend that I had to stop. 'If I look at another one of these pictures I will die,' I told him. I had reached my limit. The cumulative effect of the pornography convention in Las Vegas and four content studies – on top of the two decades of writing and speaking about the subject – had pushed me as far as I could go. I turned off my computer one day and quit. I knew enough to write the book that I wanted to write; each film I watched simply confirmed what I already knew, which is a sign that no new patterns will likely emerge and the research project can be concluded.

But beyond the intellectual criteria there was an emotional reality. I simply couldn't go on without endangering my mental health. No matter how hyperbolic that sounds, it didn't seem to me then, or now, that I was being overly dramatic. At that point, I was no longer worried about how my own training as a man in patriarchy had socialized me to find the films pleasurable. There were lingering traces of that, but by that point I was coming to understand that my concern was not that I might find the films arousing but that I might stop feeling altogether. The only way I could deal with the images was to shut off some part of myself, and I feared that I might lose that part of myself. I was afraid I might lose my capacity for empathy if I shut off too completely.

At that point I thought back to an interview I had done at AEE with Bill Ware, who was in the sales end of the business with his own distribution company. He had been touting a particular film with a particular female performer (Nikki Hunter) and I had asked him what made her so special. 'She becomes somebody different when she's got a dick in her ass and a dick in her pussy,' he said. 'She's no longer this prima donna. She's a slut whore and it's like revenge. For all these times that she's told me no, all these times she's rejected me, for all these times – I get to get her back. She gets a dick in her ass and a dick in her pussy.' I asked him if he thought that was the attraction of gonzo pornography for men, a chance to get back at women who can reject them. 'Beautiful women are intimidating to everybody,' Ware said, 'because they can take this virile American white male and just tear him to pieces, shred him up in a minute. It's all about getting back at this bitch. That's what it's all about.' I told him that seemed rather depressing. 'What about love?' I asked. 'Love?' he responded. 'What does love have to do with it?'

Later I realized I had chosen the wrong word. I didn't mean love, in the sense of romantic love. I was trying to talk about empathy. What happens to our sense of empathy, our love at a deeper level?

What's empathy got to do with it?

Empathy is the enemy of the pornographers. Men would not be able to be aroused by such material if they routinely empathized with the female performers. If the men who use pornography saw those women as fully human, as subjects not objects, the contradictions would be too obvious, forcing a choice between an erection and self-respect.

Pornography is what the end of the world looks like because pornography demands that men abandon empathy, and a world without empathy is a world without hope. Empathy is not itself a strategy for progressive social change, but it is difficult to imagine people being motivated to work for progressive social change if they have no capacity for it. Politics is more than empathy, but empathy matters. Empathy is a necessary but not sufficient condition for the work that challenges the domination/subordination dynamic of existing hierarchies, and transcending that dynamic is crucial if there is to be a just and sustainable future.

By coming to see women as fully human, we men have the chance to become fully human ourselves. When men remain trapped by the culture's toxic markers of masculinity – dominance, aggression, conquest and control – we are blocked not only from deeper and more meaningful relationships with women but also from such relationships with other men, and we also give up the chance to deepen our sense of ourselves. When we expend so much energy in the struggle to remain dominant, we have that much less to be truly human in connection with self and others. We diminish our ability to contribute to a just and sustainable future.

Men who use pornography typically see the feminist critique as a threat and see radical feminists as trying to take something from us. As a young man, that is how I understood feminism and feminists – as a set of ideas and as a group of people to be mocked, to cover my fear that they may be right about me and about men. Eventually I came to see feminism not as a threat but as a gift.[4] As a man working in a feminist movement, a major part of my task is finding ways to offer that same gift to other men.

At this point, people often ask for more detailed strategies; once we identify a problem, there is a tendency to want to move immediately to crafting a solution, which typically leads to a discussion of law and public policy. In this case I hesitate to rush to such strategizing, in part because no clear public policy solutions to the problem of pornography currently exist and none may be possible within the existing norms and structures of a liberal capitalist state.[5] Liberal ideals focus on individual freedom with little understanding of how systemic oppression structures identity and options; a predatory contemporary capitalism relentlessly commodifies everything in a supposedly free market; and concentrated state power remains a serious threat to real freedom and justice. Those are not minor considerations when trying to craft public policy, and there's no point in shaping strategies that ignore these realities.

In addition to concerns about the limits of immediate action on policy, I fear that the rush to talk strategy derails our ability to look in the cultural mirror that pornography offers. As I have suggested, looking honestly at pornography is difficult not just because of visceral reactions to the cruelty and brutality, but because of the disturbing insights it provides into the domination/subordination dynamic that structures so much of our lives, from the intimate to the planetary. Those insights are indeed painful, but never has it been more important to confront them. The horrors of the world – both macro and micro, emotional and political – sometimes seem too overwhelming for sustained attention. We want to look and learn, but too often we look away quickly, and the demand that we take immediate action can be one justification for looking away. The 'problem with solutions' (Jensen 2007b) is that our rush to act, rooted in our fear of fully facing the depth of the problem, can short-circuit the thinking and feeling necessary to come to terms with the nature of the crisis. Especially when no short-term proposals seem viable, we have the chance to face these horrors – even linger on them – as part of a process of coming to terms with the radical nature of the changes needed if there is to be any hope for a decent future.

Facing all this requires moral courage, and I believe that courage is essential if there is to be any hope for any kind of future at all.

Notes

1 As Whisnant notes (Chapter 1, this volume), feminists have begun to use the term 'dysrotic' to describe this disjunction between physical and emotional responses to pornography, although this has yet to be seriously explored in research on pornography consumption (see Flood, this volume).

2 My first visit to AEE was in January 2005, with the documentary film crew. I also attended in 2006 and 2008.

3 Available from Media Education Foundation. Online <http://www.mediaed.org/cgi-bin/commerce.cgi?display=home> (accessed 13 November 2009).

4 Crucial to that process for me were the writings of Andrea Dworkin, especially her essay 'I want a twenty-four-hour truce during which there is no rape' (Dworkin 1988).

5 The feminist anti-pornography movement of the 1980s in the United States proposed a shift from state-initiated and -directed obscenity law in the criminal arena to a victim-initiated and -directed tort law in the civil arena. That proposal was rejected by the courts on constitutional grounds (MacKinnon and Dworkin 1997). Even with modifications to that legislation, such as dropping the expansive 'trafficking in pornography' cause of action, which would bring it more in line with contemporary US jurisprudence on freedom of expression, it is unlikely the proposal would gain political traction without a vibrant feminist movement offering a radical analysis. Such a movement would be years, maybe decades, in the making under the best conditions, which do not exist at the moment.

Chapter 8

From Jekyll to Hyde

The grooming of male pornography consumers

Rebecca Whisnant

> The feminist critique [of pornography] asks a simple but devastating question of men: 'Why is this sexually pleasurable to you, and what kind of person does that make you?'
>
> (Jensen 2002)

In contemporary mainstream pornography marketed to heterosexual men, hostile and humiliating acts against women are commonplace. Consumers of such pornography routinely see women treated in ways that most people would neither choose for themselves nor accept for those they care about. While some of these consumers may be sociopaths or utterly unregenerate misogynists, I assume that the majority are neither. Thus, many consumers must experience ethical qualms about at least some of the pornography they encounter and about themselves in so far as they enjoy such material. These qualms pose a threat to their continued enjoyment of pornography. Thus, if they are to continue consuming pornography, they must find ways to silence their ethical concerns. They must, in effect, be groomed to accept sexual dominance and sadism against women.

To groom someone for some practice or function is simply to train or prepare them for it. While this process can be benign, it becomes sinister when one is trained to accept the unacceptable. For instance, individuals who are to be used sexually on a routine basis must be groomed to regard such use as normal: the grooming process employed by pimps and molesters typically involves isolating a victim, undermining her perceptions of reality and breaking down her limits through whatever combination of manipulation and force may be needed. Not only victims require grooming, however; people of normal empathy and conscience must also be groomed to accept and enjoy abusive thoughts, emotions and actions. The abuser too must be groomed – even if he is only a vicarious abuser.

Robert Jensen has observed that 'the danger of pornography is heightened exactly because it is only one part of a sexist system and because the message it carries about sexuality is reinforced elsewhere' (2007a: 103). In a culture that normalizes male sexual aggression against females in a variety of contexts, the typical consumer is pre-groomed to accept such aggression before he ever begins using pornography. In this article, I argue that many pornography consumers undergo further and more specific grooming as they acclimate to rougher and more openly sadistic materials. This grooming is a co-operative effort involving both the industry and the individual consumer. Both, after all, have something important at stake: for the industry, continued profits; and for the consumer, an important way in which he has come to experience sexual pleasure. In this co-operative grooming process, I will contend, the male porn user becomes both abuser and abused, consumer and consumed.[1]

Content and escalation

In today's mainstream pornography, aggression against women is the rule rather than the exception. For some initial evidence supporting this claim, one need only survey lists of titles at any online porn portal, or on any website selling adult DVDs: *Border Bangers, Disgraced 18, Gangland Victims, Bitchcraft, Gag on my Cock, Animal Trainer 20, Wrecked 'em, Butthole Whores 2, Tamed Teens*. The industry further markets hostile treatment of women through publications such as *Adult Video News* (see Tyler, this volume). A content analysis of best-selling 'adult' DVDs – identified through *AVN* listings – confirms that this is not simply hyperbolic marketing: physical aggression appeared in 88 per cent of all scenes and verbal aggression in 48 per cent (Wosnitzer and Bridges 2007; see also Bridges, this volume).

Thus, both cursory observation and detailed research indicate that hostile, aggressive content is so prevalent in contemporary pornography that it would be hard for a regular consumer to avoid it. In addition, we can consult the consumers themselves, who presumably know better than anyone the content of what they are watching. In online forums, consumers frequently remark on the normality of aggressive, 'over the top' content in today's pornography. Some celebrate this trend and others decry it, but virtually all agree that the trend exists and is unlikely to reverse itself.

Thus, each pornography consumer must somehow come to terms with aggressive content, and consumers no doubt embark on their porn use with varying ethical boundaries. Some may regard any aggression (like slapping or name-calling) as out of bounds, while others may object only if they see obvious, unambiguous signs of non-consent. Still others may think that 'anything goes' as long as it does not involve children. Whatever a consumer's initial boundaries are, however, they are likely to erode over time due to a process of desensitization and escalation. The kinds of pornography he started out using will become boring and he will have to look for something new and different in order to continue getting the same charge.

Many consumers are acutely aware of this escalation dynamic. James, a college student interviewed by Maltz and Maltz, explains that

> I need things that are a little more perverse, a little more dangerous, to get the good feeling I'm after. Even just thinking: *This is bad* or *This is really*

bad, can pump me up. And nowadays it's not hard to find hard-core with people slapping, choking, cutting, urinating, and even vomiting on someone. I know it's not a good idea to watch that stuff, but I keep getting pulled in for the high.

(Maltz and Maltz 2008: 89)

In an online discussion of pornography in which women are slapped, one consumer observes

I like face slapping and I'm sure many people think that crosses the line and is misogynistic. They're probably right but I am really desensitized to it and I really love to watch the rough aggressive sex.

(Taylor Von Bailey on <adultdvdtalk.com>, posted 1 June 2009)

And in a discussion of torture porn sites associated with kink.com, another writes:

I've skimmed through Whipped Ass and Hogtied and some of Water Bondage and I'm almost blown away. For some reason I've been digging on this kind of stuff lately ... Maybe I'm just jaded to standard porn fare.

(ChodeMasterJ on <adultdvdtalk.com>, posted 18 January 2009)

The pattern of desensitization and escalation is familiar enough to have inspired a joke e-card: a man sitting at his computer says to a woman standing nearby, 'My spring cleaning involves deleting pornography links that are no longer deranged enough to titillate me.'[2]

Thus, as a man's pornography use continues, he will likely be drawn to harsher material that crosses his own initial boundaries. He will encounter portrayals of acts that *he himself* regards – or would have once regarded – as abusive and unethical. In many cases, particularly if he is already aroused, he will respond sexually and masturbate to these new materials. For some consumers, this pattern of arousal and behaviour is disturbing: as one puts it, 'I couldn't believe what was turning me on' (Maltz and Maltz 2008: 17). At stake for such a consumer are questions of identity, values and self-image. If I am aroused by this material and let myself masturbate to it, he may think, then I can't be the kind of person that I thought I was, or that I want to be.

My aim in what follows is to explore some ways in which some consumers deal with these questions. I base much of my analysis on sites such as adultdvdtalk. com, where an outsider can listen in on consumers discussing the material they are using and how they feel about it.[3] This methodology has both advantages and limitations. The main advantage is that, because the discussions are anonymous and occur in a context that is broadly supportive of pornography, it is reasonable to think that consumers will be relatively honest about their thoughts and preferences – more so, at least, than they might be in speaking to a researcher (particularly a female one). Granted, these are also spaces where the consumers perform for each other and so there may be reason to doubt the absolute truth of all their statements; even so, the discussions reveal common ways in which men relate to one another through pornography and how essential the group dynamic is to the grooming process. The method's main disadvantage is that it is hard to know how representative forum participants are of porn consumers generally. It seems likely that most participants are more than occasional porn users, and men who feel ashamed of their porn use and/or are trying to quit may be less likely to participate. With these caveats in mind, however, the online forums provide a rich vein of material for analysis.

I will also discuss some of the ways that the pornography industry itself encourages men to disregard their own ethical concerns about the treatment of women. These two aspects of the grooming process – how the industry grooms consumers and how consumers groom themselves and each other – are deeply intertwined. It is easy to see how profoundly consumers' thinking about pornography (as expressed in online forums) has been shaped by pornography itself, and the very sites on which these discussions take place are not independent spaces free of industry influence. For instance, the owners of adultdvdtalk.com describe it as 'both a community site and a shopping portal' that aims to 'save you money and make you proud of your love of porn – 'cause, hey, we all like porn and there's nothing wrong with that'.[4] The site makes its money from banner advertising (mostly for online porn stores) and affiliate commissions on links to porn sites.

In what follows, all consumer quotes are taken from the forums at adultdvdtalk.com unless otherwise noted and are identified by the author's screen name and date of posting. All posts are reproduced as written, unless clarity requires the correction of mechanical errors.

Criticisms and moral ambivalence

While some consumers are engaged in moral thinking about aspects of pornography's content and/or production, it is abundantly clear that some are not. Indeed, some users appear studiously determined to avoid any moral connotation to their criticisms of certain pornography. For instance, a user initiating a discussion of slapping women's breasts frames his query in non-moral terms:

> I am not sure where most people (watchers or performers) stand on the use of tit slapping, some think it spoils a scene while some think it enhances a scene.
>
> (Jettyman, 13 May 2009)

The ensuing discussion includes numerous negative comments about breast slapping, but most are non-moral, such as 'It's stupid,' 'Not my cup of tea,'

'Annoying,' and 'Does nothing for me.' Other striking examples of non-moral criticisms occur in a discussion of Max Hardcore, one of the industry's more extreme producers:

> Max's early stuff was awesome, but when he started using gynocology tools and using 5th rate girls I had to bail. Any of the Anal Visions and original Cherry Poppers are great …
>
> (DreadZep, 27 October 2003)

> another thing I really hate is how [he] puts those big metal traps jamming the girls mouths open. What a huge turn off. It looks soo stupid.
>
> (DukeAbercrombie, 27 October 2003)

The first commenter above does not articulate why he 'had to bail' from Max Hardcore's later work, but his hearty endorsement of the *Cherry Poppers* series (which portrays a paedophile grooming young girls for sexual abuse) does not inspire confidence. The second commenter is clearer about his reasons, explaining that his objection to jamming women's mouths open with metal traps is simply that it looks stupid.

Some commenters have no compunctions expressing their enjoyment of non-consensual activities. In a discussion of 'A2P' ('ass to pussy,' an unhygienic and dangerous practice that is just what it sounds like), one user enthuses:

> One of the cool things about a2p is that quite often the guy will do it and the girl will flinch and seem surprised like she wasn't expecting it … but by then it's too late!
>
> (Andy2, 2 April 2009)

Other users raise moral questions, but not of the kind we might have anticipated. For instance, the initiator of the breast-slapping discussion winds up his query by asking,

> Am I being selfish by wanting a genre of breast slapping … or should I just carry on buying and hoping that the movie contains some of my fetish. If only I could buy 'Titslapped MILFs' or 'Titslapped Teens' I would know what I was buying.
>
> (Jettyman, 13 May 2009)

His ethical worry does not concern his arousal to seeing men slap women, but rather whether it is unreasonable to want this act specifically advertised so that he can access it more efficiently. Similarly, in a discussion of 'quagging' (fellatio in which women are gagged to the point of making audible noises in their throats), one user relates his own experience:

Just to be fair, I tried it out by throat fucking a girlfriend until she started quagging. It didn't feel very good to me and she never requested it in the future.

(Walter, 20 June 2007)

It is unclear to whom this user is concerned about being unfair, but it does not appear to be his girlfriend.

Some consumers express ambivalence, indicating that they like a certain kind of scene but feel guilty about liking it. One writes directly to producer/performer Jake Malone, enthusing about a particular scene in one of his movies:

[The female performer] hadn't cleaned out her ass sufficiently and the toys got all dirty ... you then asked her to suck it and she did! It was totally crazy and I sort of felt bad for liking it but it was pretty hot in a S&M domination sort of way. Have you ever done any other scenes like that ... ?

(mediasmarts2, 30 December 2008)

In this case, although the consumer 'feels bad' about his enjoyment of a degrading and dangerous practice, he evidently does not feel bad enough not to continue seeking it out. It is also common for commenters to follow a confession of guilt feelings with an immediate rationalization, as here:

I love to watch girls do this atp thing, but I do feel a little guilty. Has the analogy ever been made to NFL football, or wrestling? These are dangerous jobs ... But we all allow it, and we enjoy watching others do it.

(Peter1, 9 December 2007)

Sometimes, however, even a consumer who admits enjoying certain content nonetheless registers an unqualified moral objection to it:

ATP should be outlawed. As much as the little head in my pants loves to see this when he is horny the intellectual brain in my head knows how bad and wrong this act is and the impact that it has on making antibiotics not powerful enough to sustain fighting infections.

(Watcher, 27 March 2005)

And occasionally a commenter expresses a global moral objection to much of pornography's content. For instance, one man complains that most male performers 'behave as if they're capable of posting high scores on the PCL-R [a tool for diagnosing psychopathy]' (spectreman, 29 June 2007). Another agrees:

adult film has gone dreadfully, horribly wrong. It's almost all about aggression and being over the top these days. Honestly, I don't think too many folks actually enjoy watching warp-speed slam-fucking, spitting, quagging, slapping, choking, every scene ending with the girl rushing to her knees so a dick can be pointed down her gullet, and the like, but that the segment of the public who does, REALLY does.

(bps, 15 February 2008)

Interestingly, this user follows up his own observation that 'over the top' content is overwhelmingly prevalent with the puzzling claim that few consumers enjoy such content. His failure to connect the dots is striking: if so few people enjoy this material, then who is buying and using it in such massive quantities?

Drawing the line

Albert Bandura has described several 'psychosocial maneuvers by which moral self-sanctions are selectively disengaged from inhumane conduct' (1999: 193) – that is, ways that people adjust their beliefs and perceptions in order to rationalize behaving in ways that they would otherwise reject as wrong. According to Bandura, one must adopt legitimizing perceptions of the conduct itself ('it's not wrong; it's good and necessary'), of the conduct's harmful consequences ('it's not really hurting anyone'), of one's own connection to those consequences ('it's not my fault'), and/or of the victims who suffer them ('they don't matter, they like it, they deserve it').

One specific 'mechanism of moral disengagement' is palliative comparison, in which one contrasts one's own behaviour with something else thought to be worse. In this way, Bandura says, 'injurious conduct can be rendered benign or made to appear to be of little consequence' (1996: 365). Lundy Bancroft, who has spent decades working with men who abuse the women in their lives, observes that such men routinely employ palliative comparison:

> An abuser minimizes his behavior by comparing himself to men who are worse than he is, whom he thinks of as 'real' abusers. If he never threatens his partner, then to him threats define real abuse. If he only threatens but never actually hits, then real abusers are those who hit. ... If he hits her but never punches her with a closed fist ... If he punches her but she has never had broken bones or been hospitalized ... In the abuser's mind, *his* behavior is never truly violent.

(Bancroft 2002: 159)

A similar manoeuvre is endemic to the thought processes of many porn consumers. In my review of consumer forums, I came to call it 'drawing the line': the consumer defines as abusive, misogynist or otherwise objectionable some kind(s) of pornography that he does not like or use, and what he does use therefore appears (to him) benign in comparison.

Terms such as 'misogyny,' 'abuse' and 'brutality' are used to describe acts that the consumer regards as beyond the pale, while acts that he enjoys are described as 'hard-core,' 'rough sex' or, as in the following comment, 'pushing boundaries':

> [Jake Malone] makes porn that we want to see – porn that is unique in that it pushes boundaries, explores new paths and is harder without being unacceptably brutal.
>
> (bigfoot, 27 April 2009)

Line-drawing becomes essential for many consumers when they assess material as extreme as Max Hardcore's, but it often proceeds on mysterious grounds. In one discussion of Max's *oeuvre*, one user draws the line as follows:

> Some things of his I love like gaping, speculums, but I have no idea why he would shoot one girl puking into another girls mouth which is being forced open, and piss in a girls mouth. Stuff like that has forced me to look for other material, such as jules jordans which is hardcore without being so male dominant.
>
> (Jules_Jordan_Saviour, 28 October 2003)

Why forcing a woman's orifices open with a speculum is merely 'hardcore' whereas urinating in her mouth is objectionably 'male dominant' remains unexplained.

Using pornography online may lend itself especially easily to palliative comparisons. Once immersed in the world of internet pornography, the user is regularly exposed to a wide range of materials, including many that (at least for now) do not appeal to him. If he is on a portal site with tens or even hundreds of thumbnails and links, and he opts for those that are comparatively innocuous, then he can feel morally superior to those who click on more extreme links. The same goes if he ignores spam or pop-up ads for more extreme material.[5] In short, the online pornography consumer is constantly reminded that, no matter what he is using, there is always something worse out there. (And once the desensitization process kicks in, he will know just where and how to find it.)

'Not my fault': diminished responsibility

Much social-psychological study of how ordinary people acclimate to wrong-doing has focused on behaviour such as soldiers' killing in war, citizens' participation in genocide and ethnic cleansing and employees' involvement in destructive corporate behaviour (Waller 2002; Grossman 1996). Other vital insights have come from research on subjects in controlled settings, including well-known undertakings such as the Stanford Prison Experiment and the Milgram studies (Zimbardo 2007; Blass 2004). Among the most consistent findings in this body of research is the importance of diminished responsibility – that is, of seeing oneself as not connected to the harmful effects of one's actions.

Responsibility can be either *displaced* onto some other person or entity, or *diffused* throughout a larger group or network.

Displaced responsibility can take a number of forms, some of which are not available to pornography consumers. Unlike soldiers, experimental subjects or corporate employees, porn consumers are not subject to any external authority; they cannot claim to be 'just following orders' or 'doing a job'. Similarly, there is no professional identity that countenances the behaviour in question as good or required (as in 'This is what a soldier must do'). Finally, unlike the soldier or corporate employee, the porn consumer's livelihood is not at stake. However, one compelling way to displace responsibility is easily available to the porn consumer: namely, reasoning that if a woman was hurt in the making of the material he is using, that is not *his* doing. He did not hurt her and is not hurting her now. All he is doing is masturbating to films and images. In seeking out and enjoying depictions of abuse, he is something more than a mere bystander, but less than a perpetrator. By viewing the producers and/or male performers as solely responsible for any abuse, he can ignore ethical questions not only about his own patterns of arousal but also about his economic and ideological support for an abusive industry.

When responsibility is diffused, the person sees himself as having, at most, a tiny share of responsibility within a large group or complex institution (such as an army or a corporation). As William Shaw puts it, diffused responsibility allows individuals to

> see themselves simply as small players in a process or as cogs in a machine, over which they have no control and for which they are unaccountable. ... 'It's not my fault,' they think. 'This would happen anyway, with or without me.'
>
> (Shaw 2008: 26)

For the online porn consumer, responsibility is diffused through the entire vast network of other such consumers, many of whom he encounters in chat rooms, discussion forums and the like. The importance of this network cannot be overstated, since it not only reminds the consumer constantly that he is only one of a huge number of men doing the same thing, but also provides him with support and reinforcement for his particular preferences. The initiator of the breast-slapping discussion provides a clear illustration of this dynamic, chiming back in toward the discussion's end with this comment: 'It's nice to see some replies that are positive ... I was starting to think something was wrong with me for admitting I like it' (Jettyman, 31 May 2009).

The anonymity of the online environment also contributes to a sense of diminished responsibility. As Phillip Zimbardo puts it, 'Anything that makes a person feel anonymous, as if no one knows who he or she is, creates the potential for that person to act in evil ways – if the situation gives permission for violence' (2004: 29). In one study, for example, subjects in a 'deindividuated' condition – with their appearance concealed, identified by numbers rather than names – delivered twice as much shock to 'victims' as did subjects in the individuated condition (*ibid.*). In this respect, clicking on a link to whoredestroyers. com while sitting alone in one's apartment is easier than checking out a similarly titled film from one's local movie rental shop. And no doubt it is easier to discuss one's appreciation of aggressive porn content as 'Jettyman' or 'Cumwhipper' rather than as Fred or Tom.

Both anonymity and diffused responsibility are powerfully suggested by the icon for another porn user discussion board, forum.yobt.com. It shows three white male figures grouped together, pictured from the shoulders up. All three faces, however, are blank and featureless. The men are anonymous and indistinguishable, but they are all in this together.

'I felt she was into it': consumers' thinking about the women in pornography

As briefly noted earlier, another key mechanism of moral disengagement is to blame and dehumanize the individuals who are being harmed (for instance, the enemy population in war, or the targets of racial discrimination). Pornography's dehumanization of women has appropriately been the target of sustained and passionate feminist criticism. Because this dynamic so powerfully shapes consumers' thinking about the women in pornography, and thus about their own responses to material in which these women are degraded and harmed, I will begin this section by briefly discussing some of pornography's most common messages about the women who are in it.

The power of dehumanizing labels to disinhibit aggression is well established. In one study (Bandura *et al.* 1975), subjects were given a plausible cover story and told to shock other individuals. In some trials, subjects 'overheard' the experimenter referring to those to be shocked (students from another college) as 'animals'. In other trials, the subjects heard the experimenter saying that the other students 'seem nice', and in still others no labelling occurred. Even this single, overheard instance of labelling had an enormous effect on the subjects' willingness to aggress, with those labelled as 'animals' being shocked the most, those labelled 'nice' shocked least. As feminists have long observed, pornography labels women in degrading and dehumanizing ways: as animals, worthless whores, cum dumpsters, fucktubes, pathetic bitches and much more. A typical consumer would encounter a number of such labels within a single session of using pornography, let alone over weeks, months and years of use.

Pornographers also shape consumers' perceptions by what I call 'interpreting the images' – that is, explaining in accompanying text (or DVD commentary) that a woman who appears not to be enjoying something actually loves it. For example, a photo of performer Jaclyn Case shows a man's hand behind her head and a penis pushing into the side of her mouth, distending her cheek. She looks sideways at the camera with an expression that is at best bored and jaundiced; to this observer she appears worried and sad.[6] The text just under the photo reads, 'Jaclyn Case looks like she loves that juicy cock!' On the site fuckherthroat.com, the text accompanying one set of promotional images reads:

> Amber Rayne almost does a good job of pretending to be a cute and inno-cent girl. That is until she suddenly has a cock shoved down her throat and her hunger for cock is too hard to resist. Watch her eyes light up as her throat is brutally pounded by his hard piece of meat!
> (<http://fuckherthroat.com/tr/index.php>, accessed 17 August 2009)

The images show Ms Rayne's face covered in semen and mascara, with penises shoved forcefully into her mouth and cheek. Her eyes, far from 'lighting up,' appear vacant and dead. Through such consistent reinterpretation of women's expressions and reactions, the consumer learns to distrust the evidence of his own eyes and ears. He learns that things are not as they seem in the world of porno-graphy and that an omniscient commentator knows better than he does (perhaps even better than the woman herself does) what is really going on.[7]

A similar dynamic can be seen even on comparatively soft-core sites. For instance, in the summer of 2008 the owners of GodsGirls, an 'alt' pin-up site in the Suicide Girls mould, sent out this message to site members:

> WARNING! Did we mention that things have gotten a little racier around the site since you last logged in? You can now see longtime favorites like Catra and Stiletto doing things that no one ever thought would be done on a site like GodsGirls. Of course, we're still keeping it classy but some girls want to push the boundaries of class now and then … Members were surprised (in a good way!) when sets like this started going live on the site.[8]

Members are thus reassured that, if the site's content has become more hard-core, that is because the 'girls', wholly of their own accord, want to 'push the boundaries'. And who are the owners – still less the consumers – to question what the 'girls' have decided *they* want to do?

Thus, pornography's near constant message is that, whatever is being done to a woman, she wants it and likes it.[9] Among other things, this message serves to deflect the consumer's attention from his own preferences to the purported pre-ferences of the women he is watching: instead of asking why *he* enjoys seeing women treated aggressively, he is repeatedly assured that such treatment is what *she* wants.[10]

The influence of this message is clearly discernible in consumers' comments. Most are convinced that at least some of the women they are watching truly enjoy what they are doing and many are confident that they can tell which ones. For instance, in an online review of *Fuck Slaves 3*, one consumer/reviewer discusses performer Jaelyn Fox:

She was flogged and verbally abused and as dirty as it made me feel, the closer I watched, the more I felt she was into it a lot more than some critics claim [is] typically the case.

(Huston 2008)

And, back on adultdvdtalk, one user responds as follows to others' criticisms of quagging:

What if gagging *is* what they enjoy? I recall Sasha Grey saying she thinks it's hot and likes doing it a lot. Judging from some scenes I've seen, I wouldn't question her sincerity.

(RandomPrecision, 26 June 2007)

Some consumers are less invested in believing that a woman really likes it, so long as she can put on a convincing act: as one puts it, 'I prefer my porn chicks to appear to enjoy what they're doing' (Mike_Rach, 21 June 2007).

Confidence in women's acting abilities is more often expressed, however, by consumers claiming that women's expressions of pain and disgust are faked. The discussion of quagging, for example, includes repeated complaints that the gagging sounds are 'fake' (and therefore 'annoying'). And in a protracted discussion of facialabuse.com, one consumer writes:

I've seen clippets of the sight … and its always showing the chicks crying supposedly due to the guys slamming them during anal sex. Is this site legit with that? Or is it just a big ol fake-o crying? Cause I'm starting to suspect its fake.

(kaiser1one, 28 June 2009)

It is difficult to tell whether this user wants to hear that the crying is fake or that it is real. Other consumers are more straightforward about their preference for women's real rather than feigned discomfort: one says of quagging that 'If it seems faked, it sucks' (Cumwhipper, 17 February 2008).

A few commenters display empathy for women experiencing abusive treatment in pornography, as well as an understanding of the constraints on such women's choices. In the discussion of facialabuse.com, one responds as follows to a typical defence of violent scenes:

Now, I know rough sex fans will cry 'She could have stopped the scene if she wanted to' … But for two seconds realize you are dealing with girls who for the most part have never done a porn before and they really need the money. They think if they refuse to do something they won't get paid. Think about it, you get throat pumped to the point of puking for 10–15 minutes, then you refuse to eat the guy's ass, and are sent home with no paycheck. If that is what you think will happen, then most likely you are gonna eat the guy's ass even if you don't want to.

(StillHope, 7 July 2009)

Another commenter follows up:

a performer, especially a newbie ... might be mentally overwhelmed or in shock. When you're already stressed ... convulsing from being choked and puking, trying to catch your breath, etc. and you've got two pricks barking orders at you, I don't think you can be expected to make the most rational decisions. How many rape victims don't scream or call out for help even though that's sort of what you'd expect a person to do?

(MrTibbs, 7 July 2009)

This level of insight into the female performers' conditions is unusual, however, and no doubt a given consumer's dedication to enjoying the materials in question renders him less inclined to pursue such lines of thought.

Some consumers demonstrate awareness of the personal histories that underlie many women's participation in the pornography industry. In a discussion of a particular performer who has said she was gang-raped earlier in her life, one user responds to others who doubt her veracity:

I tend to believe that she was raped. Porn has been, is, and will be filled with emotionally unstable girls who have suffered some sort of sexual abuse/trauma. That's what leads them to do porn ... They get sucked into the supposed 'Porn is one big happy family' ideal and continue further down the spiral.

(Rosco Fuji, 8 April 2009)

Economic pressures, too, are sometimes mentioned as a factor motivating many women. In a discussion of the relative merits of American versus Eastern European performers, one user observes that 'American girls who look as good as those Eurobabes don't do porn, because they have better options' (elgringo-viejo58, 30 May 2009). Another points out optimistically that 'if our economy goes deeper into the crapper, our Pretty Girl Desperation Index may rise to the point that more home-grown 10's will start doing porn' (Harri Patel, 30 May 2009). Despite this awareness of the conditions (both personal and economic) that drive women into pornography, all of these users remain devoted fans of the industry – as indicated by their continued presence on fan discussion forums.

Men, but not monsters

In addition to its constant messages about women and their desires, pornography includes a quieter backstory. Robert Jensen observes,

We pretend to listen to the barker shouting about women, but that is not the draw. What brings us back, over and over, is the voice in our ears, the soft voice that says, 'It's okay, you really are a man, you really can be a man, and if you come into my world, it will all be there, and it will all be easy.'

(2007a: 33)

The backstory, then, is not about women, but about the consumer's own identity; and its central message is that the consumer is, or at least can be, a real man. Not surprisingly, much pornography (and its promotional material) caters to anxious masculinity. The name of one porn studio, Anabolic, presumably refers to anabolic steroids (synthetic hormones derivative of testosterone). Sometimes it is suggested that enjoying or at least tolerating extreme aggression against women is an indicator of masculinity.[11] For instance, the text on throated.com reads, 'WARNING: Contains extreme throat fucking and deep-throating. DISCLAIMER: If you are squeamish or faint easily please LEAVE NOW' (accessed 20 July 2009). The cultural association of squeamishness and fainting with femininity is assumed, so that the text need not mention manhood explicitly.

Frequently, pornography is offered as an antidote for men who see themselves as controlled and emasculated by women. The September 2008 issue of *Adult Video News* included a review of *Fuck Slaves 3*, in which 'Nelson X' describes it as 'a misogynistic gem that will appeal to men who have survived the social castrating of their gender' (Nelson X 2008). Thus, enjoying dominance and aggression against women is cast as both a mark and an entitlement of manhood. The trick is that, despite this enjoyment, many consumers remain invested in seeing themselves as non-abusive – as men, but not monsters. Thus, for example, the above-mentioned review, which begins with a description of Jaelyn Fox 'losing her soul' as a result of her abusive and humiliating treatment (including 'having her pretty blonde head used as a toilet brush'), ends as follows:

But, don't worry. Fox did not really lose her soul. Viewers will only think so thanks to her and [performer/director Jake] Malone's ability to revel in abuse fantasy. Good porn makes everyone feel dirty.

(Nelson X 2008)

The reader is thus reassured: enjoying *Fuck Slaves 3* and its ilk makes him a real man, vicariously experiencing the control over women to which he is entitled;[12] but because this is merely 'abuse fantasy,' in which the woman herself 'revels,' he is not a monster.

Any consumer who wishes to maintain a tolerable self-image must maintain clear, insuperable boundaries between himself and those men he considers morally objectionable. In a discussion of *Jailbait 6*, several consumers go to some effort to distinguish themselves from paedophiles. One participant opens the discussion by mentioning the film's use of a standard disclaimer:

> All the performers in this video are playing the roles of adults, and should not be viewed otherwise. Nothing in this video is intended by the producer, director, or any performer to depict or portray any person or character as a minor.

He goes on to describe the film's portrayal of adult female performers playing with blocks, colouring with crayons, having tea parties and the like, with 'the sound of children playing and laughing in the background.'

> And then there is [the director] playing the creepy guy in the park trying to lure girls with a fishing rod and a lollipop. It's soo over the top! ... 'Nothing in this video is intended to depict or portray any person or character as a minor.' MY ASS.

> (007, 30 April 2009)

Another user responds quickly, offering a ready distinction: 'Age play. As long as it is truly two consenting adults, anything goes' (LubeNLuv, 30 April 2009). Several others weigh in, expressing confidence that real paedophiles would not be interested in a film of this kind because no actual children are portrayed and because the female performers have clearly adult bodies. As one user opines,

> if the women look like adults then toys, kids clothing and playgrounds aren't going to do it for a real pedophile. You might as well suggest that a guy dressing up as a girl and putting on makeup is going to get me hot for him. That's not gonna happen.

> (Hardware, 30 April 2009)

Thus, a man's enjoyment of films like *Jailbait 6* shows that he is not a 'real' paedophile and, if he is not a real paedophile, his enjoyment of such films is no cause for concern. In this way, the discussion is kept revolving narrowly around the paedophile-versus-not-paedophile distinction, without considering what it means that the sexual excitement of many 'normal' adult men is intensified by the iconography of childhood.[13] Indeed, when a female performer joins the discussion, saying that she hated shooting such films and stopped doing so because she found them 'disgusting and inappropriate', she is shouted down by male participants.

The consumer who enjoys seeing men behaving aggressively toward women may also need to manage carefully his own identification with the men on screen. On the one hand, his enjoyment depends on identifying with the male performer(s); the whole point is to experience the action *as if* he were directly involved. However, identifying too strongly with those behaving abusively may make it more difficult for the consumer to maintain his self-image as non-abusive. He must therefore maintain a fragile balance wherein he *both* identifies and dis-identifies with the men in the pornography he is using. Some very violent sites employ a technique that may help the consumer maintain this balance. In their content analysis of internet rape sites, Gossett and Byrne found that, on most, the perpetrator is wholly anonymous. The rapist, they observe, is

> an invisible man – neither shown nor alluded to in the text [describing] the rape ... the majority of the sites do not discuss or display any particular identity, relation to the victim, or social position of the perpetrator. The ones that imply some status typically make the perpetrator anonymous in other ways, such as hiding behind masks, wearing uniforms, or using a camera angle that reveals only a body part such as a hand.
>
> (Gossett and Byrne 2002: 698–9)

That the perpetrator is a hidden or masked 'nobody' makes it easier for the consumer to project himself into the former's position. But it also means that, having so projected himself, the consumer too can be 'nobody' – least of all himself.

Self-fragmentation: from Jekyll to Hyde

As we have seen, porn consumers navigate the boundary between man and monster in a variety of ways: 'drawing the line,' displacing and diffusing responsibility, believing that the women enjoy it, and so on. All of these manoeuvres, however, have their limits, and for many consumers, as their porn habits escalate and their tastes grow more extreme, the rationalizations may become difficult to sustain. For these consumers, pornography offers a different way to accept their own patterns of enjoyment – one best illustrated by the name and logo of a porn company called Jekyll and Hyde Productions.[14] The company's logo shows a face divided in half. The left side is a normal man's face, Caucasian, with a slightly smug expression and (significantly) eyes closed. The right side is the face of a monster, with greenish skin, jagged teeth and wild, sinister eyes. The consumer is thus encouraged to fragment himself – to distinguish between his everyday self and his scary, dangerous porn-using self. The ordinary, comparatively benign self can project the troublesome desires onto this alternate self who exists only in the world of pornography (or, as one site has it, in the 'Jerk Off Zone'[15]) and who indulges even very sadistic desires.

In *The Nazi Doctors*, Robert Jay Lifton argued that physicians, whose professional identity involves healing and helping, were faced with dire conflicts when called upon to do the work of Auschwitz and other concentration camps. As he explains,

> The individual Nazi doctor needed his Auschwitz self to function psychologically in an environment so antithetical to his previous ethical standards. At the same time, he needed his prior self in order to continue to see himself as humane physician, husband, father.
>
> (1986: 419)

To explain how Nazi doctors managed such conflicts, Lifton introduced the concept of doubling: 'the division of the self into two functioning wholes, so that a part-self acts as an entire self' (*ibid.*: 418). Doubling is 'an active psychological process' whose major function, he argues, is to avoid guilt by disavowing the second self that does the 'dirty work' (*ibid.*: 422). A Nazi doctor functioned in a 'death-dominated' environment by developing an 'Auschwitz self'; indeed, Lifton claims that 'If an environment is sufficiently extreme, and one chooses to remain in it, one may be able to do so *only* by means of doubling' (*ibid.*)

To claim equivalence between the activities of concentration camp doctors and those of pornography consumers would be implausible. Nonetheless, Lifton's concept of doubling can help us understand how some porn consumers manage the conflict between their self-image as decent, ethical people and their continued enjoyment of material that violates their own ethical standards. As the Jekyll and Hyde logo suggests, the consumer can create a second self, one that exists in an 'extreme environment' that he regards as a realm of pure fantasy. This second self, rather than denying or minimizing abuse, can name it and revel in it. Such gleeful nihilism is suggested in the names of a number of porn companies and web sites, including Mayhem, Wicked, Sin City, Evil Angel and Lethal Hardcore. (One Evil Angel site, evilondemand.com, features a man yanking a woman's head out of the toilet by her hair, with the accompanying slogan 'Life's too short for soft porn!') The banner for porn-devil.com comes complete with horned devil and pitchfork, and that of twistedzones.com – advertising 'twisted sex, extreme sex' – features a skeletal head with hands displaying raised middle fingers. Thus, the consumer is provided with a ready-made 'second self,' a cartoonish and faux-rebellious alter ego on to which he can project his enjoyment of what even he recognizes as 'twisted' material.

Moral damage: from consumer to consumed

Pornography use can yield significant harm and suffering in the lives of consumers themselves (Paul 2005; Maltz and Maltz 2008). For many, over time, pornography consumption leads to isolation, damaged or lost relationships and an impaired capacity to relate sexually to real partners. For some consumers, their porn habits have negative professional or even legal consequences. One man who faced such consequences discusses the fatigue, depression and intense anxiety that he suffered as a heavy pornography user: 'I don't think I even thought about [my symptoms] as possibly being related to porn use until I went to prison and actually experienced some relief' (Maltz and Maltz 2008: 74).

While many factors contribute to the damaged lives and psyches of some pornography consumers, the grooming processes I have described here constitute a partial explanation for these men's suffering. Norman Care has argued that 'morality's most precious good is moral personality itself – and damage to moral personality is ... unpardonable' (1996: 25). The pornography industry damages its consumers' moral personalities at every turn, by hooking them on material that undermines their self-respect and integrity. According to therapists Larry and Wendy Maltz, who have worked with many men with heavy pornography habits, 'One man shook with tears telling us porn had turned him into a "pervert" and a "visual rapist"' (2008: 88). Another client told the Maltzes, 'I just don't like who I've become ... And my relationship with porn has become the vortex of my self-hatred' (*ibid.*: 86).

The pornography industry plays an active, often knowing role in undermining the moral personalities and capacities of consumers. This is not surprising, since retaining the men as paying customers depends on perpetrating a kind of moral violence against them. While many examples I have cited herein could support this point, it is perhaps best illustrated by some promotional text on the site of JM Productions, a company specializing in sadistic material. On a page advertising the *Anal Full Nelson* DVD series, the text reads:

> What's an ANAL FULL NELSON? It's a wrestling hold in which both hands are thrust under the whore's arms from behind and then pressed against the back of the neck while she gets ass fucked. ... It takes a special (AKA stupid) kind of whore to allow herself to be submitted to the most brutal ass fucking position ever ... Face it – this is the type of porn you enjoy. You may not like yourself for it, but so what. Now get ready to JACK OFF![16]

In this text, the consumer's guilt feelings are anticipated and, in a diabolically manipulative turn, exploited as a way to draw him further in. The consumer is urged to face how terribly women are being hurt and how sadistic his own sexuality has become – and not to care about either. The moral emotions that could provide him with a road map out of this empty, amoral world are acknowledged, only to be mocked and set aside. To maintain the pornographer's profits, the consumer's very humanity, his capacity for empathy and solidarity with other human beings, must be snuffed out.[17]

Relatedly, the consumer must be led to doubt his ability to change his behaviour – to believe that, even if his habits are disturbing, he is beyond help or hope. At the ironically named porn site pornisevil.com, the consumer is told to 'Bookmark Porn is Evil ... you'll be back soon anyways.'[18] Thus another aspect of moral personality, the ability to make choices according to one's own values, is denied and undermined. Some sites make mocking reference to pornography addiction; for instance, the tag line on searchextreme.com is 'Helping you beat your addiction since 1999.' On the *Anal Full Nelson* page, the series' most recent release is advertised with the following text:

> When I see shit like this I have to ask myself ... 'WHY? Why do these girls allow themselves to be treated like this? Why do the people who own porn companies finance filth like this. And why can't I stop myself from jacking off to it? Why? Why? Why?'[19]

Here, the company appropriates the consumer's own voice to reinforce his belief that he can neither control his actions nor reconnect with a self that is worthy of his own respect.

At this far end of the grooming process, and indeed at many prior points, the male pornography consumer is a target for ruthless corporate exploitation that goes much deeper than the picking of his pocket. As I have suggested throughout, however, consumers are far from passive victims in this process: if a porn user's moral personality has been damaged, he himself has played a key role in damaging it. By ignoring his qualms, tuning in to the industry's legitimizing messages and stifling his capacities for empathy and critical reflection, he has acquiesced and co-operated in his own ethical deterioration. As Lifton observes of the Nazi doctors, '[D]oubling is the psychological means by which one invokes the evil potential of the self. ... To live out the doubling and call forth the evil is a moral choice for which one is responsible, whatever the level of consciousness involved' (1986: 423–4).

The contemporary pornography industry is a wasteland of lost and damaged humanity – one for which men, both as producers and as consumers, are primarily responsible and from which primarily women and girls suffer. To recognize that many men are also steamrollered by this corporate juggernaut does not, I hope, undermine this central point. In fact, the good news is that what women and girls need from male pornography consumers – that they resist the industry's grooming and reclaim their own humanity – is also the men's own best hope for healing, connection and moral regeneration.

Notes

1 I refer throughout to 'male consumers' and to 'men,' since adult men remain the industry's main constituency. As pornography use becomes more common among under-age boys, it is vital to consider how it affects their sexual and ethical development; however, I do not pursue that line of enquiry here. Similarly, while some women use pornography, the associated grooming dynamics would require a distinct analysis beyond the scope of this chapter.

2 <http://www.someecards.com/card/my-spring-cleaning> (accessed 10 August 2009).

3 I gathered material from these sites over a period of roughly three months during summer 2009.

4 <http://www.adultdvdtalk.com/adtalk/info/about.asp> (accessed 11 August 2009).

5 See Paasonen (this volume) for a discussion of porn spam.

6 The photo was accessed through <http://www.clubjaclyncase.com/> (17 August 2009) but includes the logo of <www.fuckherthroat.com>, where it presumably originally appeared.

7 For a vivid example of such reinterpretation in a porn DVD commentary, see Jensen (2007a: 92–4).

8 This e-mail was shared with me by a student. I made a record of its content but have since lost or deleted the e-mail itself.

9 Wosnitzer and Bridges' study (2007) confirmed this pattern, showing that in 95 per cent of all coded instances of aggression the response of the person being aggressed against was either neutral or pleasure.

10 This, too, is a form of displaced responsibility.

11 In a twist on this theme, sometimes excessive aggression is thought to indicate a deficit of masculinity. In a review of *Gangbang Auditions 18* consumer reviewer Roger Pipe advises, 'Look fellas, if the ED meds aren't working and you need to choke or hit a girl to get wood, then maybe it's time to give grad school or rocket science a closer look' <http://www.rogreviews.com/reviews/read_review.asp?sku=3860 > (accessed 22 August 2009).

12 See Johnson (this volume) for a more detailed discussion of male entitlement as a motivation for porn consumption.

13 For further discussion of how the industry uses legal material to encourage adult sexual interest in children and teens see Dines (2009a).

14 See <http://www.jhpxxx.com/aboutjhp.aspx> (accessed 10 August 2009).

15 The phrase appears on the site of JM Productions, <http://www.jerkoffzone.com/> (accessed 15 July 2009).

16 <http://www.jerkoffzone.com/jmcatalog/series.php?sid=7> (accessed 29 August 2009).

17 On porn's destruction of empathy see also Jensen (this volume).

18 Accessed 19 July 2009.

19 <http://www.jerkoffzone.com/jmcatalog/series.php?sid=7> (accessed 29 August 2009).

Chapter 9

Porn consumers' public faces

Mainstream media, address and representation

Karen Boyle

The straw man

My interest in media representations of porn consumers was sparked by a throw-away comment in McKee *et al.*'s *The Porn Report* (2008: 25): 'The only porn users you ever hear from in the media,' they claim, 'are people who call themselves "addicts" and are trying to stop using it.' It was not simply the hyperbolic nature of this claim and my sense that it was at odds with own research that piqued my interest. Rather, I was curious about its discursive function in the pages of a book which draws on a range of original, empirical research about porn consumption.[1]

The comment is made in the chapter 'Dirty? Old? Men? The consumers of pornography' which opens with an extended quotation from *The Sunday Age* newspaper which presents 'Mike', an unemployed, self-identified porn addict, feeding his habit in internet cafés and his body with junk food.[2] Mike is used by the authors as a 'straw man' against which to set their research. The function of a 'straw man' is the ease with which he is knocked down, allowing a counter-discourse to emerge in his shadow. In *The Porn Report*, this counter-discourse is based on research with over 1,000 self-identified Australian porn consumers recruited through mail-order porn video catalogues and online advertising. However, as presented within *The Porn Report*,[3] the methodology and findings are effectively reduced to allowing consumers to 'speak for themselves', in opposition to the media stereotype established in these opening pages (McKee *et al.* 2008: 37). The chapter makes extensive use of quotations from interviews, often presented with little or no critical commentary, a decision the authors explain as follows:

> Of course you can never take interview responses on face value. These consumers might be liars (they might know that porn is hurting their marriages but don't want to say it.) They might be stupid or deceived (they might think that their partners like it, but in fact they don't). But asked to choose who knows themselves better – the people we spoke to, or an academic who's never met them – we're going to give the benefit of the doubt to these consumers, at least until we get any convincing evidence to the contrary.
>
> (*Ibid.*: 40)

So it's a case of *either* go with 'the media' stereotype (in which case the respondents are deluded at best, liars at worst) *or* accept what 'the people' have to say, so knocking down straw-man Mike.

To analyse what our research subjects have to tell us is *not* to assume that they are deluded and/or liars, but rather to understand that their accounts are – by definition – *representations* of their experience produced in particular circumstances for a particular purpose. As such, they can be analysed like we would analyse any other text: looking for recurring themes; examining representational strategies such as tone and language choice; identifying gaps and inconsistencies within and across individual interviews. However, in *The Porn Report* the juxtaposition between 'the media' and 'the people' seems to free the researchers from this requirement and their own framing of both the research and its presentation does not come into the equation. This is particularly striking as *The Porn Report* is, in itself, a study of (pornographic) media texts and their consumption. The implication, then, is that pornographic media are 'special', somehow divorced from an otherwise monolithic media industry and its homogenizing ways.

These criticisms aside, I share with the authors of *The Porn Report* an assumption that mainstream representations offer present or future consumers possibilities for imaginative identification and/or frameworks for contextualizing and understanding their porn use. Of course, this is not a *unique* function of mainstream media. For example, in her chapter for this book Rebecca Whisnant demonstrates how the texts and contexts created by the porn industry address consumers, grooming male users to accept ever more extreme material. Other frameworks for understanding porn consumption are offered by peer groups, religious or political discourses and regulatory frameworks, to give just a few examples. Mainstream media texts are not uniquely powerful and their representations are not universally accepted. That said, they do offer frameworks which we can draw upon when considering or rationalizing particular behaviours. And, as I will argue, porn consumers are offered considerably more choice in this respect than McKee *et al.* suggest.

In keeping with the emphasis of this book on pornography's own mainstream, my focus is the representation of the heterosexual male porn consumer. My intent is not simply to provide a typology of different character types – indeed, my mapping in this chapter is necessarily selective[4] – but rather to think about some of the ways in which representations of porn consumption *function* in particular media spaces.

'Negative' images

It is important to acknowledge up front that porn is not always celebrated in the mainstream, and negative accounts of pornography consumption do exist. The most obvious place to look for such accounts is the news media, where, as 'Mike' demonstrates, porn use is likely to become an issue when the behaviour of the user is excessive or otherwise out of the ordinary (i.e. newsworthy). As Clare

McGlynn's discussion of the public debate about the extreme pornography leg-islation (this volume) demonstrates, however, the voices of enthusiastic porn users can be assimilated into news discourse in particular contexts. A search of the BBC online news archives, for instance, finds Helen, 'who by day works in an office in the Midlands, and enjoys being sexually submissive and occasionally watching pornography, portrayed by actors' (Summers 2008) and Lucy 'a normal mum who does normal stuff but some of the things she gets up to behind closed doors wouldn't quite be seen that way' (Morrison 2008). Whilst the context for Helen and Lucy's stories is one in which the link between 'extreme' pornography and criminality is under debate, Helen and Lucy are not themselves criminalized or negatively portrayed. In other words, even in news media – at least in the UK – the porn user has more than one public image.

As Clare McGlynn argues, what was missing in the media coverage of the extreme pornography debate was a specifically *feminist* analysis of the proposals or of pornography more generally. The absence of feminist analysis is con-spicuous not only in news media but in other factual and fictional genres. A feminist critique of male demand for pornography is rarely sustained, and even critical accounts typically focus on the women within the industry. I have dis-cussed television documentaries critical of pornography in more detail elsewhere (Boyle forthcoming a), so here I will illustrate this point by way of an example from television drama: the mini-series *Human Trafficking* (Lifetime TV 2005). At the conclusion of the drama, the central character – an agent for US Immigration and Customs Enforcement, played by Mira Sorovino – ends an impassioned speech about the evils of trafficking with the following rebuke to her audience:

> And perhaps most importantly we must face the fact that none of this horror would be possible if our culture didn't create a demand for it. Ladies and gentlemen, the United States is one of the largest markets for sex slavery in the entire world, we need to realize that modern day slavery is only occurring because we choose to ignore it.

Here, demand is introduced only to be immediately subsumed within a wider critique of the culture. In the middle of final sentence the camera cuts away from Sorovino to a shot of two women in the audience, diluting any sense that chal-lenging demand might be about challenging men: this is a *women's* problem and the melodramatic tone suggests it is addressed to a female audience off-screen as well as on.

Human Trafficking is worth discussing in more detail as its extremely limited portrayal of the men who buy trafficked women and children in pornography and prostitution points to further issues I want to explore in this chapter. First, there is a blurring of roles between the porn producers and porn consumers. In *Human Trafficking*, in which porn is but one aspect of the wider commercial sexual exploitation of women and children, punters are rarely seen. Instead it is primarily the traffickers (all East Europeans) whom we see raping the women and watching their pornographic humiliation on television screens. The blurring between production and consumption contexts has a more benign face in other representations I will discuss later, but in *Human Trafficking* this process exemplifies my second point: namely that the men using women in pornography and prostitution in such contexts are unambiguously unsympathetic and are clearly not intended as a point of identification.

In *Human Trafficking* there is only one American punter with a speaking role. Dr Smith (Larry Day) appears in two scenes in the second episode. He is introduced sitting behind the desk in his spacious, wood-panelled office, talking to his wife on the telephone then moving seamlessly – and whilst his wife and children remain in-shot in framed photographs on his desk – to accessing child pornography on his computer. As he looks at the porn site – unambiguously entitled 'Child Porn' – he is framed in tight close-up, his face in partial shadow, a lascivious expression on his face. As such, Dr Smith initially embodies feminist arguments that men involved in sexual violence are, in many ways, 'normal' men (in a comparatively short scene we learn that he is a married, wealthy, professional man and a father) only to be rendered obviously and visibly monstrous (through the clarity of his tastes and the editing of the scene). He is a monster hiding in plain sight and his profession makes the play on 'Jekyll and Hyde' clear. There is no grey area here. (Dr Smith is later arrested raping a boy in a Manila brothel.)

I am hardly the first to note that men (and women) who abuse children – including those convicted of child porn offences – are widely represented as monstrous (Kelly 1996; Kitzinger 1999; Silverman and Wilson 2002). Nor is it new to argue that one of the implications of this is to marginalize discussion about the extent to which our culture encourages sexual interest in children and the childified (Dines 2009a). However, this bears repeating in the context of a discussion of mainstream representations of the porn consumer, for such representations arguably serve as a kind of 'limit case' for consumers: whatever else they may be, they are not *that*. As my discussion of the 'straw man' and Whisnant's analysis of porn-user discussion boards (Chapter 8) suggest, this is a common rhetorical device in both academic work and consumers' own accounts of their behaviour (also Kingi *et al.* 2004). And it is certainly true that variations on this sad, bad porn consumer appear in a variety of mainstream media contexts – most obviously news, crime drama and modern melodramatic forms. To extrapolate from the very specific function the porn consumer occupies in these spaces – which are, by definition, not interested in the *everyday* aspects of porn consumption, which are neither newsworthy nor dramatic – to 'the media' more generally is, however, misleading. If you care to look, porn consumers are addressed or represented in various mainstream media contexts.

Addressing the invisible man

To be fair to McKee and his colleagues, they do later acknowledge that there are 'two contradictory images of porn users in Australia' and that sitting alongside the 'media stereotype' is a more general acceptance of porn consumption, exemplified by the success of magazines like *Loaded* and *Ralph* (2008: 25). In these magazines' emphasis on 'booze, babes and birds' it is assumed that they are addressing a (male) audience familiar with pornography. Indeed, a cursory glance through magazines aimed at young men in the UK[5] reveals multiple ways in which readers are *directly* addressed as current and future porn consumers. In addition to the soft-core appeal of the magazines themselves, it is assumed that readers are using hard-core porn and so are interested in reviews of pornographic films and web sites, in receiving pornography as gifts and prizes, in articles about porn stars or the sex industry, in consuming the porn, using escorts and calling chat lines advertised in the 'adult interest' pages, in reading 'advice' pages penned by female porn stars or glamour models and in sharing their own knowledge of porn with other readers. The magazines' web sites also offer links to hard-core: from the *Nuts* home page to *Horny Teen Videos* in two clicks.[6]

Readers' desire for this kind of material is typically treated humorously and, often, self-depreciatingly. With tongue firmly in cheek, the magazines suggest that watching too much porn can involve a loss of one's critical faculties – *Front* readers, for instance, are 'numbnuts' who must be repeatedly reminded that reviewed porn sites are 'NSFW' (not suitable for work) – and across all of the magazines and their accompanying web sites men's desire for the soft-core the magazines provide, and the hard-core they reference, is described as 'dirty'. In this respect, lads' mags mirror both the language of pornography *and*, paradoxically, the language of moral campaigns against it, framing men's sexuality as something base and asocial. There is a disturbing slippage here between pornography and men's sexuality: 'dirty pictures' are desired and consumed by boys with 'dirty minds'. Men's interest in pornography is presented as an inevitable consequence of their sex and youth: pornography *becomes* (young) men's sexuality. As a result, moralist critiques of the magazines (and there have been many) are easily represented as attempts to curb young men's sexuality and can be reappropriated by the magazines themselves as a marketing tool. Similar to the approach of hard-core sites discussed by Whisnant in the previous chapter, the logic would appear to be 'if they already think we're dirty, disgusting perverts, then we might as well enjoy ourselves fulfilling their worst expectations'. Disturbingly, UK research has demonstrated that lads' magazines are typically understood by men – even those who do not read them – as 'honest', 'natural' and 'open' in their treatment of young men's sexual desires and preoccupations (Jackson *et al.* 1999).

The self-depreciating tone in which porn consumption is described in these magazines – as well as in sitcoms, teen comedies and talk shows – attempts to head off critique by laughing at the consumer in the imagined act of consumption without ever challenging his desire to consume, which is normalized and essentialized. It would not be too much of a stretch to suggest that the real 'taboo' around representing porn consumption is less about the *porn* (after all, even hard-core is routinely glimpsed in mainstream media contexts) than about the masturbation which is presumed to accompany it.[7] This might be particularly fraught in the world of homosocial camaraderie these magazines invoke. *Front*, for instance, talks about its readers as 'an army': the notion that that army might be looking at each other looking at porn for sexual arousal is an uncomfortable one.[8] Predictably, aggression is one of the ways in which the potential homo-eroticism of the lads' mags' universe is displaced. In addition to the playfully derogatory language used to describe readers (Benwell 2001), many have regular features which involve public humiliation or the gleeful abjection of the male body (e.g. 'Don't look: pictures for the stronger stomach' in *Nuts*). This arguably functions as an alibi for the group misogyny on display throughout: *everybody* is 'fair game'. However, it's hardly an even playing field: when the joke's on men, it might involve your friends taking a photo of you with your face in vomit or the self-presentation of physical injury (with cash prizes for printed photos). When the joke's on women, it rarely has that first-person quality: the joke is always at the expense of an already objectified other (Mooney 2008). More disturbingly, even the murder of women can be an opportunity for 'humour'.[9]

Although they provide some of the most obvious examples of the normalizing of porn consumption, lads' magazines are by no means unique among main-stream media in addressing their readers as porn users. In my work on television docu-porn (Boyle 2008), for instance, I argued that series such as Showtime's *Porn: A Family Business* (2003–06) court consumers of pornography whilst typi-cally stopping short of representing the porn consumer on-screen. In this show – and others like it – the viewer is invited into the porn world, where women emphasize their desire to sell sex, legitimating the consumer's purchase and providing him with enough information about the products to seek them out at the programme's end. The invisibility of consumers *on screen* facilitates this broader address: the porn consumer is everyman. This is, of course, similar to the position of the male porn performer both in these pseudo-documentaries (where he is rarely interviewed) and in porn itself, where the relative lack of character-ization and screen time occupied by the male performer, combined with the way in which he is typically framed on screen, allows the male viewer to imaginatively insert himself into the action. With this in mind, the relative invisibility of the consumer looks rather different: rather than seeing this as an issue of mis- or under-representation, might we not argue that it facilitates a mode of engage-ment which positions the prostituted, pornified woman as the object of scrutiny and titillation? Here, invisibility is a marketing strategy. And, in a pornified culture, there is a certain power in invisibility.

Porn consumers on screen

Given the well documented and debated 'pornification' of the mainstream – of which lads' mags and docu-porn are certainly part – it would be surprising if porn consumers had remained entirely marginal figures. Whilst everyday porn consumers may not be dramatically or visually interesting (unlike female porn performers), neither are they completely invisible.

First, it is worth noting that porn companies – like mainstream businesses – pay to have their products 'placed' (and used) in Hollywood films. Brandchannel. com identify ten placements for *Playboy, Hustler* and *Penthouse* in studio films from 2001–09. Whilst the *Hustler* and *Penthouse* placements are in films with age-restrictive ratings (UK 15 and 18; US 'R'), the *Playboy* placements are in comedies with less restrictive ratings (typically 12A in the UK, PG-13 in the US).[10] Brandchannel's list is by no means comprehensive: it does not, for instance, include the 2008 comedy *The House Bunny* (Fred Wolf 2008), to which the Playboy brand is central, or independent films like *Sideways* (Alexander Payne 2004) and *Little Miss Sunshine* (Jonathan Dayton and Valerie Faris 2006) (Dines 2009a).[11] Nevertheless, Brandchannel does illustrate that (in this respect at least) porn functions as a business like any other and that porn companies – Playboy in particular – deliberately target a youthful audience, placing their product in genre films with teen-appeal.

Of course, it is not only through product placement that porn has made it onto the big screen. Porn and other aspects of the sex industry have been front and centre of indie dramas such as *Boogie Nights* (Paul Thomas Anderson 1997), *The Center of the World* (Wayne Wang 2001), *This Girl's Life* (Ash Baron-Cohen 2003), *The Moguls* (Traeger 2005), *Southland Tales* (Richard Kelly 2006) and *The Girlfriend Experience* (Steven Soderbergh 2008), as well as mainstream movies for a teen audience, including *The Girl Next Door* (Luke Greenfield 2004) and *The House Bunny*. Although they take different approaches to the portrayal of the punter, all assume the viewers' familiarity with the codes, conventions and routines of commercial sex and all centre their exploration of the industry on key figures (usually women) within it. Their significance for this chapter, then, lies less in their on-screen representations of the consumer (which may be limited) and more in their address and marketing, where a knowledge of the sex industry carries a certain (counter-) cultural cachet. Recognizing porn 'stars' Sasha Grey (*The Girlfriend Experience*) and Cheyenne Silver (*This Girl's Life*) in these crossover roles creates a form of (counter-) cultural capital from porn knowledge, something director Kevin Smith – a self-confessed porn fan – is even more explicit about in relation to his casting of Katie Morgan and Traci Lords in *Zack and Miri Make a Porno* (2008).

Kevin Smith is not the only public figure to have professed his enthusiasm for porn: as porn has become increasingly mainstream so mainstream performers have embraced the porn world, at least as spectators. There is a history to this: in *Inside Deep Throat* (Fenton Bailey and Randy Barbato 2005), for instance, it is suggested that the success of *Deep Throat* was at least in part due to its very visible celebrity endorsement from film stars and television talk show hosts, amongst others. Whilst it is difficult to imagine a contemporary equivalent (not least as technology has privatized the consumption of porn films), continuing celebrity porn fandom – of which Howard Stern is most obvious proponent – refutes the notion that the lonely addict is the porn consumer's only public face.

For the male celebrity an alliance with the world of pornography can also act as a marker of distinction. Whilst for Kevin Smith (or John Waters or Jonathan Ross) this is congruent with a fan boy persona and interest in 'cult' media, being allied with porn can also connote wealth and taste in certain contexts. The 'porn connoisseur' is most obviously embodied by Playboy's Hugh Hefner. Whilst the octogenarian Hefner may seem an unlikely role model for young men, nonetheless the brand, and the associated hedonistic lifestyle, retain a seductive currency. Parties at the Playboy mansion have long been a space in which (predominantly male) celebrities endorse the Playboy brand and cement its association with wealth, exclusivity and men's sexual access to women. Similarly, fictional television shows from *Fresh Prince of Bel Air* to *Sex and the City* have envisaged mansion parties as designer accessories for privileged lives.[12] However, the stakes are very different for women in attendance who – by virtue of the 'lingerie dress code' – are always already sexualized. If the male porn user is allied with the porn producer or distributor (the porn subject), then his female equivalent finds it difficult to escape the pornifying gaze that evaluates her porn potential: even, as the Marge Simpson *Playboy* cover suggested, if she's a cartoon.

Similarly, when male celebrities talk about using porn (on radio and television talk shows, in stand-up routines, in interviews) their primary audience is implicitly other men – porn is something they can be presumed to share and becomes a kind of 'insider' language that cuts across class. Their presumed masturbation to pornography, if it is alluded to at all, is likely to be a source of humour. In contrast, when female celebrities talk about their porn consumption (in the text accompanying pictorials or the pseudo-advice columns in lads' magazines) they are often still talking to men. Even when such talk appears in reality-based women's genres it is rarely framed as something women can be assumed to share. Nor is it, typically, a source of humour. Women talking about pornography struggle to occupy a position of agency and subjectivity, not least as their speech is so often an accompaniment to the visual pornification of their bodies (Boyle forthcoming b).

American teen comedies and sitcoms – where porn features regularly as a manifestation of teenagers' and young adults' sex obsessions – provide many examples of this gendered construction of porn use in a fictional context. Two porn masturbation scenes in *American Pie* (Paul Weitz 1999) demonstrate this particularly clearly. The film opens as the protagonist, Jim (Jason Biggs), masturbates to a scrambled porn channel in his bedroom. We hear a woman's sexual moans as the camera pans across the clothes-strewn floor to Jim, sitting on the edge of his bed. Jim responds to the woman's sexual praise ('You're so good') with his first line of the movie ('Yes, I am the best, baby') as a reverse shot shows us the scrambled television image.[13] As with most teen comedies, *American*

Pie's sexual content is widely referenced in its marketing, and the film's opening seconds play on this to ally viewer sympathy with Jim: like him, the viewer has gone in search of something that isn't quite delivered (the sound track promises a woman in sexual ecstasy, the image delivers a masturbating boy). Jim is then busted by his mum and dad in a brief scene of exquisite embarrassment. His masturbation and associated porn use are a source of humour precisely because they exaggerate experiences that are assumed to be shared with the (male) audience. Jim may not be in control of his material or his body but he is nevertheless porn's subject (he uses), not its object, and we are invited to identify with him, not objectify him.

The scene when foreign exchange student Nadia (Shannon Elizabeth) masturbates to pornography is very differently framed. Nadia has come over to Jim's house to study. Knowing she will change out of her gym clothes in his bedroom, Jim has set up a web-cam so that he and his friends can watch her undress. Unaware she is being watched, Nadia strips to her panties and the action cuts back and forth between Jim's bedroom and his friend's house where he and two friends are watching. Nadia finds porn magazines on Jim's bedside table and lies back on his bed to masturbate. The web-cam images lack sound and so it is the boys' appreciative moans that we hear: Nadia is framed as a porn object even as she uses pornography for her own sexual pleasure. Egged on by his friends, a nervous Jim returns home to try to insert himself into the action. However, unbeknown to Jim, the images from his bedroom are being seen by appreciative boys across the school. As Nadia turns the tables, asking Jim to strip for her, he becomes the focus of his schoolmates' attention. Among those watching – and laughing – are a group of five young women. These women may not be framed as porn objects but nor does their viewing appear driven by desire: unlike their male counterparts they are sitting on a sofa sharing drinks and snacks and there is no suggestion that they are watching Jim (or Nadia) for sexual pleasure.

The situation goes from bad to worse for Jim as his comical striptease is followed by premature ejaculation: twice. Jim's spectacularly unsuccessful porn performance means that he is never objectified. Neither his diegetic viewers nor those in the cinema audience are invited to understand his performance as arousing; rather we are invited to share his embarrassment. At school the next day, Jim is the focus of his schoolmates' derision, although his friends are more sympathetic, particularly when they learn that Nadia's sponsors have already put her on a plane back to Eastern Europe, thus ending Jim's chances with her (at least until the sequel).

There are a number of points I want to pull out from this brief discussion. First, porn consumption is assumed to be an inherent part of teen life, particularly for boys, and is allied to their obsession with sex, which it closely mirrors. The line between sex and porn is further blurred as we experience the scene in Jim's bedroom with Nadia simultaneously as a narrative event and as live pornography. It is notable that Nadia and the women watching have no complaint about her pornification although the web-cam is activated without her knowledge or consent. Indeed, in *American Pie 2* (J. B. Rogers 2001) Nadia returns specifically to hook up with Jim. And in a further sequel, *American Pie Presents Band Camp* (Steve Rash 2005), the central character also surreptitiously films women. In short, it is expected – and to a degree accepted – that young women are porn objects and there is no language with which they can critique the perpetrators or hold them publicly accountable.[14]

Whilst Jim's school-wide celebrity is profoundly uncomfortable due to the inadequacies of his porn performance, Nadia is a 'natural' porn performer and her ability to embody the role so convincingly makes her lack of consent a non-issue. She looks and acts like a porn star, therefore she must be a porn star, and the casting reinforces this. (Shannon Elizabeth posed for *Playboy* prior to her role in *American Pie.*) There are parallels too with the leaked private sex tapes of celebrities like Paris Hilton, Kim Kardashian and Pamela Anderson, which, whilst made with their consent, were apparently distributed without it. For Hilton and Kardashian, the sex tapes launched highly lucrative media careers – including appearances in *Playboy* – which seemed to quash (and indeed call into question) their apparent non-consent to the public distribution of these recordings. Anderson, already a pornified figure at the time of sex tape, had an even tougher time eliciting public sympathy, and much of the public debate about all three was reduced to money and celebrity: if the women could share the profits and gain the limelight, where was the harm?

That said, the representation of the porn consumer in the *American Pie* films is not straightforwardly celebratory: porn consumption is a sign of male sexual immaturity. The *American Pie* films are hardly alone in this: the opening of *Superbad* (Greg Mottola 2007) provides a more recent example, whilst, on television, the first episode of UK drama series *Skins* (Channel 4 2007–?) is one of many linking male porn use with sexual immaturity and relative inexperience. This is also true of comedies featuring adult male consumers, where porn consumption is a marker of a kind of arrested development – the central characters' co-workers in *The 40 Year Old Virgin* (Judd Apatow 2005) and Joey and Chandler from the television series *Friends* (1994–2004) providing classic examples. However, mirroring the discussion of lads' mags earlier in this chapter, porn consumption remains wedded to the construction of male sexuality in these examples. It is something which is beyond the control of the hapless males whose sexual misadventures are the narrative centre, making any kind of female (or feminist) resistance within these generic spaces utterly futile. The naturalizing of porn use also means that the *industrial* character of pornography is largely invisible: so naturally does it chime with men's sexual preoccupations that there is no sense that it is a commercially constructed product. It just is. That, despite their greater sexual knowledge and maturity, young women are represented both as consumers and as unwitting, but not protesting, porn objects, further validates porn's value and its apparent inevitability. Women accept porn (and sex) on heterosexual men's terms.

Conclusion

Mike in his internet café starts to look rather different when placed next to Jim in his spacious suburban bedroom, Joey and Chandler on their leather recliners in their New York apartment, or Kevin Smith enthusing about porn to international journalists at junkets for his new movie. The men of *Little Miss Sunshine*, Hugh Hefner, Howard Stern, Helen, Lucy, Nadia and even Dr Smith further complicate the picture. Alongside the lonely, unemployed addict, then, we have the cult fan, the wealthy connoisseur, the hedonistic man-boy, the sex-obsessed teen and the sex criminal, not forgetting the sexualized female-consumer whose sexual interest in pornography and apparently willing (self-)pornification is the ultimate validation of men's porn use. Porn use is an in-joke, a homosocial experience, a 'natural' expression of youthful sexuality, even a mark of distinction and source of cultural capital. Taken collectively, these examples demonstrate that there is no such thing as 'a' media stereotype of the porn user. All these functions are, however, gendered. Women porn consumers – particularly as represented in audio-visual media – rarely escape a level of pornification, and this finding resonates with broader arguments about the ways in which the production of a pornified self is being sold to (and sometimes embraced by) women and girls as a substitute for sexual subjectivity.

Counter to McKee *et al.*'s claim with which I opened this chapter, it is the porn *refuser*, and not the consumer, who is truly marginalized, particularly in genres aimed at young people. Having researched and written about mainstream representations of the sex industry in a number of contexts (Boyle 2008, 2010, forthcoming a, forthcoming b), it is precisely this absence of feminist resistance and critique and, indeed, the generic *impossibility* of such resistance that strikes me most. Critique is headed off through the assumptive address of lads' magazines (we're all in this together), their self-depreciation and arrogance (we know we're dirty little sods and we don't care), as well as the naturalization of young men's porn use here and across popular culture (boys will be boys). On-screen, sympathetic characterization and the encouragement of identification with youthful male porn users further discourages critical engagement on this issue, as does the situation of pornography – and porn use – in everyday generic contexts.

Most disturbing of all is the way in which porn consumption and production have become interchangeable in certain contexts. Whilst this arguably mirrors the experience of many young people in an era of increasingly mobile and accessible technology, it is the casual disregard for consent which is most worrying. The logic would appear to be that there's no such thing as bad publicity: for a young woman to be pornified, even without her knowledge or consent, is a recognition of her sexual desirability for men and confers a degree of celebrity, however local. It is telling, for instance, that the term 'porn *star*' is almost universally (and uncritically) adopted in talking about women performing in pornography: who doesn't want to be a star? Men filming women without their knowledge or consent aren't, therefore, abusers: they're star makers. This depends on a lack of empathy with the pornified and a sense of entitlement that involves the extension of porn's world view into interpersonal relationships. Examining and critiquing some of the ways in which porn consumption is made meaningful in contemporary popular culture offers one way to begin the work of changing, challenging and expanding those meanings. Making a genuine *choice* – to consume or appear in pornography – is possible only where alternatives are imaginable.

This leaves me wondering what is really at stake for the authors of *The Porn Report* in sidelining media examples like those discussed in this chapter and zeroing in on Mike. Without Mike as their straw man, might the accounts of porn consumption produced by their interviewees appear less revelatory and more formulaic and generic? This is not to suggest that these porn consumers are deluded about their practices or suffering from false consciousness, but rather to acknowledge that their accounts do not come from nowhere, but, rather, intersect with broader discourses about pornography and its consumption.

Notes

1 The book is published by Melbourne University Press, although intended for a broad readership. Responding to an earlier version of this chapter (Boyle 2009), Alan McKee accepted that their claims about 'the media' were hyperbolic, but justified this with reference to the book's intended readership, for whom, he suggested, a more nuanced understanding of 'the media' would render the argument unnecessarily complex. Such detail is saved for articles in academic journals which are referenced in the endnotes.

2 The full quotation from *The Sunday Age* is as follows: 'Mike likes to get a particular computer station in the back corner of the 24 hour internet café he visits often – more often than a man without a job can afford. The cubicle feels familiar and is marginally more secluded than others that line the walls. Late at night, which is when Mike usually arrives, the cafe is not busy or bright as during the day. He finds his spot, logs on and starts looking at pornography. And sometimes he's still there 24 hours later. "They have snack food in the place, and that's all I feed myself on – a soft drink, a packet of chips," he says. ... Mike believes that he's addicted to pornography ... [and that] his dependence on porn is impacting on his ability to lead a normal, balanced life' (McKee *et al.* 2008: 24, ellipses in original).

3 Elsewhere (e.g. McKee 2004) the authors are more careful in their presentation of this material. However, the framing of their research in this more 'populist' account performs precisely the kind of over-generalization about pornography and its consumption – at least as filtered through popular debate – that their use of 'Mike' is intended to critique.

4 I draw on examples from print, film and television media and fictional, factual and entertainment formats. Examples were identified through keyword searches of film and television databases as well as links suggested in previous academic work and are limited to Anglo-American media. The 'survey' produced here is by no means scientific: rather, it offers some initial propositions which later critics may choose to test empirically in relation to one or more medium or format.

5 This is based on a reading of weeklies *Nuts* and *Zoo*, *Front* (which is fortnightly) and monthlies *Loaded* and *FHM*, between April and June 2009.

6 <http://www.nuts.co.uk/> (accessed 9 August 2009).

7 Responses to the initial cover design for this book were telling in this respect. I was keen to have an image that focused attention on what pornography is *for*

without, in itself, reproducing pornography and the tissues fulfilled that brief. Canvassing responses from colleagues, students and friends, it was striking that gut reactions were either to find it disgusting or funny. In contrast, the numerous covers of academic books which feature images of women in the sex industry are rarely seen as controversial or even noteworthy.

8 Male masturbation *per se* is sometimes argued to be an implicitly homosexual act. In this reading, pornography becomes a way of heterosexualizing masturbation, inserting a compliant female into male self-pleasuring (Maltz and and Maltz 2008).

9 See *Zoo* magazine (24–30 April 2009: 36) and *Loaded* (May 2009: 90, 146) for examples. As this book was going to press, a controversy broke out about advice given by celebrity agony uncle, Danny Dyer, in *Zoo*. In response to a reader's letter about an emotionally painful break-up, Dyer advised that the reader should 'cut his ex's face, so no one will want her'. Whilst this comment generated considerable outcry – forcing Dyer and *Zoo* to apologise – the world-view it expresses goes unremarked week-in week-out in this magazine and others like it, making the 'apology' (which attributed these remarks to an 'extremely regrettable production error') all the more disingenuous. (<http://www.zootoday.com/lateststuff/archive/2010/05/05/zoo–magazine-error-apology.htm>, accessed 6 May 2010).

10 *Penthouse* product placement: *Semi-pro* (Kent Alterman 2008). *Hustler* product placement: *Friday 13th* (Marcus Nispel 2009), *Watchmen* (Zack Snyder 2009), *The Butterfly Effect* (Eric Bress and Jim Mackye Gruber 2004). *Playboy* product placement: *Austin Powers in Goldmember* (Jay Roach 2002), *Charlie's Angels: Full Throttle* (McG 2003), *Bruce Almighty* (Tom Shadyac 2003), *Big Momma's House 2* (John Whitesell 2006), *Scary Movie 4* (David Zucker 2006) and *Borat* (Larry Charles 2006).

11 In *Sideways*, Hustler's *Barely Legal* is an unremarkable presence on two middle-aged guys' wine-tasting road trip, another marker of the friends' arrested development. In *Little Miss Sunshine*, two of the male members of the dysfunctional family – the foul-mouthed, drug-taking grandfather (Alan Arkin) and the depressed gay uncle, Frank (Steve Carrell) – are porn consumers. The initial comedy lies in the grandfather's matter-of-fact request that Frank buy him something 'nasty' and the subsequent confusion when Frank is witnessed buying heterosexual porn by his ex-lover. Later, the grandfather's magazines get the family out of a tricky situation with a police officer who assumes that the porn (and not the grandfather's dead body) is what the father is hiding in the trunk.

12 The relevant episodes are 'Fresh Prince after dark' (1993) and 'Sex and another city' (2000). Hefner also appears in *The Simpsons* ('Krusty gets cancelled' 1993), *Blossom* ('True romance' 1993), *Just Shoot Me* ('At long last, Allie' 2001), *Entourage* ('Aquamansion' 2003), *Curb your Enthusiasm* ('The smoking jacket' 2005) and *Family Guy* ('Airport 07' 2007).

13 Jim's interaction with the screen – he responds directly to the female performer's address and expresses frustration when her male partner speaks, interrupting the flow of communication – is a succinct expression of the argument that the marginalization of the male heteroporn performer encourages the male viewer to imaginatively insert himself into the action.

14 Some television teen drama series do explore other responses to this kind of pornification but usually within a context where explicit violence (e.g. drug rape, murder) has taken place or where the images are used to sexually bully or blackmail the young woman. See, for example, *Veronica Mars* (UPN 2004–07) and Season 1 of *Gossip Girl* (WB 2007–?). Susan Berridge's on-going Ph.D. research at the University of Glasgow explores these story lines more fully.

Chapter 10

To catch a curious clicker

A social network analysis of the online pornography industry

Jennifer A. Johnson

The male consumer of commercial pornography operates at the nexus of two dynamic systems of stratification – patriarchy and capitalism. He is at once a *male* who is accountable to the demands of patriarchal hegemonic masculinity and a *consumer* who is subject to the weight of modern imperial capitalism. Patriarchy emphasizes difference whereby hegemonic masculinity is established through dominance over femininity yet is routinely vulnerable to challenge and suspicion. Modern imperial capitalism is motivated by profit which is derived primarily through the colonization of new markets and consumption. These two macro systems of power interact to configure the social context within which the male pornography consumer makes choices and exercises agency. His 'choices' are therefore not completely his own, rather they are constrained by these dual systems of power, which, I argue, conspire to define the male consumer as a site of exploitation for the commercial pornography industry.

The commercial pornography industry is a capitalist endeavour designed to seek profits. As such, it is subject to the same Marxist critique as all other capitalist enterprises. As Brod (1988) points out, to take a socialist feminist position, as I am doing here, raises different questions about the pornography industry. Specifically, it allows me to ask questions about the male consumer and the *practice* of consumption rather than its putative effects. The question expands from what type (exploitive versus empowering) of sex is being sold to include *how* sex is being sold. A socialist feminist critique raises questions such as: How does the commercial porn industry extract its profit? How does the industry interact with its customer base? Is it fair and ethical in how it markets to its customers? How is the pornography industry structured to make a profit? How is power distributed among the industry's members? In other words, what is the political economic structure of an industry that culled US$24.9 billion from the pockets of primarily male consumers in 2006 (Free Speech Coalition 2007)?

To answer this question, I use a social network perspective to map the operational environment of the online commercial pornography industry as constituted by business relationships between members of the pornography industry as well as those with mainstream business. I ground my analysis in the theoretical work of Heidi Hartmann, R. W. Connell and Harry Brod, among others. These data reveal a spider-like network anchored by two main conglomerate hubs that connect to a series of producers and distributors. Through these connections, commercial online pornography is produced and distributed to 'affiliate web sites' whose goal is to cast a wide 'sticky' net to ensnare the male consumer in a never-ending series of web sites embedded with 'clicks' that are consciously designed to profit by circumscribing and limiting consumer choice. The lure of this capitalist network is patriarchy. The male consumer, primed by hegemonic masculinity, is drawn to the edge of the network by curiosity, where he finds gonzo porn sites that promise to satiate his need for masculine validation. Upon his arrival, he is entangled in a series of click manoeuvres and marketing gimmicks calculated to further reduce his agency and transform him from the 'curious clicker' into the 'member clicker'.

A co-operative union: patriarchal capitalism

Heidi Hartmann, a socialist feminist, argues that capitalism and patriarchy coexist in a co-operative, symbiotic union with the shared goal of establishing and maintaining dominance. Through this union, a gendered division of labour is constructed that allows 'men of all groups to dominate at least some women' through control over women's domestic and economic labour (Hartmann 1979:185). Patriarchy, the older of the two systems of power, is a set of materially based social relations through which solidarity among a hierarchy of men is established by shared control over women. Capitalism, as the arbiter of the material order, services patriarchy by maintaining women's economic and social dependence on men through low wages. In return, capitalism gains acquiescence to economic exploitation from lower-order men. In other words, capitalism 'buys off' men at the lower echelons of the material order by providing them patriarchal control over the domestic labour of women, thereby establishing solidarity with men at the top. By creating a symbiotic relationship, the interests of patriarchy and capitalism are aligned such that promoting the interests of either system reflexively protects and advances the interests of the other.

According to Hartmann, this union was cemented through the family wage. Though the industrial revolution had the potential to draw all labour into the work force, creating a deeper pool of cheap labour, working men quickly recognized the negative impact economically empowered women would have on their public and domestic power. Arguing that women and children needed protection from the brutalities of the industrial workplace, men actively bargained for restricting union protection and high-wage occupations to men as well as for a family wage that would enable men to 'protect' women and children at home. While a deeper pool of cheap labour was economically beneficial to the capitalists, there was also a recognition that 'women could not serve two masters' and that their long-term economic interests, both as capitalists and as men, were best suited by paying working-class men wages high enough to support a family, including an economically dependent wife. By working co-operatively and recognizing the interests of each constituency, patriarchy and capitalism were able to provide men twice the access to women's labour – once as cheap labour in the work force through sex-segregated jobs and twice through dependent labour in the home as homemakers and caregivers to children. By guaranteeing all men access to economically dependent women, this compromise reinforced the domination of each constituent group – men in the home and capitalists in the workplace – thereby solidifying each system's power in the social order.

A compromised union: modern imperial capitalism and old patriarchy

The old-style capitalism that brought forth the family wage is not the capitalism of today's post-industrial world. No longer is capitalism rooted primarily in local markets of production and distribution, it has now grown into a global set of relations which function as a 'complex structured totality' encompassing all aspects of social and political life (Hennessy 2000: 9). This new-style imperial capitalism, which emerged in the post-World War II era, is characterized by corporate strategies aimed at developing new markets for accumulation and profit-making, creating flexible forms of labour and intensifying the pressure for consumption by drawing finer distinctions in consumer culture (Hennessy 2000). By expanding markets and emphasizing consumption, capitalism has drawn women into the work force both as labourers and as consumers, thereby altering the basic tenets of the original agreement negotiated through the family wage. Women now have access to economic resources through service-sector jobs which, no matter how paltry the pay, still afford women some economic independence from men and heterosexual marriage. In the US today, 51 per cent of women live outside of a marital arrangement, as compared to 35 per cent in 1950 (Roberts 2007), and women are outpacing men in college attendance and graduation, with college degrees paying greater economic dividends for women than for men (Buchmann and DiPrete 2006). While this is not to say that women are now playing on an equal economic playing field (Bernstein 2006), these changes illustrate a broadening of women's economic opportunities for securing material resources beyond reliance on men and heterosexual marriage.

While women's economic opportunities have expanded, men's position under modern imperial capitalism has grown weak and unstable. In the US since the 1950s, male wages have stagnated or declined, traditional masculine jobs such as manufacturing and agricultural work now account for only 20 per cent of the work force (AFL-CIO 2002) and, for the first time, the US Bureau of Labor Statistics report that men's unemployment rate has surpassed that of women (Bureau of Labor Statistics 2009). Modern imperial capitalism has betrayed patriarchy by no longer guaranteeing the economic dependence of women. Such betrayal threatens the integrity of both systems, for, as Harding (1981) argues, the relationship between the two is co-dependent: 'Capitalism mediates patriarchy. Patriarchy mediates capitalism' (Harding 1981: 136–7). Capitalism needs patriarchy to establish a compliant work force in order to maintain its hold on the labour surplus of both men and women; patriarchy needs capitalism to establish the material basis of heterosexual marriage, the crucial element for conferring male privilege. Without the support of the other, both systems of dominance are compromised.

A union threatened: imperial capitalism and a general crisis in patriarchy

Patriarchal imperial capitalism finds itself in a quandary; how can this union survive if patriarchy continues to rely on the economic dependence of women for establishing dominance but such dependence is no longer profitable for the new imperial capitalist regime? How can male solidarity be achieved when capitalism has gone global, with its seats of power located beyond the local sphere of influence, yet patriarchy remains wedded to a masculinity validated through forms of dominance that need to be accessible to *all* men, regardless of their position in the material hierarchy? And, lastly, how can capitalism continue to ensure men's acquiescence to labour and consumer demands without being able to offer up women's economic dependence as a 'buy out' to all men?

The genesis of this quandary is a culture lag between the two regimes: capitalism has modernized but patriarchy has not. Capitalism, as a regime governed by the brutally rational logic of profit, has adapted to social and technological changes with limited regard to external contingencies such as male dominance in search of expanding markets and new sources of profit. The new form of capitalism – global, expansive work force and consumer-driven – has the potential to threaten institutional male dominance by decreasing *some* men's power at the micro-level (Brod 1988). Yet patriarchy remains wedded to hegemonic masculinity, a form of masculinity validated through acts of dominance that need to be accessible to *all* men, regardless of their position in the material hierarchy, in order to ensure male solidarity and protect male power.

As defined by Connell (1987), hegemonic masculinity is the dominant form of masculinity within the gender hierarchy characterized by aggression, power, authority, physical/emotional toughness, heterosexual prowess and domination. It is a collective strategy for the subordination of women to ensure male solidarity and protect male power. Hegemonic masculinity is not an identity of affirmation, rather it is an identity built around negation. A man must first prove what he is not – feminine or woman-like – in order to prove what he is: a real man. The term 'hegemony' reflects the large measure of public consent given to the cultural standards of masculinity to which all men are expected to adhere and against which all men are measured. Hegemonic masculinity is a public identity that requires demonstrable proof and validation from others, with the most valuable affirmations coming from other men (Connell 1987; Kimmel 2005).

However, legitimate opportunities for the public display and validation of masculinity are shrinking while sanctions for failure are increasingly punitive.

An 'ornamental' culture seized by commercialization, consumerism and celebrity, in other words modern imperialist capitalism, does not offer men tangible, unquestioning public tools of masculine display such as land ownership, traditional marriage and/or loyalty to country (Faludi 1999). While men continue to have access to marriage (Nock 1998), sport (Messner 1992) or fraternities (Boswell and Spade 1996), these are no longer enduring or permanent access points across the life course. Yet, hegemonic masculinity maintains its power through the capricious use of 'threatening spectres' such as the label 'fag' (Pascoe 2007) and stiff penalties for failure such as violence, public humiliation, psychological trauma and/or social marginalization to guarantee conformity (Messner 1992; Kimmel 1994; Pollack and Pipher 1999). While the union between patriarchy and imperial capitalism maintains male power at the macro-level, it creates a quiet sense of desperation among individual men as they search for increasingly scarce avenues to prove their masculinity.

Brod (1988) calls this dilemma a 'general crisis of patriarchy', reflecting a broad depersonalization of patriarchy, with power residing closer to the individual man in pre-capitalist patriarchy whereas now men's power over women is collectively positioned and individual men increasingly fall under the domination of the larger rubric of imperial capitalism. This crisis produces the male paradox of power where institutional male power coexists with a personal sense of powerlessness among men. If left unresolved, this crisis could threaten the union between the two systems of dominance. The power of any system of dominance rests on a well cultivated sense of legitimacy among its constituents. If groups of men no longer feel empowered inside systems in which they are ostensibly afforded such power, the door is opened for personal divestment and the legitimacy and authority of the respective hierarchy comes into question. It is therefore in the best interests of both capitalism and patriarchy to resolve the 'general crisis in patriarchy' by creating a sense of male empowerment at the micro-level.

A reconstituted union: commercial online pornography and hegemonic masculinity

Seeking to resolve this paradox, men look for power inside their immediate sphere where the transformation to modern imperial capitalism has commodified the body and elevated its role in the 'identity projects' of men and women (Gill *et al.* 2005; Tiefer 1994; Foucault 1978). Micro-power is now offered to men through the most immediate and personal site possible – their bodies and sexuality (Gill *et al.* 2005; Potts 2000). Brod (1988: 403) describes this as 'imperialism of the body' where capitalism colonizes the body in its search for new markets. Work by Brubaker and Johnson (2008) illustrates how online erectile enhancement ads reconstruct a healthy functioning penis as a landscape for product development through the marketing of hegemonic masculinity. Men are offered more powerful tools of domination and masculine display, i.e. bigger, stronger and longer-lasting erections, through the use of a commercial product. By offering up a commodified body as a source of micro-power for men, capitalism once again upholds its end of the bargain by providing men a tool of dominance through which they can establish and validate their masculine identity.

As the commodified male body and its sexuality increase in symbolic value, the construction of a hegemonic masculine identity is once again democratized, affording *all* men access to points of control, power and dominance. Bowser (1994) illustrates how economic and personal frustration among African American men can translate into an exaggerated investment in the body and sexuality as they seek more accessible methods for 'doing' hegemonic masculinity. This democratization of hegemonic masculinity through a commodified body/sexuality alleviates the 'general crisis in patriarchy' by reconstituting inter-strata male solidarity to include an easily accessible form of domination – the sexual domination of women – to augment the increasingly unstable economic domination of women. The lynchpin of this new form of domination is that it must be available to *all* men regardless of their social location in other hierarchies. The most available, accessible and affordable means for accessing hegemonic masculinity through the body/sexuality is online commercial pornography.

My argument is that online commercial pornography plays a pivotal role in maintaining the hegemonies of both patriarchy and capitalism. By providing *all* men reliable and accessible means for the validation of hegemonic masculinity through a commercialized venue, men's interests are aligned both as men and as capitalists. Just as economic dominance aligned *all* men with the priorities of family wage capitalism, sexual dominance aligns *all* men with the goals of modern imperial capitalism. This alignment creates a win/win for both macro-systems of power because the legitimacy and authority of each are mutually reinforced. But, as I will show, individual men, under both iterations of the union, are faced with a win/lose scenario. Just as most men traded collective economic power for individual domestic power under family wage capitalism, so too do they trade collective consumer power for individual sexual power under imperial capitalism. Just as traditional capitalism offered the economic dependence of women as validation of the patriarchal order so too does imperial capitalism offer male sexual dominance as validation of the patriarchal order. Just as traditional capitalism ensured compliant access to men's labour surplus through the family wage, modern imperial capitalism gains such yielding access to men's economic surplus through commercial pornography. Either way, men win – or at least they appear to do so – as members of the dominant group in the patriarchal order, but they remain economically exploited to the tune of US$24 billion a year.

Much of the work on pornography has focused on the ways in which men win inside patriarchal capitalism; less work has focused on the losing side of the equation (Jeffreys 2009b).[1] My goal in this chapter is to begin to outline the way in which men lose in this system by illustrating how the imperatives of a rigid structure of hegemonic masculinity make them vulnerable targets for economic exploitation by the online commercial sex industry. Through a structural analysis of the online commercial pornography network, I will show how capitalism and patriarchy collaborate to construct the male consumer as a ripe target for economic exploitation. Through the lure of hegemonic masculinity, men are drawn into the online commercial pornography network, where they find themselves enmeshed in a well constructed set of relationships designed to extract maximum profits through the circumscription of consumer choice. The structure of the network is designed to prevent 'leavers' – those who engage through curiosity but leave before becoming members – by restricting and/or obfuscating (male) consumer choice.

My argument rests on the assumption that there is a connection between pornography and hegemonic masculinity. I do not intend to re-establish how the content of online commercial pornography is heavily embedded with the text and symbols of hegemonic masculinity. This connection has been well established in the literature (e.g. Jensen 2007a; Kimmel 2008). I assume that men are drawn to pornography because it provides them with a vehicle through which they can enact, relive and anticipate the demands of hegemonic masculinity and that the particular power of pornography lies in linking this process to sexual arousal and pleasure. Instead, I will describe the political economy of the online pornography industry to illustrate the way in which the political context of patriarchy, specifically hegemonic masculinity, contours the ways in which the consumer capitalist market place of online commercial pornography extracts its profits from the pockets of primarily male consumers.

Methodology

The methodology which I will use to map the political economy of online pornography is social network analysis (SNA). Social network analysis is a descriptive social science methodology which maps networks, reveals patterns among connections and quantitatively identifies powerful constituents or what are called 'nodes' in the network. This methodology produces two forms of data – visual renderings of a network and quantitative metrics which measure patterns of ties and rank nodes in terms of network power. SNA data are comprised of nodes and edges. In this analysis, nodes are business entities involved in the production, distribution, marketing and sale of online commercial pornography. These nodes are connected to each other through edges representing a variety of types of connections, including joint ventures for website launch/development, production or distribution agreements, technology use and development, financial connections, e.g. affiliate cash sites, marketing and subsidiaries.

Data were gathered through online business reports published in 2007 and January 2008 on both pornography trade sites such *Adult Video News* (*AVN*) and *X-Biz* and mainstream sites such as *Lexis-Nexis* and *Yahoo Business*. These reports documented connections between and among both pornography and mainstream companies. Coders culled through each report and extracted the connections between all organizations listed in the report. For example, on 19 December 2007 *X-biz* published a report stating:

> NEW YORK – Late-night mobile content provider WAAT Media has entered into a deal with mobile video solutions provider Vantrix to facilitate the distribution of video over WAAT Media's mobile media platform.
>
> (Yagielowicz 2007)

A connection was coded between WAAT Media and Vantrix. Other parts of the text documented multiple connections. For example, further down in the WAAT Media report, the text states:

> WAAT Media has on-deck agreements with more than 70 major mobile carriers, distributing images, video, mobile TV and mobile games through its Twistbox Games subsidiary.
>
> Vantrix overcomes the technology hurdles of providing video-on-demand, live TV, video alerts, user-generated content, video share and any other type of multimedia in mobile and other digital platforms for companies like ABC News, Orange, T-Mobile and The Weather Channel.
>
> The deal will bring video from publishers such as Playboy, Penthouse, Vivid, Mr. Skin and others to more than 100 carriers worldwide.
>
> (*Ibid.*)

Coders extracted multiple connections from this text, including a connection between WAAT Media and its subsidiary Twistbox Games, Vantrix and several connections to ABC News, Orange, T-Mobile and the Weather Channel as well as connections between both Vantrix and WAAT to Playboy, Penthouse, Vivid and Mr. Skin.

Two more rounds of coding cleaned, validated, normalized and categorized the data. Organizations were categorized according to their function in the network. For example, a business that is involved in the production of pornographic material is categorized as a producer; a company that processes payments for purchases or membership fees is coded as financial; a web site that organizes webmasters for the construction of end-user web sites is an affiliate; end-user web sites where consumers become members and purchase pornography are coded as web sites; and a large organization that performs all of these functions is a conglomerate. The edges were not categorized. Because the purpose of this analysis is to gain a better understanding of the structure of the entire network, as opposed to measuring the strength of the relationship between individual nodes, multiple connections between two organizations were collapsed to a single non-directional link. Lastly, organizations and associated links using the same moniker in the title of the business were rolled up into one organization; so all organizations and links associated with the 'Playboy' moniker fall under the 'Playboy' node.

The current analysis uses a visual rendition constructed by a 'spring embedded algorithm' which uses force-directed placement to co-locate those nodes with the shortest distance between them. Essentially, this layout algorithm places those nodes that are closest to each other in terms of function in the network as defined by patterns of ties, closer to each other on the physical space. This allows a picture of the overall structure of the network because the visual map clearly illustrates which organizations are working most closely with each other and which are on the periphery of the network.

The current analysis also utilizes three metrics – degree, betweenness and closeness – to identify the central players or hubs in the network. *Degree* measures the influence of a node by number of connections it possesses; in other words, how many lines radiate out from the node in the visual map. *Betweenness* is a measure of influence based on the number of network paths that cross through that node; in other words, how many paths must go through a particular node to access other nodes. *Closeness* measures influence based on the level of access a node has to other nodes in the network; in other words, how quickly a node can reach other nodes in the network.[2] These measures combine to indicate 'hubs' or nodes that are critical centres of power in a network.

Analysis

The data produced a main component[3] containing 508 nodes and 712 edges, making it a relatively sparse network, with only 3 per cent of all possible ties present. Of these 508 nodes, 70 per cent were pornography businesses and 30 per cent were mainstream companies. Table 10.1 shows a categorical breakdown of the nodes. The first visual rendition (Figure 10.1) reveals a spider-like network with long arms radiating from a pseudo-centralized core. The primary strategy of modern imperial capitalism is the colonization of new markets through a constant refinement of consumer culture to intensify consumptive pressures. The online commercial pornography industry has a very active core which functions to

Table 10.1 Number and types of nodes in the online pornography network

Node type	n	%
Conglomerate	6	0.010
Producer	91	0.180
Distributor	115	0.230
Affiliate programme	38	0.070
Financial	15	0.030
Marketing	49	0.100
End-user web site	93	0.180
Technology	74	0.150
Personals	22	0.040
Other	5	0.001

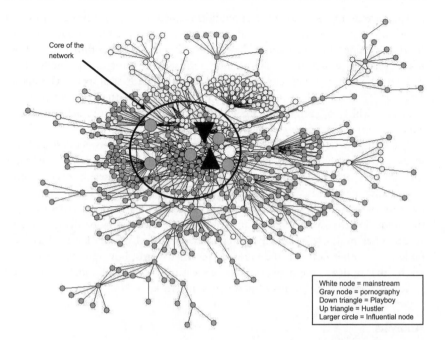

Core of the
network

White node = mainstream
Gray node = pornography
Down triangle = Playboy
Up triangle = Hustler
Larger circle = Influential node

Figure 10.1 Structure of 2007–08 online commercial pornography business network.

diversify product development, production and distribution processes. The core is surrounded by marketing tentacles designed to infiltrate and cultivate niche areas of the market. Johnson compares the business model of the pornography industry to that of an amoeba using its pseudopods (fake feet) to continuously shapeshift the organism forward in search of new sustenance (in Coopersmith 2006). The core of the network, like the amoeba itself, dispatches the tentacles as its pseudopods to constantly identify, cultivate and infiltrate new and existing consumer markets, the hallmark characteristic of modern imperial capitalism.

The core of the online commercial pornography network is a pseudo-hub structure dominated by two powerful nodes (Figure 10.1). Hub networks are characterized by a network's dependence upon a limited number of powerful nodes (Barabasi 2003). As shown in Table 10.2, Playboy and Hustler exercise the greatest influence on the overall network, making them the 'hubs'. These two conglomerates are connected to the most nodes (degree), most other organizations use them to connect to others in the network (betweenness) and they are able to connect to the most organizations in the fewest number of steps (closeness). The primary strength of 'hub' networks is that this centralization provides the ability to broadly co-ordinate across the network. Playboy and Hustler operate as 'bridges' co-ordinating different regions of the larger commercial market (Wasserman and Faust 1994). While Playboy focuses on the mainstream, with 54 per cent of its ties to mainstream companies, Hustler's ties are almost

Table 10.2 Centrality measures: most influential organizations

Node	Degree	Closeness	Betweenness
Hustler (conglomerate)	45	1.0000	0.8419
Playboy (conglomerate)	43	0.9898	1.0000
Sugar VOD (distributor)	31	–	–
Penthouse (conglomerate)	24	–	–
Yappo.com (distributor)	23	0.9077	0.3163
Naked Sword (distributor)	18	–	0.3945
Xbiz (marketing)	18		
Private Media Group (conglomerate)	–	0.8788	0.3840
NetCash (affiliate)	–	0.8719	–
PornoTube.com (website)	–	–	0.3747
Network mean	2.80	0.6134	0.0214
Standard deviation	4.66	0.1150	0.0780

Note – Not highest-ranked on that measure

exclusively embedded in pornography, with just 0.07 per cent of ties to mainstream business. This market specialization by the two dominant players extends the reach of the network, thereby expanding access to more niche markets. In spite of Playboy's efforts to separate itself from the hard-core elements of the pornography industry, its central role in the larger network indicates that it offers significant support to the entire industry, hard-core pornography included.

While the online commercial pornography network takes advantage of the co-ordinating ability of the two major conglomerates, it does not rely exclusively on their activities, thus avoiding the main vulnerability of hub structures, which is that they are easy to fracture through the targeted removal of the hub nodes (Barabasi 2003). As Table 10.2 shows, other organizations also play disproportionately large roles in the network when comparing the organization's metric to the network mean. For example, Yappo.com, a distributor, has influence across all three dimensions, with scores that are five or more standard deviations above the mean. There is functional diversity in the other influential nodes as well: two are conglomerates, two are distributors and there is a marketer, an affiliate programme and a web site. Furthermore, there are numerous organizations specializing in one or two functions providing overall organizational redundancy to the network (Table 10.1). By building diversity and redundancy into the core, the network not only protects itself against easy dismantlement, it also provides a strong foundation to support the arms of the network in their quest for new consumers through niche marketing.

While the core serves to stabilize the online industry by anchoring it to the more established pornography industry, the tentacles, like pseudopods, extrude out from the core in search of new customers hiding in small pockets of the market (Figure 10.2). These tentacles work to promote and distribute pornography primarily through affiliate programmes and the affiliated webmasters and end-user

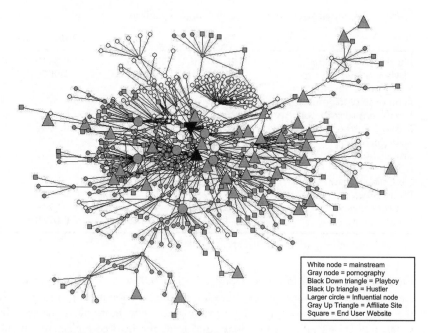

White node = mainstream
Gray node = pornography
Black Down triangle = Playboy
Black Up triangle = Hustler
Larger circle = Influential node
Gray Up Triangle = Affiliate Site
Square = End User Website

Figure 10.2 The affiliate structure of the online commercial pornography network.

sites. Affiliate programmes are organizational tools for the producers/distributors at the core of the network. Core producers/distributors develop or sponsor affiliate programmes to recruit individual webmasters as new affiliates to build end-user web sites focused on a niche or specialized sexual 'kink' using content provided by the sponsoring producer and/or distributor. In return, the webmaster receives a 'payout' or a percentage of any fees paid out by the consumer. Various types of payouts include pay-per-click, where the webmaster receives a small payout, e.g. 0.05¢, for each unique click on a particular banner; pay-per-lead, which pays out for trial memberships, and/or pay-per-sale, with payouts for new full memberships. The more money the consumer pays, the greater the payout to the webmaster.

The goal of the webmaster is to 'convert' the casual surfer of online pornography, or what I call the 'curious clicker', into a paying member of the affiliate programme. To push this conversion, the affiliate webmasters use manipulative technology designed to constrict consumer choice. Such technology includes 'blind clicks', where a click will take the surfer to a different site than what was intended. Webmasters refer to this as 'mousetrapping'. Exit consoles are pop-ups which appear when a surfer tries to leave the site. The pop-up asks if the surfer is sure they are sure they want to leave; if Yes is clicked, they are taken to another pornography site, where another series of exit consoles will continuously redirect to other pornography sites, if No is clicked then they are returned to the original page. Push technology is used to deliver pornography content to the desktop without the active request of the surfer. Pass-through linking allows pornography companies to share customers, further boxing the consumer in, and cascading billing ensures that all credit cards will find approval. While each of these technological tools is common practice among both pornography and mainstream online industries, pornography has been a leader in the creative use of such choice – constricting technology to maximize profit (Doyle 2000).

While this technology is designed to entrap the male pornography consumer and limit his agency inside the network, what draws him into this capitalist web is patriarchy. My central argument is that commercial pornography plays a pivotal role in the restructuring of the new union between patriarchy and capitalism because it provides *all* men an accessible tool to validate hegemonic masculinity through dominance – in spite of the growing independence of women – in a way that is economically profitable and maintains capitalism's access to men's economic surplus. Affiliate programmes are the crucial link in building and sustaining this modern union, because they are manifestly designed to capture the economic expenditures of the male consumer, using hegemonic masculinity. As the organizational tools of the network, affiliate programmes provide the webmasters the tools for pursuing the curious clicker. Such tools include differing payout structures to reward conversion, software webmasters can use to track conversion rates (how many curious clickers become member clickers) and resources such as banners, pics and other membership perks.

However, the most compelling selling point for affiliate programmes is how gonzo or niched the affiliated end-user sites are; in other words, how much degradation of women can be found exclusively in the affiliated sites for that particular programme. For example, IncredibleDollars.com markets itself to prospective webmasters as 'promoting the most unique sites on the net'. Webmasters are told that the 'unique content [of IncredibleDollars.com] is proven to maximize conversions and make you money! This crazy and exclusive content is [guaranteed] to convert and retain members, maximizing your revenues.'[4] This unique content includes the affiliate end-user site HumanToiletsBowls.com, where consumers get to 'watch first timers swallow it like a toilet'. The site finds 'the prettiest, perfect, innocent chicks and [fucks] the shit out of them' by getting them to do 'the most vile [human] things caught on tape' with a toilet bowl over their head. Once the 'hot girl gets totally destroyed' she is stamped 'degraded', indicating that the 'hot bitch has now been treated like the human toilet bowl she is'.[5]

The ways in which gonzo pornography uses acts of male dominance to degrade women is well documented (Dines *et al.* 1998; Jensen 2007a). However, with regards to the structure of the online commercial pornography network, the dehumanization and degradation of women are a means, not an end. The purpose of the degradation of women is to capture the economic expenditures of the male consumer looking for verification of his masculinity.

The content is described in terms of how addictive or captivating it is to the curious clicker. For example, VirtualGirlHD markets its product – desktop strippers – to the webmasters as 'very addictive' because the product uses push technology so the stripper is automatically pushed at random intervals to the desktop of the consumer.[6] Videosecrets.com uses a glue bottle to describe how its affiliate end-user site, Flirt4free.com, keeps the members 'glued to your site'.[7] Content that is unique to a particular site, highly specialized and hard-core is marketed as more likely to convert. For example, PerfectGonzo.com states that it is 'easier to convert your traffic and get big checks with Perfectgonzo' because its sites are 'high quality hard-core content that we produce in house'.[8] Perfectgonzo.com affiliate sites include Fistflush.com, where women fist each other as 'their holes are stretched to the maximum',[9] AssTraffic.com, which markets its product as 'big gaping assholes, big butts & thigh asses, double penetration, double anal, ass to mouth and more'[10] and SpermSwap.com, where one movie clip is described as 'A couple cute babes get their holes fucked hard. The guys drop two huge loads in one chick's mouth which delivers it to the other one for complete swallowing.'[11] Freakbucks.com tells webmasters that its content can reach 'traffic that is hard to target' with its 'rich assortment of high-quality niche and micro-niche sites for you to promote'.[12]

Using terms such as 'traffic' or 'conversions' as euphemisms for the male consumer obfuscates the way in which online commercial pornography deliberately targets men for economic exploitation. There are numerous community forum sites such as YNOT.com, where webmasters discuss how best to target 'traffic' and gain 'converts'. *AVN* and *X-Biz* post articles advising webmasters on how better to pursue and exploit customers. For example, an article by industry insider Jack Morrison (2004) advises webmasters on how they better target consumers. Referencing a study done by Cooper (2002), which found that 20 per cent of male online pornography users consider themselves addicts, Morrison states:

> there's little doubt that certain consumers are very heavy users and collectors of online sexual materials and experiences, and that those behaviors are not healthy – not because of the content – but because of the addictive nature of the personality … These consumers are particularly important because of the significant financial resources that they pour into the online erotica industry.
>
> (Jack Morrison 2004)

The industry clearly recognizes that its product is unhealthy and addictive to a segment of consumers, yet it works consciously to offer an unhealthy product to men who are made vulnerable both by addiction and by the social pressure to validate an increasingly outdated sense of masculinity. By disguising the health risk of its product as individualized and divorced from actual content, the pornography industry is able to maintain the legitimacy of the profits extracted from men. At its core, online commercial pornography is a business directed at exploiting the male consumer; the content – gonzo degradation of women – is simply the bait used to hook his money.

Summary and conclusion

Using the work of Heidi Hartmann, I argue that the online pornography industry plays a pivotal role in sustaining the new union between patriarchy and capitalism. Hegemonic masculinity is the sole logic for 'doing' gender available to men. Men are required by this dominant logic to publicly validate their masculinity primarily through the domination of women. Failure comes with significant social penalties that are specious and random, creating instability and insecurity in masculine identity. This insecurity is exacerbated by the fact that public proving grounds for validating masculinity have become increasingly scarce since the economic domination of women, the traditional source of male power, is no longer guaranteed, leaving men desperate in search of available bastions of masculine display. This desperation is ground zero for capitalist exploitation by the online pornography industry. Men are vulnerable to the imperialist consumer demands of capitalism because patriarchy chains men in to a rigid and punitive form of masculinity. Patriarchy creates the demand from which capitalism extracts a profit.

The 'Triple A engine' of online commercial pornographic use – available, anonymous, affordable – provides the illusion of collective power to men who feel individually powerless (Cooper 1998). But, as Soble (1986) and Brod (1988) illustrate, pornographic fantasy is in fact an expression of male powerlessness in the face of the strengthening imperialism of personal life by consumer capitalism. Pornography is offered to men as compensation for their individual powerlessness by an imperialist capitalist system that requires the support of patriarchy to maintain power. Imperialist capitalism not only pacifies men through a temporary salve of artificial sexual dominance in order to access their compliance, it deliberately extracts a profit from the very power paradox individual men experience inside patriarchal imperial capitalism. In the end, men are boxed in either way – as male consumers they are burdened with an antiquated hegemonic masculine order *and* an imperialist system of economic exploitation.

Let me be very clear here: my goal in this chapter is to expand the lens of exploitation to include the male consumer. I do not intend this work to result in a rank-ordering of oppression whereby the discussion centres on who is more exploited by commercial pornography, men or women? Pecking order discussions like that are a red herring that lead us away from the vital questions of how the mechanics of oppression and exploitation work. Furthermore, my intent is not to argue that men's choices are completely devoid of agency. As Whisnant (2004) points out, choice is not a dichotomy; rather, choice operates on a socially contextualized continuum that is layered with differing realities. Choices are influenced by race, class, gender, education and sexuality, just to name a few. Some of these can enhance agency while others may limit it. Nor is choice the final arbiter of what is good, moral or just. Simply being able to make a choice does not mean that those choices do not have larger social, political or economic consequences. To argue that men's choices are circumscribed through a joint venture between patriarchy and capitalism does not equate men's exploitation to women's exploitation. Women are harmed through men's choices even if those choices are bounded by systems of power that also diminish and harm men. In the end, commercial pornography residing at the nexus of patriarchal imperial capitalism is harmful to all.

The most significant limitation of my study is the question of how representative this network picture is of the larger reality of online commercial pornography. The reality of online pornography is that the network is constantly changing and consists of possibly millions of nodes. Fully capturing a picture of such a large and nebulous structure is difficult if not impossible. However, while an accurate real-time accounting of the nodes may be difficult to capture, I believe that the shape and function of the network are accurate. A network anchored by a core set of very active, strong conglomerates surrounded by numerous extensions designed for cultivating new markets fits with the strategic goals of modern imperial capitalism (Castells 2000). In other words, online commercial pornography is a perfect exemplar of a modern imperial capitalist network.

Future work is focused on developing a better understanding of the connections between the functionalities and expanding the boundaries of the network. Ongoing data collection includes fleshing out the ego networks of the affiliate programmes, identifying the end-user web sites of each programme and the affiliated webmasters. Does the boundary of the network expand with these new data or does it fold back in on itself? If it expands, this would indicate that the network is indeed very sparse and loosely connected, with little co-ordination between functional nodes. If it folds back in on itself, this would suggest a more enmeshed network with tight co-ordination between the central actors. Each of these characteristics would inform how the money flows through the network. A loose network would have a linear path back to the core, with money becoming centralized in the hands of a few large conglomerates. A tight organization may mean greater dispersion of the profits.

By describing the structure of the online commercial pornography network, my work offers a new way of envisioning the exploitation of pornography that does not centre exclusively on content. My research looks at how the industry makes a profit through a Marxist lens, asking questions about economic exploitation at the level of the consumer. What I show is a systematic set of business relationships and practices that consciously cultivate addiction, dependence and entrapment. In this way, the pornography industry operates much like the tobacco industry or the drug trade; it offers potential customers a small free taste of the product, knowing that the potential for addiction is clear and present. That the male consumer ostensibly does not mind such economic enslavement does not negate the organized exploitation of the market. Instead, his acquiescence is a testament to the strength of the new union between patriarchy and capitalism, which has once again 'bought out' men with a false sense of empowerment. Pornography is a paradox of power for men where they are provided individual masculine authentication in return for collective economic exploitation. Resolution of this paradox will not come through a search for more niched or hypergonzo porn. Rather, resolution comes through men's withdrawal from patriarchy and consequently the collapse of the new union.

Notes

1 See Jensen, Whisnant and Flood (all in this volume) for further discussion of the costs to men of their porn consumption.
2 See Wasserman and Faust (1994) for an in depth discussion of the methodology of SNA.
3 The main component is the largest set of connected nodes in the network. By extracting it, sets of nodes that are small and disconnected are peeled away, leaving the central activity network.
4 <http://www.incredibledollars.com> (accessed 12 May 2009).
5 <http://www.humantoiletbowls.com> (accessed 12 May 2009).
6 <http://www72.virtuagirlhd.com/us/> (accessed 12 May 2009).
7 <http://www.videosecrets.com/programs.php?tracker_logged=&_referrer=&sales_id=> (accessed 6 July 2009).
8 <http://www.perfectgonzo.com/> (accessed 12 May 2009).
9 <http://www.fistfluch.com> (accessed 12 May 2009).
10 <http://www.asstraffic.com> (accessed 12 May 2009).
11 <http://www.spermswap.com> (accessed 12 May 2009).
12 <http://www.freakbucks.com/index3.php> (accessed 12 May 2009).

Chapter 11

Young men using pornography

Michael Flood

Most everyday users of pornography are heterosexual men. Looking at, and masturbating to, pornography is the routine practice of large numbers of men. And most of the commercial pornographic industry caters to heterosexual men. These men – and their consumption of pornography – are the subject of a growing body of research. This chapter offers an overview of what we can learn about heterosexual boys' and young men's use of pornography, focusing particularly on quantitative studies of the extent, nature and meaning of pornography consumption.

Pornography plays an increasingly significant role in boys' and young men's peer cultures and sociosexual relations. Consumption of pornography is exacerbating some males' tolerance for sexual violence, intensifying their investments in narratives of female nymphomania and male sexual prowess, and shifting their sexual practices and relations. Among boys and young men, effective efforts to limit or shape the use of pornography will address the powerful appeal of such materials and the cultural contexts in which pornography consumption is given meaning.

Patterns of pornography use

Males are more likely than females to use pornography, including among younger age groups. Different studies define 'pornography' in varying ways or allow research participants to do so: some do not distinguish between different kinds of pornographic media (videos, internet sites and so on) and some do not distinguish between accidental and deliberate exposure. Nevertheless, it is clear that large numbers of boys and young men in particular are growing up in the presence of sexually explicit media.

In general, men are significantly more likely than women to view pornography frequently, to be sexually aroused by it and to have favourable attitudes towards it (Johansson and Hammarén 2007: 60–4; Lo and Wei 2002: 16; Sabina *et al.* 2008: 69; Wallmyr and Welin 2006; Walsh 1999: 779). Of course, women too consume pornography (Juffer 1998; Walsh 1999), although image-centred pornographies have not developed mass appeal among women.

One of the few nationally representative surveys of pornography consumption comes from Australia. A national survey of 20,000 individuals aged sixteen to fifty-nine years found that about one-quarter looked at X-rated videos or internet sex sites in the last year. More than twice as many males (37 per cent) as females (16 per cent) watched an X-rated film in the last year. Males are almost seven times as likely as females to have visited an internet sex site on purpose in the last year: 16.5 per cent of men did so and only 2.4 per cent of women (Richters *et al.* 2003: 185–6). US data are similar. One study found that 23 per cent of men and 7 per cent of women have visited adult web sites, and getting access to adult sites is most popular among men aged eighteen to twenty-nine (Lenhart *et al.* 2001: 33). Among undergraduate internet users at a Texas university, 57 per cent of men and 35 per cent of women had used the internet to search for sex-related information (Goodson *et al.* 2001: 106). However, some males are more likely than others to use pornography. The national Australian survey found that pornography consumption is more common among young men, with close to half of males aged between sixteen and twenty-nine using pornography.

A wide range of studies in Western countries document both that significant proportions of boys and young men consume pornography and that they do so in greater numbers and with much greater frequency than their female peers. For example, a Swedish study found that 30 per cent of adolescent boys and only 3 per cent of adolescent girls watched pornography at least once a week (Forsberg 2001: 161). In an Australian study among sixteen- and seventeen-year-olds, 73 per cent of boys had watched an X-rated video, with one in twenty watching them on a weekly basis, while more than a fifth watch an X-rated video at least once a month. Only 11 per cent of girls had watched an X-rated video, all of them less often than once every two to three months (Flood 2007). Similar findings come from other countries such as Taiwan (Lo *et al.* 1999; Lo and Wei 2005). Some studies do find that girls and young women are not far behind boys and young men in the extent to which they have *ever* seen pornography, although gendered patterns in their frequency of consumption are likely to persist (Bonino *et al.* 2006: 273; Fleming *et al.* 2006: 145; Johansson and Hammarén 2007: 60; Sabina *et al.* 2008: 691–2; Wallmyr and Welin 2006: 291).

Gendered patterns of sex-related internet use also can be found among queer and same-sex-attracted individuals. An Australian survey of same-sex-attracted young people aged fourteen to twenty-one found that over 80 per cent of young men had downloaded sexual materials from sex sites, compared with under 50 per cent of young women. And close to 40 per cent of males had used sexual materials to get aroused before sex, compared with just over 10 per cent of females (Hillier *et al.* 2001: 13–14).

There are further gender contrasts in patterns and contexts of pornography use. Boys and men are more likely than girls and women to use pornography for sexual excitement and masturbation, to initiate its use (rather than be introduced to it by an intimate partner), to view it alone and in same-sex groups, and to view more types of images (Cameron *et al.* 2005; Flood 2007: 51, 56; Flood and

Hamilton 2003: 13–14; Nosko *et al.* 2007: 2). Such patterns have been documented also in older studies among young people in Canada (Check 1995: 89–90) and the US (Bryant and Brown 1989: 46). On the other hand, in a study at a Texas university, while males were more likely to report accessing explicit materials out of sexual curiosity and to become sexually aroused, there were no differences in the frequency of masturbation (Goodson *et al.* 2001: 108–13).

Effects and significance

What is the significance of this pervasive pornography consumption among boys and young men? While there is considerable controversy regarding any claims that media have 'effects', I wish to argue that pornography consumption has a series of identifiable effects among boys and young men. There is debate regarding the methods used to demonstrate that pornography has effects, so I begin with this, before offering some caveats for my own claims.

Research into pornography's effects can be divided into various types, according to two dimensions: the study design, and the type of effect being studied. In terms of study design, some studies are experimental, often in laboratory conditions, and involve testing the impact of exposure to pornography on participants' attitudes or behaviour. Other studies are correlational and involve the investigation of possible relationships between 'naturalistic' pornography use (in everyday life) and attitudes or behaviour. Longitudinal studies examine the use of sexual media and its correlates over time. In terms of the type of effect being studied, much research focuses on attitudes, while some focus also or only on behaviours (Malamuth *et al.* 2000: 41–2).

Laboratory-based experimental studies on pornography have been criticized as excessively artificial and formal (Boyle 2000: 188; McNair 1996: 65–7). Pornography is often defined by the particular effect it produces in the spectator, that is, sexual arousal and masturbation to orgasm. Yet masturbation is usually absent in experimental studies. The experimental context is very different from the natural setting of pornography consumption, for instance where a young man masturbates to internet pornography in his bedroom or a group watch an X-rated video in the living room. Masturbation and orgasm, as powerful physical and emotional experiences, are central to the pornographic experience and influence the interpretation and effect of the material. It is therefore possible that experimental studies in fact *under*estimate the effect of pornography (Jensen 1998b: 105). Experimental studies have also been criticized for focusing on measures of physiological arousal rather than affective or emotional responses such as pleasure or shame, and neglecting long-term effects, given that their definitions of 'massive' exposure may be as small as five hours' worth (Jensen 1998b: 104) and their time scales may be only weeks long (Thornburgh and Lin 2002: 156).

Correlational studies do not allow determinations of causality: associations between exposure to sexual media and particular attitudes or practices may go either way, be reciprocal, or shaped by other factors such as sexual interest

(Hald 2006; Janghorbani *et al.* 2003). And few studies are longitudinal, tracing the use of sexual media and the formation of sexual and gender identities over time.

Nevertheless, existing empirical research is robust enough for us to be able to claim that pornography consumption does have discernible effects. It suggests too that at least three types of factor mediate the impact of exposure of pornography: the characteristics of the viewer, their own engagement with the material, and the character and context of exposure.

First, the likely effects of viewing sexual content among young people are moderated by such variables as age, gender, maturation, sexual experience and parental involvement. Age and maturation influence children's levels of understanding of, comfort with and interest in content such as sexual humour and innuendo. In a study of eleven- to fifteen-year-old girls, girls who were more physically mature and had been in an intimate relationship with a boy were both more interested in and more critical of portrayals of sex in the media (Huston *et al.* 1998: 15–16). Research on the relationship between pornography and sexual aggression finds that important moderating variables include the individual's cultural background (emphasis on gender equality or inequality), their home background (sexually permissive or restricted), their personality characteristics and their current emotional state (Malamuth *et al.* 2000: 55).

Second, pornography's effects are shaped by the user's sexual, emotional and cognitive responses to the material (Fisher and Barak 2001: 317–20; Jensen 1998b: 157–9; Malamuth and Impett 2001). There is evidence that the effects are greater for people who are more active and involved viewers, who watch the media in question with specific purposes in mind and who attribute greater realism to the portrayals (Ward 2002: 3). At the same time, little is known about children's and young people's active engagement with pornography, although children and young people are known to be active and agentic consumers of media, using critical skills and perspectives in interpreting sexual content (Buckingham and Bragg 2003).

Third, the character and circumstances of exposure are important: the type of material involved, the duration and intensity of viewing, and the context (voluntary or involuntary, solitary or collective) (Thornburgh and Lin 2002). For example, when a young man watches an adult video or views a pornographic web site alone and masturbates, the powerful physical and emotional experiences of arousal, masturbation and orgasm may lend greater intensity to the sexual images (Jensen 1998b: 104–5). Mixed effects may occur when boys watch an X-rated video or look at internet pornography in a group. On the one hand, the intensity of the experience may be lessened, as there are distractions, taboos apply to open displays of sexual arousal and group interaction may be characterized by sexual banter, playfulness and sarcasm rather than sexual absorption. On the other hand, watching pornography in groups may enhance collective acceptance of the value systems embedded in pornography and normalization of the particular sexual practices shown.

Some of pornography's impacts are innocuous or even desirable, but others are problematic if not deeply troubling. Below, I move from effects more likely to be perceived as the former to effects more likely to be seen as the latter. Among boys and young men, pornography provides information about sex and sexualities, tends to liberalize sexual attitudes and shifts young men's sexual practices and repertoires. Its use, particularly when secret, can harm female partners' sense of intimacy and trust and can take compulsive and obsessive forms. Pornography encourages sexualized and sexually objectifying understandings of girls and women. Finally, pornography consumption can intensify boys' and young men's tolerance for, and participation in, sexual violence.

Pornography as sex education

Sexual knowledge and attitudes

Pornography is a significant source of young men's information about sex and sexualities (Measor 2004). Pornography's teachings take place in the context of both limited formal sexuality education and young men's reliance on peers for sexual information (Gelder 2002). A series of reviews document that regular and frequent exposure to sexual content, at least in mainstream media, produces greater sexual knowledge among children and young people (APA 2007; Strasburger and Wilson 2002; Thornburgh and Lin 2002; Ward 2003). Children and young people exposed to sexual media content have greater sexual knowledge (about such topics as pregnancy, menstruation, homosexuality and prostitution) than the control groups (Huston *et al.* 1998).

There is evidence too that pornography in particular is a significant source for many boys' and young men's formative sexual knowledge (Allen 2001). For example, some men report that pornography helped them to learn about female and male bodies and sexual techniques (MacDonald 1990). Some male users describe early encounters with pornography as 'educational', in that it provided information about biology and sexual practices, demystified and destigmatized sex, and taught them about sexual positions, practices and techniques, thus increasing their sexual competence (McKee 2007b). It is worth asking, however, exactly what males learn about bodies and sex from pornography, given that in much heterosexual mass-marketed pornography

> sex is divorced from intimacy, loving affection, and human connection; all women are constantly available for sex and have insatiable sexual appetites; and all women are sexually satisfied by whatever the men in the film do.
>
> (Jensen and Dines 1998: 72)

Consumption of pornography and other sexual media also shapes the liberalization of boys' and young men's sexual attitudes. The reviews of exposure to sexual content in mainstream media also document that this produces more liberal sexual attitudes among children and young people. In experimental studies, for example, children and young people exposed to sexual media content are more accepting of pre-, extra- and non-marital sexual relations (Huston *et al.* 1998). Correlational studies find associations between greater exposure to sexual content on television and the belief that one's peers are sexually active and a more favourable attitude towards recreational sex (Strasburger and Wilson 2002).

Similar if not greater effects are likely for pornography, given its explicit and decontextualized depictions of diverse sexual relations. For example, fifteen- to eighteen-year-olds in a Swedish study who had ever watched a pornographic film were more likely than others to be less ashamed about masturbation and to see prostitution, pornography and sex without love as 'okay' (Johansson and Hammarén 2007). Pornography use also shapes the acceptance of pornography itself: young men (and to some extent women) exposed to large amounts of explicit sexual content often become more supportive of and less offended by such material (Thornburgh and Lin 2002).

Another dimension of pornography's role in male sex education concerns male bodies and bodily processes. Some men argue that pornography has played a therapeutic role in helping them develop healthier sexualities (Kimmel 1990: 21). Pornography has allowed men to feel less shame about ejaculation and semen and to accept themselves as sexual beings (MacDonald 1990). These effects are one aspect of the allegedly 'sex-positive' contribution afforded by pornography. For some feminist and queer commentators, pornography has challenged sexual repression, heterosexist and erotophobic sexual norms and thus benefited women (Duggan *et al.* 1988: 82). However, others argue that while pornography oppresses women, it also limits men. Pornography has helped to homogenize men's sexual tastes, narrow the range of male sexual satisfaction, channel all men's intimate needs into genital sexual activity and promote myths of perpetual male sexual readiness and penis size (Brod 1990).

The limited evidence available regarding men's pornography use and their sexual self-esteem and body image is contradictory. A Canadian study among students on college campuses found that men with higher rates of exposure to internet pornography had lower levels of genital and sexual esteem (Morrison *et al.* 2006). On the other hand, a study among heterosexual university students did not find this relationship, although it did document an association between pornography use and higher sexual anxiety (Morrison *et al.* 2004). In fact, one study among male undergraduates finds that frequent readers of soft-core pornographic magazines report more positive body esteem than other men (Schooler and Ward 2006: 37). However, it may be that frequent reading of pornography here acts as a proxy for a specific type of masculinity which itself is related to certain body image attitudes.

Pornography has further influences on sexual attitudes which I address below, as they concern attitudes towards particular sexual practices.

Sexual practices and relations

Given its influence on sexual knowledge and attitudes, it is not surprising that pornography also may shift boys' and young men's sexual expectations, practices and repertoires. While these are shaped by a wide variety of interpersonal and contextual influences, there is some evidence that males' consumption of pornography is informing increased interest in, demand for and participation in particular sexual practices such as anal intercourse and extra-vaginal ejaculation, both of which are pornographic staples.

While one should not expect that the depiction of sexual practices in pornography will match their prevalence in the population, it is worth noting just how wide the gap can be. For example, Australian studies suggest that anal intercourse – a feature of *most* pornographic features according to Jensen and Dines (1998: 80) – is a relatively uncommon practice. Among all Australians aged sixteen to fifty-nine, in their most recent heterosexual sexual encounter only under 1 per cent practised anal intercourse. Over their lifetimes, about one in five (21 per cent of males and 15 per cent of females) had ever had heterosexual anal intercourse, including 4 per cent of people aged sixteen to nineteen (de Visser *et al.* 2003: 151–2).

Evidence that pornography is shaping young men's sexual practices comes from three sources. First, some young male pornography users themselves report this, either for themselves or for others. For example, in a study among 300 young men aged sixteen to twenty-four visiting a genito-urinary clinic in Stockholm, Sweden, 53 per cent agreed that pornography had had an impact on their sexual behaviour (Tyden and Rogala 2004). Close to half described this as only 'Yes, a little,' and 4 per cent said, 'Yes, much.' However, more men believed that pornography influenced *others'* sexual behaviour. This 'third-person effect' – the belief that others are more affected by media messages than oneself – is a common finding in studies of media effects (Hald and Malamuth 2008; Lo and Wei 2002). Asked how they might be influenced by porn, the young men responded that they had been inspired or influenced to try particular acts or positions.

The second source of evidence concerns associations between pornography consumption and sexual behaviour. Various studies find correlations between young people's actual sexual behaviour and the consumption of sexual media content (Huston *et al.* 1998; Strasburger and Wilson 2002; Ward 2003). These findings hold for pornography in particular from the few studies examining naturalistic pornographic consumption among minors. In a Swedish study of 1,300 high-school students, Johansson and Hammarén (2007) report that young pornography users are more likely than non-users also to have had sexual intercourse, masturbated, had same-sex sex and a one-night stand. A survey of 522 African American females aged fourteen to eighteen found correlations between viewing X-rated movies and having multiple sex partners, having sex more frequently and testing positive for chlamydia (Wingood *et al.* 2001). One of the most well documented associations concerns young men's pornography use and their practice of heterosexual anal intercourse. Five studies among Swedish young people find that young men who are regular consumers of pornography are more likely to have had anal intercourse with a girl and to have tried to perform acts they have seen in pornography, and that girls who have seen pornography also are more likely to have had anal intercourse (Tyden *et al.* 2001; Rogala and Tyden 2003; Tyden and Rogala 2004; Haggstrom-Nordin *et al.* 2005; Johansson and Hammarén 2007).

A third source of evidence comes from experimental studies. When adults engage in prolonged consumption of pornography showing particular sexual practices, their estimation of the prevalence of such practices in the population increases (Thornburgh and Lin 2002: 153; Zillmann 1989: 135).

It is likely therefore that consumption of pornography among boys and young men is shaping their actual sexual practices, including their involvement in anal intercourse. Young men may be learning from pornography that anal intercourse is normal, desirable and enjoyable for women (even though most young women in the Swedish studies above who had had anal intercourse did not enjoy it and did not want to do it again). Given heterosexual pornography's obsessive pre-occupations with extra-vaginal ejaculation, double and triple penetration, multiple-partner sex and other 'esoteric' sexual practices, these too may be increasing in erotic salience among boys and young men.

However, the relationship between pornography use and sexual behaviour also is likely to be complex. For some young men, both their use of pornography and their involvement in anal sex may represent a broader, sexually adventurist or experimental orientation. Pornography by itself is unlikely to influence an individual's entire sexual expression, and its consumption may be part of 'a larger sexual space and sexual experimentation' (Johansson and Hammarén 2007: 66).

An additional form of influence on young people's sexual relations concerns pornography's representation of same-sex sexualities. Research among same-sex-attracted young people in Australia finds that internet pornography has played a role as 'one way to address the invisibility of same sex desire, sexual performance and behaviour in Real Life' (Hillier *et al.* 2001: 20). In the context of a silence about homosexuality in their everyday lives, young men and women use pornography to learn what to do when having sex, to improve their knowledge about sexual behaviour or as a substitute for sexual relationships.

Pornography as betrayal

Pornography arguably can be a healthy part of sexual intimacy in couple relationships. For this to take place, the use of pornography should be freely chosen, mutual and open, and the sexually explicit materials themselves should be ethical (although there is considerable debate over the ethical status of depictions of sex). In such circumstances, couples may watch pornography together, or make it themselves.

However, it is likely that for most heterosexual men who use pornography and are in relationships, these conditions are not met. Instead, their pornography use is hidden from their partners. There are no data regarding the extent to which women are aware of or indeed share their male partners' pornography use. I suspect that there is a widespread denial and dishonesty in heterosexual relationships in which women do not know of their partners' use of pornography. Among those women who *do* know of their partners' pornography use, some experience significant distress at this.[1]

Studies among women who are aware of their male partners' use of pornography find that most have largely neutral attitudes to this use. They 'don't mind' and see it as 'normal'. However, a substantial proportion have much more negative attitudes, experiencing their partners' pornography use as damaging both for their relationships and themselves. In a US study, one-quarter of women saw their partner's pornography use as a kind of affair, one-third felt that it had had negative effects on their sexual lives and relationships, and over one-third agreed that they felt less attractive and desirable and more like a sexual object (Bridges *et al.* 2003). Other studies find that partners of adult pornography users report decreased sexual intimacy, lowered esteem and demands that they participate in activities they find objectionable (Manning 2006).

Some heterosexual men use pornography in their sexual relations in ways which women find coercive or abusive. A representative survey of 4,446 college women in the US found that 6 per cent of the young women had been exposed to pornographic pictures or materials by someone when they did not wish to see them (Fisher *et al.* 2000: 31). Some women are coerced by sexual partners and others into looking at pornography, and pressured or forced into unwanted sexual acts inspired by the man's use of pornography (Jensen 1998b: 108–19). There is no doubt that some women freely choose to consume pornography, and some consider pornography a positive force in their lives. At the same time, other women experience distress and harm in relation to their male partner's use of pornography.

Pornography as addiction

An emerging scholarship on sexual, internet and cybersex 'addiction' suggests that some pornography consumers come to use pornography in ways which are obsessive, compulsive and have damaging consequences for themselves or others (Cooper *et al.* 2004; Young 2008). Seen through the prism of traditional understandings of drug use, the term 'addiction' implies that pornography consumption necessarily is compulsive, escalates over time and has harmful personal effects, and these can be mitigated only by abstinence. The internet is seen to play a particularly potent role here, with one text referring to its role as 'the crack cocaine of sexual addiction' (Schneider and Weiss 2001).

The analogy between pornography use and drug use is dangerous if we assume a model of 'one taste and you're hooked'. On the other hand, other models of illicit and licit drug use provide more useful ways of conceptualizing pornography consumption. For example, there may be 'recreational' users, occasional users, and habitual users: some individuals will use pornography for years with little negative effect, while others will find it highly destructive.

Some men's (and women's) use of pornography clearly is habitual, compulsive and has negative effects on other areas of their lives, resulting for example in social, occupational or financial difficulties. Such patterns of use may be less well framed as 'addictions' and more accurately described as impulse control disorders, akin to eating disorders or pathological gambling (Heron and Shapira 2003). While there is no research on 'pornography addiction' among minors, some argue that similar patterns may emerge among younger users (Sussman 2007).

At the same time, we must be wary of problematic norms of behaviour which can guide the medicalization and pathologization of certain forms of pornography use, for example in which any adolescent sexual behaviour and any powerful interest in sex are defined as problematic. In addition, notions of pornography use as 'addictive' or 'compulsive' may divert attention from questions regarding users' agency and responsibility.

Pornography as sexist education

Pornography's influence on boys' and young men's attitudes includes the encouragement of sexist and stereotypical understandings of gender and sexuality. Evidence for this comes in the first place from research on mainstream media. Both correlational and experimental studies find that adolescents' and young adults' exposure to mainstream media which sexualize girls and women is associated with greater acceptance of stereotyped and sexist notions about gender and sexual roles, including notions of women as sexual objects (Ward 2002; Ward *et al.* 2005). Adolescents and young adults who have frequent, regular exposure to media genres high in sexualized content (such as music videos) are more accepting of attitudes that sexualize and sexually objectify women (APA 2007: 31–32). For example, in a study among undergraduates aged 18–22, Ward (2002) documented both experimental and correlational connections between TV viewing and students' sexual attitudes and assumptions. Students' support for sexual stereotypes typical in television content (dating is a recreational sport, women are sexual objects whose value is based on their physical appearance and men are sex-driven creatures who have trouble being faithful) was associated with more frequent and more involved viewing.

Among media with sexual content, pornography may be particularly effective in encouraging adherence to sexually objectifying understandings of and behaviours towards girls and women. Pornography shows a much higher degree of sexual explicitness (by definition) than other sexual media. More than this however, much contemporary pornography offers a decontextualized portrayal of sexual behaviour, a relentless focus on female bodies, and sexist and callous depictions of women (Flood and Hamilton 2003). As various experimental studies among adult men find, exposure to narrow ideals of female sexual attractiveness in pornography constrains men's appreciation of and intimacy with female partners:

> exposure to pornography ... leads men to rate their female partners as less attractive ... to indicate less satisfaction with their intimate partners' attractiveness, sexual performance, and level of affection ... and to express greater desire for sex without emotional involvement.
>
> (APA 2007: 29)

A correlational study among over 600 US undergraduates found that men who regularly viewed pornography were more likely than others to see women (but not men) in sexualized ways, to endorse gender-stereotypical statements about themselves and others and to perceive men as more masculine and women as more feminine (Frable et al. 1997).

Men's consumption of sexualized media also influences how they actually treat and respond to real women in subsequent interactions. At least three studies find that when men are exposed to sexualized content they are then more likely to treat women in sexualized ways (APA 2007: 32). In these experiments, effects were strongest among stereotypically masculine men, suggesting an interaction between media exposure and pre-existing orientations.

While pornography appears to be influential in shaping men's sexualized and sexually objectifying understandings of women, its significance for sexist attitudes per se appears to be complex. A series of studies have found that relationships between pornography consumption and attitudes towards women are either weak or non-existent (Garos et al. 2004: 71–2). Attempting to explain this, Garos et al. examined more complex measures of sexist attitudes. In two studies among US university students, they report, there was no relationship between pornography use and more hostile, overt measures of sexism, although pornography use was related to more benevolent, 'modern' forms of sexism. The authors suggest several possible explanations for this. One is that the forms of pornography examined were 'mainstream' rather than those depicting women experiencing pain or suffering, limiting a relationship with hostile attitudes towards women. Another is that both pornography use and favourable attitudes towards women are shaped by a third factor, a general liberal orientation (Garos et al. 2004: 89–90). This may also explain the finding in an Australian study of self-selected pornography users of no relationship between the extent of pornography use and attitudes towards women (McKee 2007a).

Pornography as rape training

The final area of pornography's impact I consider is the most troubling, its relationship to sexual violence against women. The application to existing empirical studies of summary techniques or 'meta-analysis' finds consistent evidence that exposure to or consumption of pornography is related to male sexual aggression against women. This association is strongest for violent pornography and still reliable for nonviolent pornography, particularly by frequent users (Malamuth *et al.* 2000: 53).

In experimental studies, adults show significant strengthening of attitudes supportive of sexual aggression following exposure to pornography, such as acceptance of rape myths, sexual callousness and adversarial sexual beliefs. Across sixteen experiments with 2,248 participants, the association between pornography and rape-supportive attitudes is evident as a result of exposure to both nonviolent pornography (showing consenting sexual activity) and violent pornography, while the latter results in significantly greater increases in violence-supportive attitudes (Allen, Emmers *et al.* 1995: 19). Exposure to sexually violent material desensitizes male viewers to sexual violence, diminishing their emotional response to the stimulus, eroding their empathy for victims of violence and informing more callous attitudes towards female rape victims. According to a meta-analysis of thirty-three experimental studies involving 2,040 participants, adults also show an increase in behavioural aggression following exposure to pornography. Exposure to non-violent or violent depictions of sexual activity increases aggression, and the effect is stronger in the case of exposure to violent pornography (Allen, D'Alessio *et al.* 1995: 271).

What about correlations between pornography use in everyday life and attitudes supporting sexual aggression? An early meta-analysis did not find these (Allen, Emmers *et al.* 1995: 18), although analysis of the differences between non-violent and violent pornography was not possible (Malamuth *et al.* 2000: 47, 53). However, a more recent meta-analysis, correcting for problems in the 1995 effort and including more recent studies, did find an association between men's everyday pornography consumption and their attitudes supporting violence against women (Hald *et al.* 2009). Across nine studies with 2,309 participants, violence-supportive attitudes correlated more strongly with the use of sexually violent pornography than with the use of non-violent pornography, although the latter relationship was also found to be significant.

There are correlations too between everyday pornography use and actual sexually aggressive behaviour. Studies among men in the general population find significant associations between the use of at least certain forms of pornography or habitual pornography use and levels of sexual aggression (Malamuth *et al.* 2000: 50). In addition, men who use 'hard-core', violent or rape pornography and men who are high-frequency users of pornography are also significantly more likely than others to report that they would rape or sexually harass a woman if they knew they could get away with it (Malamuth *et al.* 2000: 51–2).

There appears to be a circular relationship between pornography and sexual aggression, in which men at higher risk for sexual aggression (given their attitudes and so on) are more likely to be attracted to and aroused by sexually violent media and may be more influenced by them (Malamuth *et al.* 2000: 55).

Most of the research on pornography and sexual aggression has been conducted among young male adults. While its findings cannot simply be extrapolated to younger males, there is evidence of pornography's role in sexually aggressive attitudes and behaviours among adolescent and older boys. Looking first at non-pornographic sexual media, experimental studies among young adults find that males (and females) exposed to sexualized or objectifying content are more accepting of rape myths, violence-supportive and adversarial beliefs (Kalof 1999; Lanis and Covell 1995; Milburn *et al.* 2000; Ward 2002), while correlational studies among adolescents also show such associations (Cowan and Campbell 1995; Kaestle *et al.* 2007).

What about pornographic media? In a study of Canadian teenagers with an average age of fourteen, there was a correlation between boys' frequent consumption of pornography and their agreement with the idea that it is acceptable to hold a girl down and force her to have sex (Check 1995). Among US boys and girls aged eleven to sixteen, greater exposure to R- and X-rated films was related to stronger acceptance of sexual harassment (Strouse *et al.* 1994). There are behavioural associations too. Among Italian adolescents aged fourteen to nineteen, there were associations between pornography use and sexually harassing a peer or forcing someone into sex (Bonino *et al.* 2006).

Pornography is not the only important source of sexist and violence-supportive discourses and representations in our cultures (Segal 1998: 49–51). Other media such as television and film are also effective teachers of gender-stereotyped and rape-supportive attitudes (Strasburger and Wilson 2002: 164). At the same time, pornography warrants particular attention, given its pervasiveness, accessibility, functionality and the extremes of hostility and callousness towards women it often betrays.

Fifty ways to leave your lover

If we agree that boys' and young men's use of pornography, or particular forms of consumption and/or of particular forms of pornography, is harmful, what do we do about it? I focus here on social and educational strategies rather than legal and regulatory ones, for two reasons. First, the former have been neglected while the latter have been widely canvassed. Second, they have several advantages over technological strategies such as filtering. They encourage young people's moral and ethical development and resilience, they are more effective than technological solutions in the long term and they minimize the negative effects of exposure if and when it does occur.

The most prominent response to the problem of men's pornography use centres on abstaining from its use. Christian pastors, centres and texts exhort men to abandon pornography, seek the forgiveness of their wives and of God and renew their spiritual and marital vows. This faith-based response to pornography is the logical extension of traditional Christian hostility to masturbation, sex for sex's sake, sex outside the boundaries of married heterosexual monogamy and infidelity. It overlaps with strategies which frame pornography use and abuse as 'addiction'.[2] This abstinence-centred strategy is the most well developed of existing social strategies. At the same time, its reach is limited. It appeals primarily to conservative Christian adherents and its narrow sexual proscriptions are confronted by the contrary tenets of a powerful sexual culture.

A very different call for abstinence comes from pro-feminist men. Committed to the feminist critique of pornography and the sex industry as patriarchal, brutalizing and misogynistic, they call on men to quit pornography and forge ethical sexual and gender relations. The most prominent advocate is Robert Jensen (2007a), with others including Jackson Katz and John Stoltenberg. Pro-feminist frameworks too must confront the weight of powerful, patriarchal sexual norms, although they are more in step with contemporary destabilizations of rigidly heterosexual and masculine identities, assertions of female sexual agency and increasing norms of gender equality (Flood 2009).

Given that young people turn to pornography in part for information on sex and sexuality, the provision of alternative, more age-appropriate content on sexuality is an obvious strategy. Sexuality education for children and young people, both face-to-face and through the internet and other media, is desirable in its own right and in reducing the appeal of pornography (Thornburgh and Lin 2002: 250–1). To be most effective, sexuality education will need to address the negotiation of sexual and intimate relations and include explorations of lust and desire.

However, even the most compelling sexuality education will not satisfy young people's, and particularly young men's, interest in sexually explicit materials for stimulation and masturbation. Indeed, asked what they would like in sexuality education, some young men call for the inclusion of pornographic depictions of bodies and sex (Allen 2006). Still, pornography will not help to foster young men's sexual development, as it does not prepare them for the emotional complexities and bodily diversities of lived sexual experience.

There are two further strategies which, while very rare thus far, are promising ones. Given that boys and young men are likely to continue to consume pornography, an important strategy is to teach them the skills with which to read it more critically. 'Pornography education' centres on encouraging critical skills in media literacy, such that viewers are more resistant to sexist and violence-supportive themes in pornography (Strasburger and Wilson 2002: 346–63; Thornburgh and Lin 2002: 248). Support for this strategy comes from experimental studies, which find that adults shown violent pornography can be 'inoculated' against its negative effects through pre-briefing or 'cured' afterwards through debriefing (Allen et al. 1996). There are fledgling efforts to incorporate pornography education into school curricula in Australia and the UK (Crabbe and Corlett 2008).

One significant resource among boys and young men here is their resistance to pornography. Various studies find that significant proportions of boys and young men have critical attitudes towards pornography. In a Swedish survey of young people aged fifteen to eighteen, 23 per cent of males (and 67 per cent of females) disagreed with the statement that 'porn is sexually exciting' and 37 per cent of males (and 69 per cent of females) agreed that pornography is degrading (Johansson and Hammarén 2007: 61–2). Two other studies document both complicity and resistance in young men's relationship to pornography (Thomson 1999: 194; Dean 2007: 48–9).

A final strategy is encouraging the use of more ethical pornography and more ethical forms of use. Ethical pornography would eroticize consent, respect and intimacy and be produced without participants' coercion or harm. While this strategy is the most marginal of all those I have canvassed, its value is in finding ways to inform and inspire men's and women's erotic lives and relations without also entrenching inequalities.

The effectiveness of these efforts in helping boys and men to quit or rework their pornography use has not been tested empirically. Still, there are some general principles which should guide any such endeavour. Among boys and young men, more effective efforts will address the powerful appeal of such materials and the cultural contexts in which pornography consumption takes place and is given meaning. They will avoid intensifying the stigma of masturbation or pathologizing sexual interests and desires. They will mobilize some young men's discomfort and guilt regarding the sexism of pornography. And they will be complemented by wider efforts to foster egalitarian sexual cultures among young people.

Notes

1 See Dines, Whisnant, Thompson and Boyle, this volume, for anecdotal accounts of women's distress at their male partner's pornography use.
2 A typical example is the web site Through the Flame, a 'pornography and sex addiction support group' on line at <http://www.throughtheflame.org/> (accessed 16 November 2009).

Chapter 12

'Students study hard porn'

Pornography and the popular press

Mark Jones and Gerry Carlin

While researching a contribution to another volume on contemporary pornography, we found it necessary to browse some hard-core pornographic web sites
using our office computers (Jones and Carlin forthcoming). Negotiating a
somewhat fraught route between the university's information technology policy,
research sub-committees, ethics committee, and various harassment, civil rights
and academic freedom agendas, we were reminded that the alleged ubiquity of
pornography in the contemporary environment is in fact continually and vigorously resisted by multiple administrative, legal, moral and technological constraints. The supposed mainstreaming of pornography – through visual
quotation, allusion, and appropriation in music, fashion, advertising and celebrity
culture – has been discussed, bemoaned and lauded for over a decade.[1] But
despite the ease with which porn can now be privately accessed, and its increasing
familiarity in mainstream discourses, hard-core pornography itself remains largely
obscured from public display. Frequently cited, but seldom actually sighted
unless deliberately sought out,[2] hard-core pornography remains an object for
primarily private consumption.

It was transgressing this rule of solitary and private viewing that landed the
authors of this chapter in trouble in January 2004, when we suddenly found that
our single session on pornography on a final-year English module had become
front-page news in the local Sunday tabloid newspaper. 'Students study hard
porn' was the banner headline, while the report inside directed the outraged, but
perhaps reasonable, question 'What the Dickens are they teaching?' at a course
which in one semester degenerated from James Joyce to hard-core video pornography (Wells 2004). It was not, however, the ostensible subject of our session
which caused this eruption of moral outrage; after all, we had been teaching a
class on pornography, in various modes and media, since the mid-1990s. Rather,
it was our specific pedagogical practice, involving the communal screening of
pornographic material, which so enraged the popular press. 'Students *watch* hard
porn' would have been the more accurate, if less surprising or newsworthy,
headline. Weekly 'lad' magazine *Nuts* more accurately summarized the essence of
the situation, with the headline 'Students watch mucky movie – For their degree'
(Anon 2004c). It seems that what is at issue in minor moral panics such as ours is

not the presence of pornography as such, but the highlighting of the act of consumption, even in artificial and distinctly non-erotic circumstances.

The distinction in public perception between pornography and its use was indicated more recently in the differing histories of two other moralistically inclined UK news stories. The tabloid press – when they eventually found out about it – were outraged by a segment on Jonathan Ross's late-night BBC Radio 2 show which broadcast a telephone message left by Ross and comedian Russell Brand on the answer-phone of venerated comedy actor Andrew Sachs in which Brand boasted of his sexual encounter with Sachs's granddaughter, Georgina Baillie. Throughout the series of escalating outraged responses by the press and public, the reporting in the *News of the World* of Baillie's career as a pornographic per-former had no apparent effect on the public mood, and was not followed up by other news outlets or bloggers (Anon 2008b). However, much more interest in specific pornographic texts was evinced in the story of former Home Secretary Jacqui Smith's inadvertent expenses claim for adult films watched by her husband in her absence (Anon. 2009). While the more respectable news producers largely concentrated on the issue of Members of Parliament's unacceptable expense claims, the tabloids, bloggers and porn industry were much more concerned with identifying the actual films viewed by Richard Timney. What distinguishes these two stories is not the issue of legitimate public interest or the public purse – both involved persons paid from public funds – but the different roles played by pornography. Baillie is employed within the commercial sex industry and the revelation of her filmed work was an excuse for reproducing a few titillating images, but was of no apparent consequence in the context of the story. The legal production of pornography for the adult market no longer has any parti-cular news value, whereas the consumption of the same material is apparently still newsworthy. Pornography, so long as it is for the heterosexual market and does not feature animals, children or extreme fetishistic behaviour, seems to be approaching a state of moral neutrality in the public sphere; masturbation, on the other hand, is not.

In this chapter we will discuss the presence of pornographic quotation in the mainstream media in order to explore contemporary public attitudes to porno-graphy. Our contention is that the mainstream is not, as often claimed, itself becoming increasingly 'pornographized'; rather, it is negotiating a complex path between a marked liberalization in public attitudes towards pornography and continued strictures in the public display of explicit sexual material and anxieties over media effects. With the recent liberalization of censorship, the increased availability of hard-core pornography and the rapid expansion of the British porn industry, the legitimate commercial production and distribution of pornography itself are, for most of the population, apparently no longer of particular importance. Other than in the somewhat marginal broadcast of late-night, minority-channel porn documentaries, pornography enters mainstream *debate* only when its obscured ubiquity is foregrounded by its juxtaposition with another, apparently incongruous, issue. This was the case with the political expenses row, as it was with the debate over educational standards and 'Mickey Mouse' degrees which provided the subtext in the news stories detailing our pornographic pedagogy. We will use the various media responses to our class on pornography as our principle examples of mainstream pornographic quotation, along with other cases where the intersection of porn and the academy has emerged into the media spotlight.

Serious research into visual pornography in fields other than psychology and legal studies dates only from the late 1980s, when a handful of American professors of film studies, cultural studies, English and cognate fields began to respond to allegedly reductive analyses by Andrea Dworkin and Catherine MacKinnon (Winkler 1989). A few years later, most of these researchers had translated their research into classroom practice and were regularly showing pornographic materials to students.[3] And since the early 1990s there has been a steady stream of 'porn prof' scandals hitting the local and, occasionally, national and international news outlets.[4] While it is likely that these stories are themselves examples of cultural pornographization, giving fairly staid and traditional publications the opportunity to put 'porn' in a headline, the generator of these stories is clearly the apparently incongruous juxtaposition of pornography and the university syllabus. The typical justification for the newsworthiness of these reports comes from complaints made either by anonymous students or by named local politicians. The nature of the complaint can vary: students tend to highlight personal, political or moral offence; politicians often focus on the expense of the state contribution to the funding of higher education. Students other than the complainant usually, though not invariably, support the beleaguered professor and testify to the interest, importance and relevance of the course. Contributions solicited from other persons – parents, 'vox pops', professional commentators – are more likely than those directly involved to cite the degradation of educational and cultural standards. These stories, then, are figured as skirmishes in the 'culture wars' that have dominated the recent discourse around university education in the humanities and social sciences in the United States in particular.

This cultural conflict becomes clearer in the moralistic feature articles, commentaries and overviews of the 'porn profs', which usually cite porn studies as an example of the post-1960s collapse of American social morality and equate it with a range of social problems including sexual assault and abuse, promiscuity, drug addiction, political correctness, postmodernism and anti-patriotism.[5] These articles indicate the continuation of the obscenity agenda among American conservatives despite four decades of virtually unrestrained hard-core production: the location of pornography with other 'self-evident' social ills attempts to suggest a continuity of attitudes to the issue which, although clearly inaccurate, does indicate the continued efficacy of porn in initiating public debates over moral standards. The feminist critique of pornography is largely absent from these attacks on porn profs, signalling the cessation of the brief alliance between moralists and civil right campaigners exemplified by the Dworkin and MacKinnon ordinances of the 1980s (Downs 1989) and reflecting a more general marginalization of feminist discourses in public debates about pornography (McGlynn, this volume).

It is the functionality of pornographic representation, and particularly the history of changing attitudes towards it, as an indicator of how social context alters the meaning of textual materials that prompted us to address it in our final-year English module and thus led to our becoming part of the same public debate that we conduct more privately in class. The module on which we teach pornography is called Unpopular Texts and is comprised entirely of problematic 'limit' texts in various genres and media. As well as pornography, the sometimes graphic content of the texts on the syllabus includes depictions of nuclear apocalypse, the Holocaust, cannibalism, racism, genocide, child sexual abuse, rape, drug use, terrorism and domestic violence. The material we disseminate to students on the course is not merely gratuitous, but is used to illustrate the historical and social contexts of offence, providing means of analysing our own and our society's responses to what is typically hidden, ignored or suppressed. On our module, therefore, hard-core pornography is only one aspect in a nexus of representational modes, all of which challenge the mainstream media's implicit claims of normalization. After traversing the gamut of genocidal racism and extreme violence, it might be thought that pornography becomes contextually less offensive. However, we have always been conscious – if not quite able to explain why – of pornography's particular problems, even when set against proven animal cruelty (Fenton *et al.* 1999: 63) and provable incitement to racial hatred (Sutherland 2000), and so we have always left it to the final session on the module when students have already assembled a variety of strategies for dealing with extreme representations.

Of course, it is not only pornography's possibly problematic nature that locates it as the last session – its dubious attraction is a useful counter to falling attendance figures as essay deadlines draw near. But it is only for the past eight years, since hard-core pornography has been legally available in Britain, that we have shown explicit video clips of pornographic films to students. Still, though, pornography seems to require special treatment. It is the only class on the course in which we draw a clear distinction between levels of explicitness in the available textual material. The first half of the session uses clips from various television documentaries describing the production, consumption, censorship and potential harm of pornography. We then have a short break during which people can leave if they wish. The second part of the session consists of two pornographic shorts, one a stag film from the 1930s, the other a fifteen-minute-long 1990s production shot on video-tape, followed by about forty minutes of discussion. The majority of the students on the module attend the entirety of the session each year.

Our typical classroom experience of pornography seems to suggest that such care is unnecessary. For the first few years of screening porn we still had the occasional student who professed to have never before seen hard-core pornography. Now, though, all students claim some familiarity with hard-core imagery, and seem to accept it as a legitimate form of representation and topic of discussion. Our experience of pornography in the classroom shows that the tone and approach typically adopted by most populist metadiscursive material on pornography is perhaps an appropriate one, as most students find the subject both amusing and titillating, and they often stubbornly resist attempts to problematize it, except in its most extreme and illegal forms. Despite lecture and documentary material testifying to actual physical and psychological degradation and harm among both users and producers of pornography, the involvement of organized crime, trafficking in people and drugs, the cycle of addiction and dependence, etc., students tend to view porn as at worst inevitable and often as harmless or desirable.[6] In discussions about pornography as a cultural phenomenon, the contributions of students range through testimonies to its use, indifference to its existence, and an oscillation between amused acceptance of it as a furtive pleasure and a vague sense of unease about its percolation into the mainstream through magazine and newspaper pin-ups and hip-hop videos.

So ingrained is the tolerance of pornography amongst young students that we count it a success if we persuade them that it may be a cultural inevitability – supported by and supporting socialization, economics and gender politics – rather than an expression of natural conditions and relations. Students' blasé indifference to pornography, if not always to pornographization, has been noted by most of the academics who have written about their pedagogical practice in the area.[7] This being the case, it is perhaps surprising that reports of pornographic pedagogy have so frequently leaked out of the groves of academe into the public sphere. The fact that whenever they do some local news provider finds it worth while to print the story is perhaps the most marked indicator of contemporary academia's distance from the ostensibly prevailing public morality. Ironically, when cultural studies is most engaged with the hidden habits of the populace, it is most pilloried for its apparent alienation from the views of the people.

A handful of the cases of curriculum pornography are probably genuinely newsworthy. When unsupervised students at the University of California, Berkeley, devised their own sexuality course, including a visit to a strip club and an orgy, newspapers all over the world reported on the story (Burress 2002; Poole 2002). Most of the news stories, though, are clearly inflated. A plan to offer 'Topics in Communication Studies: Critical Pornography Studies' at the University of Iowa in 2005 provoked responses by *Time*, MTV and David Letterman, and a threat from the Iowa House Speaker to reduce the university's funding. The storm subsided when it emerged that no pornography would be viewed in class (Zimmerman 2006).

Our case and its reporting were more conventional than Berkeley or Iowa. Typically, the original story was justified by reference to a student complaint and bolstered by solicited expostulations by the student's father and a local Member of Parliament (Wells 2004). Unusually for 'prof porn' stories, there are no contributions from other students on the course, though the student body is alluded to through a claim that the complainant raised a petition signed by twenty of her peers. The anonymous student's problem with the course was both educational and moral – 'It seemed irrelevant to the course I was doing, let alone disgusting' – and she made her objections known to the department head. Her father was more pragmatic, allowing that 'If people want to look at pornography in their own time then that is one thing ... [but] I cannot see how pornography will help [my daughter's] career at all.' Bill Cash, MP, labelled the course 'gratuitously unnecessary' and 'not the kind of thing that ought to be conducted in any self-respecting academic environment'. The course was defended by a university spokeswoman, who stated that 'the object of the session was to consider whether or not porn is offensive to the majority'. While the news report itself was fairly lurid, claiming 'English undergraduates at the University of Wolverhampton were shocked when they turned up for a lecture – and discovered it was on hard-core PORNOGRAPHY', the newspaper editorial carried the bulk of the condemnation, citing 'trendy lecturers', 'self-important artspeak' and 'educational obscenity' (Anon. 2004a). The story was illustrated by a screen-capture of the module web site, featuring a slightly risqué 1950s postcard and low-resolution photographs of us taken from the university web site, resembling those which tend to accompany news reports on dangerous sexual perverts. All the standard reference points for this kind of story were therefore present, albeit more exaggeratedly tabloid-esque than in most US versions.

The close conformity of the *Sunday Mercury* report to the 'porn prof' template established by many previous news stories is perhaps surprising, as most of the story was fabricated. There was no complaint by a student to the head of department and no petition, though we cannot testify to the presence or otherwise of an irate father. Once the core of the story had been invented, though, the rest of the pieces fell into place. The generic nature of the 'porn prof' story is clearly demonstrated by its functionality even when largely fictional. And its efficacy as pornographic quotation can be shown by the publicity a minor local Sunday tabloid managed to subsequently generate.

The day after the front page splash, the story was repeated in the local evening daily newspaper (Rea 2004). As the *Express and Star* encompasses a broader demographic than the 'red-top' *Sunday Mercury*, the story was somewhat less hysterical. The *Sunday Mercury* had informed the university that it was running the story at only just before 5.00 p.m. on the previous Friday. By Monday the university had mobilized its public relations more effectively, correcting some errors in the original report and managing to downgrade the pornographic display to soft-core. As our photographs (and all our contact details) had been removed from the university web site, the portraits of us accompanying the *Express and Star* story were from a library picture released by the university to publicize a conference on the 1960s we had organized a few years earlier; the newspaper removed keynote speaker Germaine Greer from the photo before printing it.

At this point, with the story not being picked up by other news outlets, and no further interest being evinced, we were sure that the minor scandal had run its course. Once we had demonstrated to the university that we had taken due care and attention in the planning and delivery of both the course and the pornography session the treatment we received from the institution was benign, aside from the cautionary measures taken which prevented our harassment by journalists or others. However, on Friday afternoon the university was again contacted by a Sunday newspaper seeking comment for a planned story. This time, though, it was a national paper – the *Mail on Sunday*. Knowing the *Mail*'s typical stances on obscenity, media studies and former polytechnics, we feared the worst. However, when the report appeared it occupied only half a column. Repeating some of the *Sunday Mercury*'s inaccuracies – without which the event was almost certainly a non-story – the only addition was a quotation from Eric Hester, 'retired English Literature chief examiner and now vice-chairman of the Family Education Trust', who professed himself 'quite indignant' (Anon 2004b). As the *Mail* group is notoriously the most condemnatory commentator on the various aspects epitomized by our minor moral panic, we breathed a sigh of relief and again believed that the story was over.

It was at this point that the liberal media took up the baton and showed that they were much more interested in the opportunities for pornographic quotation than even the conservative media. The day after the appearance of the *Mail on Sunday* story, we were contacted by *The Guardian* and asked to write a response to the controversy, placing the study of pornography in the context of the course and the degree. This resulted in a full-page article in *The Guardian*'s compact supplement 'G2', illustrated this time by a small commissioned photograph of the two of us looking like a minor and superannuated indie duo and a large stock photo of an alluring erotic dancer clutching her breasts (Jones and Carlin 2004a). Only the latter can be found on the *Guardian* web site. Despite the somewhat salacious accompaniment, we, of course, used the opportunity to vigorously defend our critically informed approach to a pervasive cultural phenomenon and emerged from our brief and unwelcome role as irresponsible degenerates to become respectable social commentators. Somewhat triumphantly, and certainly naively, we again believed that this would be an end to the matter and that we had succeeded in having the last word.

It did prove to be our last word on the matter, at least on paper, until now. But *The Guardian*'s publication of the story, in a relatively serious form but with an erotic illustration and a somewhat coy title, merely served to prompt a wider variety of pornographic allusions. A popular weekly magazine for men labelled a photo of the university 'School of Porn', and countered quotations from Bill Cash and the Dean of School with ' "Look at the Shakespeares on that," said a spokesman for *Nuts*' (Anon. 2004c). At the other end of the media spectrum, *The Times* asked us to answer questions about the course in its online 'Student talking point' (Jones and Carlin 2004b). Also unexpected, despite our prior experience with blogs as a form of student assessment, was the number of salacious and cynical commentaries which appeared on blogs worldwide. Because the university was diverting our internal calls to the school secretary, we heard only at second-hand about most of the requests to appear on radio discussion shows and call-ins, including one on Irish radio we were told was called *The Gender Agenda*.

Despite the possibilities for self- and institutional promotion, we refused all these requests; apart from wishing to avoid the same kind of media ambush which began the story, we genuinely believed that our *Guardian* article and *Times Online* Q&A contained everything we wanted to say about our pedagogical practice we had pursued in a solitary seminar session. We were not researchers into pornography, and there was nothing further we wished to contribute publicly to the debate.

As we had expected, our absence from the airwaves meant that most of the proposed shows did not go ahead. One which did, though, was BBC Radio 4's *The Message* (a regular magazine programme examining the media). Listening to the discussion focused on a class we had taught two months earlier was a strange and somewhat alienating experience. As noted by Henry Jenkins in his useful warning to the unwary pornography teacher, 'You can act responsibly, make intelligent decisions, create a comfortable classroom climate, develop a thought-ful pedagogical rationale and avoid legal pitfalls, and still find yourself in the midst of a media circus' (Jenkins 2004: 7). Jenkins' essay, like ours, includes personal testimony of becoming the object of media scrutiny. And, like us, having prepared carefully for possible recriminations, he was fully supported by his institution. In fact, what both Jenkins' and our experience bring to the fore in the responses of colleagues and other academics is that as long as the lecturers in question have a secure reputation, or are able to submit a reasoned defence of their programme and method, whatever happens in the local or national press, most of the academic community will publicly close ranks around the belea-guered educators. This demarcatory pact over the primacy of upholding academic freedom is perhaps brought most manifestly into focus by the clear distinctions that can be drawn between the voices from higher education, united almost without exception in support of this key principle, and the media intelligentsia, who, however liberal and well informed, tend to be notably more suspicious and cynical. In our case, this was exemplified by the polarized debate on *The Message* between *Granta* editor Ian Jack, who could see no worth in our session, and Sally Feldman, head of the School of Media, Arts and Design at the University of Westminster, who, whatever her personal opinions, expressed her support for academic enquiry.

We were immensely grateful at the time for the support that we were offered by our peers, but we are not now certain that we especially deserved it. Almost all of the criticism of 'porn profs' comes from outside of the academy and for aca-demics it seems to become automatically disqualified for this reason. While even the most committed pornographic pedagogue would generally accept that teaching pornography is a more ethically sensitive issue than writing about it ever will be, the majority would claim that as long as it can be demonstrated to occur within an appropriate critical frame its study at degree level can be shown to be legitimate. The frames applied by individual educators may vary according to discipline, ideological background, or personal preference, but are typically based on theories of genre, modes and histories of production and consumption, sexuality and gender. However, there is perhaps a valid criticism that while these critical frames provide the study of pornography with academic legitimacy, the theoretical discourses around pornography are themselves, in fact, meta-pornography. Much like the 'docu-porn' (documentaries on the porn industry, Boyle 2008) which proliferate on cable television or on minority network channels, academic meta-commentaries can be as titillating as their notional objects of study. As our experience showed, they can, in fact, be recuperated to provide a validation for the generation of further pornographic discourse. At one end of the scale, this was demonstrated by *Nuts*' joke that our university would soon be renamed '*Penthouse* Poly' (Anon. 2004c). More respectable, but still marginally pornographic, was the six-part television series *Pornography: The Secret History of Civilisation*, justified by the producer through reference to books by Walter Kendrick and Lynn Hunt, along with university courses by Constance Penley and Linda Williams (Bailey 1999: 10–11). A potential relationship between the mainstream acceptability of hard-core porn and the work of 'academic women who breathlessly defend pornography' is suggested by Catherine MacKinnon (2005: 19). It seems that pornography is able to stubbornly retain its pornographic features, whatever frames it is surrounded by, and that there is a complex interdependence between the academic and media meta-discourses on pornography, together with a further reticulation of both with the thing-in-itself.

It is this recalcitrant generic persistence which uniquely problematizes pornography, even in the context of university teaching, and which means that the classroom treatment of porn is under threat from agencies more serious than moral righteousness and tabloid opinion. While it was a relaxation in the application, if not the letter, of British obscenity laws which allowed us to screen hard-core pornography to students without being arrested, new laws restricting certain types of sexual expression have been implemented. The limits of permissible speech are once again being reinscribed, and the notion that the university occupies some kind of meta-social space in which the testing of representational limits is legitimized by the project of intellectual enquiry is directly challenged by the laws on 'extreme pornography' (see McGlynn, this volume).

In this moral and legal climate, it might be thought that, given our pedagogical practice and our tabloid exposure, we would be securely behind attempts to defend the teaching of pornography to students. However, we feel that the disproportionate attention given to porn by both propagators and detractors of university courses on the topic might be a distraction from other serious issues of social relations and the politics of representation. While porn's pervasiveness is reason enough for a detailed consideration of it in appropriate contexts, it can easily become a mere signifier of cultural radicalism rather than a real touchstone for academic significance and educational augmentation. Indeed, we are more than a little embarrassed that our carefully devised syllabus of Unpopular Texts is indelibly associated with pornography rather than with the other, arguably more offensive, material on the course. We provide the students with an early shock with extracts from Enid Blyton's long unavailable *The Three Golliwogs*

(1944); *Cannibal Holocaust* (Ruggero Deodata 1980) prompts a number of walk-outs every time we show it, despite detailed warnings; and the only text that we know to have prompted a traumatic reaction from a student is Sidney Lumet's *The Offence* (1972), with its depiction of a suspected paedophile beaten to death in police custody. But most contentious of all is the white supremacist and genocidal novel *The Turner Diaries* ('Andrew Macdonald' [William Pierce] 1978), clearly indictable in the UK under incitement to racial hatred and, potentially, the glorification of terrorism. Placed next to the issues raised by the gross hatred of this novel, the graphic and composed brutality of *Cannibal Holocaust* and the inept racism of Enid Blyton, most pornography is, as our students usually see it to be, unproblematic and uninteresting.

For our students the consumption of porn is largely a matter of private choice; they are generally more concerned with the public aspects of pornographization, which, despite the immense scale of the porn industry, seems to them to be more pervasive and intrusive. Whatever the intrinsic interest of textual and generic analysis of pornography, and the potential revelations over such aspects as subjectivism, objectivism and identification, the concerns of our students indicate the most vital work in porn studies needs to be social research into its increasing normalization. We do, though, continue to teach it, and screen it in class, and discuss its formal conventions. Textual analyses of porn can at least provide evidence of its repetitive narratives and tableaux of power, and lead to an informed examination of its ideological constructions. Removing porn's manifest use value, as achieved through communal viewing, is the only way to make it available for analysis rather than consumption, and is a prerequisite for any form of ideological investigation.[8]

Textual analysis can be only a starting point in exploring the cultural importance of porn, but is an important ingredient in constructing any critique of its alleged effects. And only through a reliable and sustained analysis of its specific elements can we arrive at a satisfactory definition of porn. While immutable demarcatory generic categories are anathema to academics, at some point in the near future such an articulation of pornography's distinguishability from non-porn might be required. We know that, despite our ambush by the media, we are legally secure in our exhibition of pornography. However, under the recent legislation on extreme porn our display of the sexually violent *Cannibal Holocaust* might not be so protected. We believe the film to be clearly distinguishable from pornography, and can show this through an analysis of its formal properties, its address to its audience and its manner of consumption. We are not, though, impressed by the possibility that some day we might have to demonstrate this in a further media circus, or in a court of law.

Notes

1 In 1996, Brian McNair was already claiming societal sexual saturation. Similar claims have been made more recently by Feona Attwood (2009b). Meanwhile,

authors and publishers compete to effectively signify the pervasiveness of pornography by forming neologisms combing porn with various suffixes: pornification (Paasonen *et al.* 2007b), pornified (Paul 2005), porning (Sarracino and Scott 2008), pornocopia (O'Toole 1998), pornographication (McNair 2002), pornographisation (Edwards 2003), pornotopia (Poyner 2006), and pornucopia (Todd G. Morrison 2004).

2 The tension between hardcore pornography's ubiquity as an object of public debate and mainstream representation, and its relative scarcity as a sighted object (for women in particular) is also discussed by Dines, Whisnant, Thompson & Boyle (this volume). The online industry has, however, worked hard to close down consumer choice *not* to see hardcore images (Paasonen and Johnson, this volume).

3 Surveys of the various uses of pornography in the university, the educators who use it, and some of the moral panics it has generated, can be found in Curry (1996), Atlas (1999), Gumbel (1999), Abel (2001), Cullen (2006), Andrews (2007). The prominence of women among the professors who teach pornography, mentioned by most commentators, is discussed by Lord (1997).

4 A sample of scandal stories and their repercussions: 1991, University of Iowa (Anon 1991); 1992, San Bernardino Valley College (Leatherman 1996, O'Neil 1996); 1993, University of Michigan Law School (Austin 1999, pp. 310–11); 1993, University of California, Santa Barbara (Kirkham and Skeggs 1996); 1994, University of Colorado at Boulder (Wilson 1994); 1999, School of Art Institute of Chicago (Leatherman 1999); 1999, Wesleyan University (Rich 1999); 2001, Arizona State University (Bozelka 2007); 2001, Massachusetts Institute of Technology (Jenkins 2004); 2003, University of Kansas (Anon 2003); 2004, University of Wolverhampton (Wells 2004); 2004, College of Charleston (Adcox 2004); 2005, University of Iowa (Tecson 2005); 2006, New York University (Anon 2006); 2006, Cornell University (Brewster 2006).

5 Horrified, disgusted, or resigned exposes of porn studies include Jarrard (1998), Dial (2001), Jablonski (2001), Bockhorn (2002), Carlson (2003), Reisman (2003), Young (2003).

6 In this respect, our experiences chime with those of Gail Dines and Rebecca Whisnant (Chapter 1, this volume) in the US who report that students are typically familiar with pornographic texts but not with critical approaches – and, specifically, *feminist* approaches – to thinking about pornography.

7 Self-confessed academic exhibitors of hardcore pornography who have publicly pondered on their practice include Lindgren (1993), Straayer (1994), Durbin (1996), Kane (1996), Kleinhans (1996), Jenkins (2004), Jones and Carlin (2004a, 2004b), Williams (2004a), Reading (2005), Lehman (2006a), McNair (2009), Smith (2009) and Waskul (2009).

8 This is as true for censorship decisions as it is for academic analysis, as was seen when the British Board of Film Classification proposed ending its practice of having 'sex works' scrutinised by at least two examiners (Robinson and Brook 2009).

Chapter 13

Marginalizing feminism?

Debating extreme pornography laws in public and policy discourse

Clare McGlynn

The regulation of pornography is a topic which has long divided feminists, but it is also a subject which demonstrates the richness and pluralism of feminism. This diversity should not be interpreted as constituting a lack of common ground or purpose for feminists. Indeed, in this chapter, I hope to outline what unites us in this field. Unfortunately, however, this story of shared experiences is not a positive one. It is, in fact, a lesson in shared marginalization.

Feminist arguments, from all perspectives, were marginalized in public and policy discourses which led to the introduction of a new law in England and Wales criminalizing the possession of what is called 'extreme pornography'. At its most basic, my argument is that we must not assume that the fact that pornography regulation is on the policy table represents a feminist victory. While it could be argued that the extreme pornography laws were initially inspired by feminist activism, this was soon forgotten as the arch-liberals and moral-conservatives took up their usual positions, dominating debate and parliamentary discussion whilst the voices of feminists faded into the background. Indeed, in the debates over these new measures the old, familiar battle lines were redrawn. Thirty years on from the Williams Commission report (Williams 1979), debate continues to focus on futile causal effects debates (Boyle 2000) and supposed state control of morality, with feminist arguments and interventions falling on deaf ears.

The end result is legislation which does not meet feminist demands – from any feminist perspective. What feminists may share, therefore, is a sense of déjà vu; of having witnessed a debate in which feminist and women's voices *should* have played a significant role – but they did not. While in scholarly debates we may take as axiomatic the advances and developments in our understandings of pornography and culture, this richness of thinking and debate has had almost no impact on the nature of politico-legal debates. What we have seen is a policy process in which the classic terms of debate about the regulation of pornography have been reinforced, as if feminist debates did not exist.

Criminalizing extreme pornography

Before developing this argument more fully, it is important to briefly outline the nature and content of the new law on extreme pornography. In England and

Wales, the primary legal measure governing pornography is the Obscene Publications Act 1959. This Act criminalizes the production and distribution of 'obscene' materials: defined as those which may 'deprave and corrupt' the consumer (subject to a defence for materials deemed to be in the 'public good') (McGlynn and Rackley 2009). The number of prosecutions under the Obscene Publications Act has been falling in recent years, to only thirty-five in 2005 (Ministry of Justice 2007: 90), though of course this Act continues to govern and regulate conduct.

It was in this context, of the apparent desuetude of the Obscene Publications Act, that the sexual murder of Jane Longhurst sparked national controversy and debate (e.g. Pook 2005; Branigan 2006). Longhurst was asphyxiated and sexually murdered by Graham Coutts in 2003, with the case attracting national media attention largely due to evidence admitted in court regarding Coutts's proclivity for internet pornography featuring images of necrophilia, asphyxiation and forced sex (R. v. Coutts 2006). Motivated to 'do something' by the public outcry over this murder, and the nature and prevalence of these forms of pornography, the government proposed new legislation to criminalize the possession of extreme pornography, thereby extending the law to capture the activities of not just producers and distributors but also viewers (Home Office 2005, 2006a).

The government's first proposal – in 2005 – defined 'extreme pornography' to include images of 'serious sexual violence', as well as images of necrophilia and bestiality (Home Office 2005: paras 37–9). The justification was the government's professed desire to 'protect' those engaged in the pornography industry and to 'send a message' that these materials have no place in society, as they might exacerbate problems of sexual violence (*ibid.*: para. 34). To that extent, the government could be seen to be favouring a feminist agenda concerned about possible links between pornography and sexual violence (McGlynn and Rackley 2007: 679–80). However, by the time the new legislation was enacted, in the Criminal Justice and Immigration Act 2008, things were very different. The government had faced a barrage of criticism, from all sides and perspectives, and debate retreated on to very familiar territory, as we will see. But first an outline of what the new Act contains.[1]

The extreme pornography provisions (section 63) of the Criminal Justice and Immigration Act 2008 came into effect in January 2009.[2] The Act provides that it is a criminal offence (punishable by up to three years of imprisonment) for a person to be in possession of an 'extreme pornographic image'. The image must be 'explicit and realistic', thereby excluding cartoons, drawings and the written word. It is 'pornographic' 'if it is of such a nature that it must reasonably be assumed to have been produced solely or principally for the purpose of sexual arousal' (section 63(3)). In determining whether an image satisfies this test, the overall context or narrative (including the producer's intention) will be relevant, but the test remains what the magistrate or jury will consider was 'reasonably' produced for the purposes of sexual arousal. A pornographic image is 'extreme' if it is 'grossly offensive, disgusting or otherwise of an obscene character' and portrays, in an explicit and realistic way, acts which are life-threatening or result, or are likely to result, in serious injury to a person's anus, breasts or genitals. 'Extreme' also covers images of bestiality and necrophilia.

The applicability of the new law to images of life-threatening or serious injury gave rise to considerable debate for two main reasons. First, the scope of the measures had changed considerably from the original proposals, which defined 'extreme' images as including those depicting 'serious sexual violence'. The government narrowed the scope of the measures, adding the instantiation that the depiction of any 'serious injury' must only be to 'anus, breasts and genitals'. For many who already criticized the timidity of the government's proposals, the reduction in scope was a serious concern, not least as it is unlikely that pornographic pro-rape web sites (McGlynn and Rackley 2007: 686; Gossett and Byrne 2002), which are freely and easily accessible on line, will now be covered. This is a surprise, not least because the 'extensive availability of sites featuring violent rape' (Home Office 2005: para. 5) was within the initial purview of the government. Although some rapes may be covered – if they involve weapons or result in serious injury to the anus, breasts or genitals – most images of rape will be excluded, creating a dubious distinction between 'violent' and 'non-violent' rape.[3]

While many, particularly feminist groups, objected to the *limited* scope of the measures, the other major criticisms came from the bondage domination sadism masochism (BDSM) community. They argued that defining extreme images to include those which depict life-threatening or serious injury meant capturing many consensual BDSM activities (Backlash 2007). While the intention of those involved in such BDSM activities is not to threaten or endanger life (though this may not be apparent when the images of these activities are viewed in isolation), many such images, for example of asphyxiation, may well satisfy the definition of 'extreme'. The organization Backlash, established to campaign against these measures, was successful in focusing debate largely around the issue of consensual participation in BDSM activities and the potential threat of the new law to this community. Not only did this lead to the sidelining of issues of representation, it also meant that the inclusion of images of bestiality and necrophilia within the scope of the law largely went unnoticed. Indeed, there appeared to be a general consensus that such measures *should* be subject to regulation (Home Office 2006a: para. 35; Jerome Taylor 2008).

One further threshold must be satisfied before an image is considered to be 'extreme': it must be 'grossly offensive, disgusting or otherwise of an obscene character'. This provision was added during the final stages of the parliamentary process and was acknowledged by the government to constitute the 'most significant' change to the original proposals (Hunt 2008b). This new clause was taken, apparently, from a dictionary definition of what constitutes 'obscene' and was intended to 'clarify the alignment between this offence and the Obscene Publications Act' and ensure that 'only material that would be caught by' the Obscene Publications Act is caught by the new Act (Hunt 2008b). The last thing this clause will do is to clarify the scope of the measures, as it introduces yet more criteria to be satisfied and uses terms which are open to considerable interpretation.

Finally, it must be emphasized that the criminal offence is 'possession', the creation and distribution of obscene materials being covered by the Obscene Publications Act. 'Possession' is nowhere defined in the Act, and the same terminology has given rise to considerable problems in the field of child sex abuse images. Modern technology has challenged traditional definitions of possession with there being a distinct lack of clarity surrounding the status of those who have deleted images (which can be recovered), or 'just looked' at them on screen (without knowingly storing them) and whether the computer-illiterate should be more immune from prosecution (as they have little or no knowledge about the storing of images on hard drives) than those who do understand and use computers (McGlynn and Rackley 2009). There are also a number of exclusions and defences. Material classified by the British Board of Film Classification is specifically excluded (though in practice this would be unlikely to pass the 'pornographic' or 'explicit' thresholds). There are also defences mirroring those available in relation to the offences of possessing child sexual abuse images: legitimate possession (for example, by the police), unsolicited images which are not kept, and unaccessed images (the person had not seen the image and did not know it to be extreme pornography). In addition, there is a defence where the individual possessing the images consensually participated in the acts portrayed. This defence was introduced during the latter stages of the parliamentary process in an attempt to allay fears about the impact of the law on the private sexual practices of consenting BDSM participants.

Debating extreme pornography

In 1979 the Williams Commission published its report into the regulation of pornography (Williams 1979). This Royal Commission debated pornography regulation from two conflicting positions, namely the religious, moral perspective in favour of pornography regulation because of its apparent threat to the well-being of society generally, and the liberal, advocating legal reform based on Mill's harm principle (Mill 1985; Feinberg 1983). The liberal approach held sway and the Williams Report claimed there to be no harm in pornography (or at least none that was sufficient to meet a 'harm' threshold) and therefore little justification for obscenity laws and any prohibition on pornography. These two dichotomous perspectives, of moralism and liberalism, hold a tenacious grip on public and policy debates about pornography. While the Williams Commission claimed that the women's movement was 'dormant' (Williams 1979: 1–3) when it was carrying out its investigations, this is certainly no longer true. Yet, when examining debates around the recently enacted extreme pornography laws, it would be possible to think that such was indeed the case. While many women's organizations did respond to the government's 2005 consultation, and there were feminists involved in campaigns both for and against the laws, there was a distinct absence of feminist perspectives in discussions in Parliament and in the media. The voices of feminists were heard only when they chimed with the prevailing arguments of moralism or anti-censorship. This co-option of feminist arguments is not new to pornography debates (West 1987; Luff 2001) but nonetheless surprising and disappointing.

To begin with, as noted above, the government did appear to be concerned with what might be called a 'harm to women', or feminist, perspective. However, as opposition to the measures grew, the government took two steps which undermined any feminist credentials. First, they retreated to the familiar language of moral outrage and disgust-based justifications for the measures. For example, Jack Straw, the Minister of Justice, referred to the 'vile' material being discussed (Straw 2007); the government's explanatory notes referred to 'aberrant' sexualities (Home Office 2007: para. 803); Home Office Minister Vernon Coaker described the extreme pornography covered by the law as 'deeply abhorrent' (Home Office press release 2006b), and other Members of Parliament who supported the government referred to the 'sickening internet images' being proscribed (Salter, quoted in BBC 2006). The government were not alone, of course, in deploying morality justifications. The main opposition party, the Conservatives, were equally condemnatory, describing the material at issue as 'deeply depraved and corrupting' (quoted in McGlynn and Rackley 2007: 682).

Second, they attempted to play the liberals at their own game by entering the causal effects debate. While the government had originally eschewed the need for effects-based evidence before regulating pornography (Home Office 2005: par. 31), on the back foot, they entered this terrain (Hunt 2008a), relying on a 2007 report which purported to demonstrate 'some' adverse effects on 'men' of using extreme pornography (Itzin *et al.* 2007: iii). But this was controversial territory and, more important, territory on which the liberal establishment felt very safe. The research evidence on which the 2007 report is based is open to criticism, or at least acknowledged as not providing a sufficient basis for regulation.[4] Thus, while some feminists do argue that there is a direct link between pornography and sexual violence, to claim that it is a unidirectional, causal link is problematic and lacks satisfactory evidential justification (also Boyle 2000). Ironically for the government, the studies used in the 2007 report are almost exclusively on attitudes to rape pornography, which, as noted above, is largely excluded from the new laws. Furthermore, much of the 'evidence' used by others to suggest direct effects is religious and/or morality-based and not generally favourable to feminist interests (Fagan 2009).

In retaliation to the causal links suggestion, the liberal opposition repeatedly maintained that there is no evidence of any causal link between pornography consumption and sexual violence (Liberty 2008; Miller 2008b). In addition, there was an emphasis on the key role of freedom of speech in liberal democracies and suggestions that the regulation of pornographic materials has a 'chilling effect' on the broader culture of free expression (Dworkin 1985). Debates in Parliament, therefore, became focused again on the dichotomous choices of liberalism and moralism.

Arguments about an invasion of privacy (and breach of privacy rights) were routinely made, with the Campaign against Censorship, for example, challenging the proposals by raising the spectre of an 'Orwellian victimless crime enforced by Thought Police' (quoted in McGlynn and Rackley: 677–8; see also McGlynn and Ward 2009). The proposed legislation, Julian Petley advised, 'puts Nanny firmly into jackboots' (2008a) and the government, he concluded, was 'happy' to align itself with the regimes of 'Saudi Arabia, China and South Korea' (Petley 2007). The supposed cultural effects were also raised, with the regulatory body of barristers in England and Wales, the Bar Council, worried that those who perused images of anal rape in video recordings of Howard Brenton's *Romans in Britain* might find themselves up before the bench (quoted in McGlynn and Rackley 2007: 684–5). While such material would not actually come within the scope of the measures – not being explicit or pornographic or involving life-threatening or serious injury – the argument about the 'chilling effect' on art was made. As well as these more conceptual critiques, liberal opposition focused on some of the specifics of the measures, with the organization Liberty castigating the 'carelessly drafted, over-broad' language of the statute (Liberty 2008: para. 25). The Joint [parliamentary] Committee on Human Rights similarly objected to the measures on the basis that they were 'vague' and that the concept of 'extreme' pornography was 'inherently subjective' (Joint Committee on Human Rights 2008: para. 1.50).

The liberal and moral domination of the legislative debates was also matched in the media. For example, an article in the broadsheet *Independent* newspaper referred to 'artistic creativity' being stifled, to regulation of what goes on in 'people's bedrooms' and to unfair 'protective legislation' criminalizing 'previously law-abiding people who have a harmless taste for unconventional sex' (Jerome Taylor 2008). Carol Sarler, writing in the *Observer* newspaper, similarly deployed classic liberal arguments, castigating the lack of 'proof' that there is any 'cause and effect' between pornography and sexual violence and the unjustified interference in the privacy of individuals (Sarler 2006). In *The Sun* (2006) the images to be covered were referred to as 'vile', the *Telegraph* called them 'perverse' (Pook 2005) and the *Daily Mail* 'depraved' (Fisher 2009). The *Guardian* discussed the moralists' condemnation of extreme pornography, balanced with the concerns of 'libertarians' (Branigan 2006). Where the liberal, anti-censorship approach did move beyond the more abstract arguments about privacy, human rights and chilling effects, the focus was on the sexual practices of the BDSM community, not on any specific feminist concerns, or, indeed, on pornographic *representations*. Similarly, the only role which women played in the moral, religious accounts was of outraged wife, mother or victim.

Feminist interventions

There was only one news report which did focus on feminist arguments – an online article in the left-wing publication *New Statesman* (Katy Taylor 2008).

This article considered the radical and anti-censorship feminist arguments about the extreme pornography law. Being *feminist*, these perspectives differed from those generally deployed in the mainstream press and Parliament because of their very specific focus on feminist arguments, strategy and overarching debates about the position of women in society. While there are a great variety of feminist approaches to the legal regulation of pornography generally, and to these measures in particular, the focus on these two broad perspectives provides a good starting point to consider the marginalization of feminist perspectives in the extreme pornography debates.

Radical feminism and the legal regulation of pornography

A radical feminist approach to the regulation of pornography generally favours regulation in order to reduce the various, and gendered, harms of pornography. In some general ways, therefore, these measures were welcomed by feminist organizations which might be characterized as radical feminist in approach. However, I want to suggest that, in the cold light of day, and when we have seen the final version of the legislation, radical feminists have much to be concerned about.

When the government first consulted on the proposals (Home Office 2005), there was considerable support from a wide constituency of feminist groups such as Rights of Women, Justice for Women, the Women's National Commission, Object and Eaves (McGlynn and Rackley 2007). What united these groups was their broad support for the proposed measures and their general concern that the ubiquity and misogyny of pornography is implicated in the prevalence of violence against women. Despite differences in opinion regarding the empirical evidence, all the supporting feminist organizations agreed that there is strong experiential evidence of the adverse harms on women of pornography. In this light, it is perhaps no surprise that these organizations, while welcoming the government's 2005 consultation, suggested that far more pornography should be regulated. In particular, concerns were expressed that a category of materials that are deemed 'extreme' creates unfortunate distinctions between different types of pornography, rendering non-'extreme' pornography harmless or less serious.

At a very general level, therefore, the fact that the government was looking to regulate in the field of pornography suggests an approach in sympathy with that of radical feminism. Furthermore, the government's reference to the Home Office research report, which purported to show some causal links between viewing pornography and sexual violence (Itzin *et al.* 2007), suggests approval of this aspect of the radical feminist argument.

However, the government's attraction to radical feminist arguments was only skin-deep. First, the government's chosen method of regulation is the *criminal* law and, in particular, the criminal law of obscenity. Radical feminists Catharine MacKinnon and Andrea Dworkin (1997) proposed the regulation of pornography via the civil law precisely to avoid state control via the criminal law. More specifically, using the civil law was to empower women who took legal action, putting them in control and in receipt of any damages. In deploying the criminal law, the government has placed the power over the enforcement and implementation of the legislation in the hands of the criminal justice system – a system which has proved largely ineffective in challenging sexual violence (Fawcett 2009). Thus, while anti-censorship feminist Avedon Carol has criticized the extreme pornography laws as being part of a 'police state' (quoted in Katy Taylor 2008), this argument is in fact close to radical feminist concern over the patriarchal state and use of the criminal law to (purport to) solve social problems.

Further, while this new offence was originally proposed as a stand-alone offence, separate from the obscenity laws, under pressure the government made an explicit link with the Obscene Publications Act by introducing the added threshold of 'grossly offensive, disgusting or otherwise of an obscene character' into the legislation. This phraseology was designed to ensure compatibility with the Obscene Publications Act (Hunt 2008b). This was a retrograde step for all feminists. Feminists are united in their objection to obscenity legislation which is inspired and underpinned by conservative and conventional views of 'appropriate' sexuality (Strossen 1993). Obscenity legislation has been used to restrict access to feminist materials and is generally concerned about certain forms of sexual expression, rather than harm or violence in particular. It is, in essence, a paternalistic legislative regime, which seeks to protect the *consumers* of the obscene materials from themselves. The enactment of the extreme pornography measures, with their explicit link to the obscenity legislation, reinforces the existence and import of the obscenity approach to regulating pornography, with adverse effects for all feminists, especially radical feminists who would wish to focus on the harm of pornography to women.

On the specifics of the legislation itself, there is also much to worry the radical feminist. As anticipated, the Act has created a dubious distinction between extreme pornography – bad, criminalized – and the non-extreme, thereby legitimized. Further, it will be recalled that an image is defined as extreme if it displays serious injury to the 'anus, breasts and genitals' alone. This could lead to absurd results, with some images being proscribed, others not, simply because of the body parts injured. This completely overlooks the nature of the harm of pornography which has most concerned radical feminists. If there is a harm portrayed in violent pornography, it is not a physical harm to specific body parts. It is the harm of forced sex, the psychological harm of rape or the loss of autonomy and the cultural representation of women as enjoying violence.

In a similar vein, radical feminists will recognize the incongruity of pornographic images of intercourse or oral sex with animals being criminalized but not pornographic images of forced sex. To all intents and purposes, pornographic rape images will not now come within the scope of the measures. The failure to include such paradigmatic images of sexual violence says much about the policy process and aim of the legislation. It further confirms that, for all the government's warm words in the initial consultation, it feared the disapprobation of liberals and moralists rather more than that of the anti-pornography feminists.

Finally, it is clear that this new law is not a keynote policy of the government. The government does not include pornography within its definitions of 'violence against women' and therefore does not list the extreme pornography laws among its actions in this field (HM Government 2009). Neither does the government include these measures in its achievements and priorities for the Ministers for Women and Equality (Government Equalities Office 2008). This should tell us much about the government's approach. For radical feminists, pornography is integral to the reality and prevalence of violence against women: but for the government it gains no mention. This signals that the government does not share the radical feminist perspective and adds weight to the critique of the government that, in this area, its perspective is a conservative, moral one, at the expense of any concerns shared with feminists (McGlynn and Rackley 2009). In summary, therefore, if radical feminists were to draft new laws on pornography, the extreme pornography measures are not what they would look like. In fact, they would be radically different.

Anti-censorship feminism

Anti-censorship arguments played an important role in challenging the adoption of the extreme pornography laws, as noted above. However, while there was much anti-censorship opposition to the new regulations, there is little evidence to convince that it was feminist-inspired.

Feminist Nadine Strossen argues against censorship on the basis that 'sweeping' censorship laws pose particular dangers for 'women and women's rights causes' (Strossen 1995: xvi). Women, she argues, are 'relatively disempowered' and their rights are 'unpopular causes' (*ibid.*: xvii). Therefore, defending freedom of sexual expression is 'especially essential for advocates of women's rights, as well as equality rights more generally' (*ibid.*: xix). Making reference to radical feminists, Strossen notes that she 'shares the fears, frustration and fury about the ongoing problems of violence and discrimination against women' but censorship, she argues, would not reduce 'misogynistic violence or discrimination' but would likely 'aggravate those grave problems' (*ibid.*:13).

In relation to the sex industry in particular, Avedon Carol of Feminists Against Censorship argues that anti-censorship feminists 'do have genuine concerns about the production of sexual materials: in television, film, written material, there has been a history of androcentrism, insensitivity to women's views, misrepresentation of women's attitudes and tastes, stereotyping and just plain sexism' (Carol 1993: 187). This is an approach shared by Anne McClintock, who expresses concern over the lack of opportunities for women working within the pornography industry to define and create their own sexual imagery which might challenge the misogyny of much mainstream pornography (McClintock 1992).

Anti-censorship feminists, therefore, oppose censorship not because of attachment to an abstract ideal, but because they fear that it will harm their overall goals of reducing violence against women. Similarly, the anti-censorship agenda does not leave the sex industry unchallenged: it is the subject of detailed criticism for its adverse treatment of many women and its stereotyped portrayal of women's sexuality. Alison Assiter and Avedon Carol also argue that the focus, for feminists, should not just be on sex, or sexual expression, but on all the other ways in which women are disadvantaged in society from the assumptions about motherhood and family to inequalities of pay, to interference with our reproductive capacity (Assiter and Carol 1993b).

There are, therefore, shared goals amongst feminists such as challenging sexual violence and improving women's labour conditions; it is the means of achieving these aims which are hotly contested. It is this decidedly feminist approach which differentiates anti-censorship feminism from other general liberal arguments against pornography regulation. Ann Orford, for example, writes that concerns about the wages or conditions of employment of women in sex industries are '[c]onspicuously absent' from most liberal works (Orford 1994: 90). Orford warns that liberalism resists the 'subversive tendencies of feminism' and operates to 'naturalise and depoliticise the subordination of women' (*ibid.*: 74). Much liberal debate, therefore, presents a rather simplified picture of 'the forces of freedom and liberty battl[ing] the opposing armies of conservatism and feminist repression', portraying all feminists as 'puritanical, repressive and dangerously powerful' (*ibid.*: 87). We see glimpses of this in the extreme pornography debates, with Julian Petley describing the arguments put forward by feminist supporters of the proposals as 'dogmatic and intellectually dubious' (Petley 2007) and radical feminists engaged in pornography debates as 'not exactly people with open minds on the subject' (Petley 2008b).

A further aspect of the general liberal objection to the extreme pornography laws is the deployment of arguments based on the concepts of human rights, privacy and freedom of speech. While some feminists have embraced rights rhetoric as an essential strategy, there is much for feminists to be concerned about in the 'turn to rights'. The entrenchment of civil and political rights in many Western constitutions, and their enforcement as part of English law through the Human Rights Act 1998, has given rise to many feminist critiques (Palmer 1996; McColgan 2000). In essence, civil and political rights, with their privileging of the individual, the privacy of the home and freedom of political expression, have all been interpreted in ways which often hinder women's claims. Women, where they are vulnerable members of communities, do not generally benefit from excessive individualism; women routinely suffer violence and abuse in the 'privacy' of their own home, and freedom of political speech may not mean much when there are few opportunities for women to have their voices heard. In other words, there is no necessary coincidence between the classic liberal objection to the extreme pornography measures and feminist anti-censorship arguments.

Indeed, it may be the challenge which all feminists make to the dominance of masculine perspectives on sex and sexuality which is perceived as a threat to (male-dominated) liberalism – although this is not necessarily directly expressed. For example, as noted above, the Joint Committee on Human Rights objected to the extreme pornography measures on the basis that they were 'vague' (Joint Committee on Human Rights 2008: para. 1.50). Nonetheless, the same body, in the same report, welcomed the introduction of a new offence of incitement to hatred on the grounds of sexual orientation on the basis that it was a 'human rights enhancing' measure (*ibid.*: para 1.62). It justified this approach on the basis that there was clear evidence of harm (thereby satisfying the Mill standard for regulation) in that there is 'considerable evidence that gay people in particular are often the subject of material inciting people to violence against them' (*ibid.*). It is not clear why there appeared to be satisfactory evidence for a 'human rights enhancing' measure restricting speech which expressed hatred against gay men and lesbian women, but not for controls on extreme pornography (often expressing hatred of women). Indeed, there are a myriad of 'vague' criminal laws. The laws on rape, based on the concept of 'consent', could be said to be extremely vague (one of the reasons, possibly, for the low conviction rate), yet attempts to move beyond a consent standard are generally strenuously resisted on the basis of liberal arguments of autonomy. One further example: the entire basis of the law of theft rests on the concept of 'dishonesty', which is left to juries to determine. There is no common understanding of what constitutes honesty (BBC 2009). It is a 'vague' provision, but has been an established part of the criminal law for decades. Therefore is it not plausible that some of the liberal objections to the extreme pornography laws, while purporting to be based on supposedly objective criteria such as vagueness or harm, may in fact just be more general political objections to the regulation of sexual imagery? It is pornography regulation to which some liberals may object, not regulation *per se*.

One further aspect of anti-censorship feminism must be considered. Some feminists object to censorship not just because it may harm women in often unintended ways, but because pornography itself benefits women. In this way, Wendy McElroy provocatively states that: 'Women benefit from pornography, both politically and personally' (McElroy 1995: viii). This approach is positive about the role of pornography in women's lives, most particularly by freeing them from traditional conceptions of feminine sexuality (Wilson 1992). This 'pro-pornography' approach had little support in the public debates about the measures. The lone female voices expressing a desire for pornography were part of the more general campaign of sexual freedom organizations championing the BDSM community and characterizing the extreme porn provisions as an attack on that community.[5]

Indeed, it was commonplace among the liberal opposition to state clearly a dislike of pornography generally before detailing any objections to the measures. The approach of Baroness Miller, a key architect of opposition to the new law, was common. She stated that violent pornography was 'dangerous as regards the well-being of society' and 'very distasteful' (Miller 2008a) but she objected to the measures for other reasons (also Sarler 2006). Also an objector, Lord Faulkner referred to letters he received from users of pornography as 'frankly quite disturbing' (Faulkner 2008) before expressing his concerns over pornography regulation. This 'I don't like pornography, but … ' approach has strong antecedents, with political philosopher Ronald Dworkin stating that:

> Pornography is often grotesquely offensive; it is insulting, not only to women but to men as well. But we cannot consider that a sufficient reason for banning it without destroying the principle that the speech we hate is as much entitled to protection as any other.
>
> (Dworkin 1996: 218)

Feminist objections to pornography regulation are as diverse as those which are in favour of regulation. Nonetheless, for the purposes of my argument in this chapter, the anti-censorship approach has been highlighted, with more limited reference to what might tentatively be called 'pro-pornography' feminism. My argument is that the liberal opposition to the extreme pornography laws, while sharing some elements of anti-censorship feminism, was not feminist in orientation. While some might suggest that, for feminists, liberals make better bedfellows than conservatives (Dyzenhaus 1992), an empty bed may be best of all, giving freedom and space to advocate a specifically feminist agenda.

Marginalizing feminism

What unites feminists, in general, is our concern with the position of women in society. When feminists debate pornography, we are similarly united in our shared concerns over violence against women in society, the dominance of masculine perspectives on sex and sexuality, the disadvantaged status of many sex workers in the industry, and so on. What is evident, therefore, is that feminists seek an end to the endemic disadvantage and discrimination which many women face. Where the unity breaks down is in how this is to be achieved. In the area of pornography regulation, radical feminists consider that restricting pornography will help in the fight against sexual violence, while anti-censorship feminists fear that it will further limit women's sexual choices and that it is a distraction from other, generally costly, policy options. But what is clear from such debates is that the focus is very much on women's lives and experiences. And it is just such a perspective which was largely absent in the public and policy debates over the extreme pornography measures.

Thus, while it might be assumed within the academy that feminists have 'reoriented the moral and political debate' (Nussbaum 2004: 191) and challenged the 'coherence of liberal discourse itself' (Cameron 1990: 785), such transformations appear to have remained within the scholarly community. Indeed, my preliminary analysis of the public and policy debates surrounding the adoption of the extreme pornography laws suggests that we have advanced little from the days of the Williams Report in the late 1970s. Feminist arguments are sometimes co-opted where helpful, but neither the moral proponents of reform, nor liberal opposition, have women's status and disadvantage as their concern.

This was a debate in which the old battle lines were simply redrawn. In so doing, we have a situation in which obscenity-based provisions have been entrenched, in which the causal effects debate took central stage, where the government relied on morality and disgust-based justifications and the (often gendered) ideas of privacy, freedom of speech and anti-censorship were reified. We may talk about the need to craft a feminist politics which is attentive to differences and necessarily complex. But even the most caricatured feminist positions barely got a chance in these debates. Feminist voices were little heard in this politico-legal debate, even when a measure has such an obvious connection with feminism.

Notes

1 For a more detailed discussion of the legislation see McGlynn and Rackley (2009).
2 At the time of writing (December 2009), there have been a small number of prosecutions under the Act, though official figures are not yet available. The prosecutions have generally arisen in the context of other criminal proceedings rather than being instigated solely on the basis of the possession of extreme pornography.
3 The Scottish Parliament is currently debating whether to introduce a law criminalising the possession of extreme pornography. The proposal before the Scottish Parliament would extend the remit of the law, beyond the position in England and Wales, to cover images of 'rape' and 'non-consensual penetration'. For more information see <http://www.scottish.parliament.uk/s3/bills/24-CrimJustLc/b24s3-introd.pdf> (accessed 16 December 2009).
4 Michael Flood, in this volume, is more positive about the potential of effects research but, in his conclusion, he too is sceptical about the utility of this work in shaping legislation.
5 See <http://www.backlash-uk.org.uk> for examples.

Epilogue

How was it for you?

Karen Boyle

In his chapter for this book Robert Jensen discusses the emotional toll of researching pornography from an anti-pornography perspective. Anticipating and ameliorating the impact of research on researchers, students and teachers is far more embedded in feminist work in the social sciences, particularly around violence,[1] than it is media studies and related fields where recent scholarship on pornography has been concentrated. As Jensen suggests, when we're dealing with pornographic media – which are, after all, designed to arouse – the emotional impact of research can be even more difficult to untangle, not least as it may be accompanied by physical arousal.

Even at one remove from Jensen's research, reading his chapter for the first time left me feeling depressed. It crystallized for me not only the difficulties of the research Jensen and other contributors to this book have undertaken, but also the difficulties of being in the audience for that research. Sometimes, I wonder if it's better (it's certainly easier) not to know this stuff, not to hear or believe the blatant misogyny and enthusiastic embrace of degradation by many of those who make and sell pornography, packaging it up as what 'sex' is about. It's tempting to get angry with the messenger, to find ways to not believe the evidence of their research because it's too uncomfortable, because it says difficult things about a culture in which we are invested, possibly about the people we love or the choices we have made or do make. So to those reading this epilogue I first want to say thank you for sticking with it. Whether you agree with me (or any of the other contributors) or not, thank you for taking the time to read our arguments and – I hope – engage with them intellectually, critically, politically. And if you've found it hard going it's OK to take some time out: you don't have to put the book down and go change the world (though if you can then great!). As Jensen suggests, before we move to solutions, sometimes we need to get in touch with how we feel about the evidence before us and allow ourselves to be angry, hurt, confused, sad, dismissive – possibly even turned on – and think about what that means about our society, our culture and ourselves.

The last sentence would look absurd in many contemporary accounts of pornography and its position in the mainstream. Resistance (as anything other than a postmodern, individualistic reading strategy) doesn't have to be addressed in accounts accepting of pornography because the culture is already pornified. Porn is part of dominant culture. Its position on university curricula may be less secure, but even within the academy research into pornography is well established and understood as legitimate (Jones and Carlin, Chapter 12); which is no bad thing. However, feminist anti-pornography work has become increasingly marginal within the academy whilst more celebratory accounts of pornography proliferate and flourish. Porn studies has become a (sub-)discipline in which feminism is constantly 'taken into account' (McRobbie 2009) in ways that are not necessarily feminist. I am not interested in extending acrimonious (and intellectually point-less) debates about who can or cannot (should or should not) call themselves 'feminists'. Rather my concern is that in studies of popular culture (including pornography) the debate has become fixated on being feminist rather than doing feminism in ways entirely in keeping with the post-feminist, individualistic ethos of the culture more generally.

As I have argued in more detail elsewhere (Boyle 2005), we are living in an essentially post-feminist culture where questions about women's choices, desires, pleasures and representations seem to dominate the academic agenda for femin-ists working in media-centred disciplines. Increasingly, we study what we like and we like what we study. We interrogate ourselves and each other about these pleasures, losing sight of some of the bigger questions and issues which have long defined feminism as a movement. Those of us who have continued to study things we don't necessarily like are fairly used to being thought of as, at best, 'worthy', quite possibly masochistic and most probably missing the point. (Work should be *fun!*) Those of us who take a political position anti pornography are quite used to being thought of as not only joyless but also sexless or, worse, anti-sex.

In Chapter 1, Gail Dines makes it clear how absurd such criticism is. If we were critiquing McDonald's, she argues, it would be widely understood that we were critiquing a business or a mode of producing and selling food rather than arguing against food *per se*. Yet I am aware that at least some readers will have – quite understandably, given the tenor of much contemporary debate – picked up this book in the expectation that it's about sex. If you've been invited to think about porn as part of your degree course, you might have anticipated something to amuse, shock or maybe even disgust you, something you could talk about with your friends afterwards whilst they marvelled at your good fortune that you get to think about sex whilst they have to work out mathematical equations or read weighty Victorian novels. Academics teaching various forms of popular culture regularly grapple with such anticipations and disappointments, as well as with accusations that our academic reading 'spoils' a particular text for those who have previously appreciated it, especially when their investment in that text is bound up with their sense of who they are (Doty 2000). But in relation to pornography the stakes are slightly different because it can be perceived that we are not simply 'spoiling' your enjoyment of a film but of (hetero)sex itself. This is why it's imperative that we unravel the ambiguous relationship between pornography and sex.

To describe the relationship between pornography and sex as ambiguous might seem ridiculous: what is porn if not sex? Whatever one's personal or political response to pornographic texts, we can probably all agree that they are, in the main, about sex: sex is what is represented and what is supposed to be at the forefront of the consumer's mind. Radical feminists in the 1980s took this further, demanding that a critique of porn be tied to a critique – if not outright rejection – of (hetero)sex. For Andrea Dworkin (1981, 1987), for instance, pornography is the expression of male sexuality in a male supremacist culture and, to the extent that such a culture makes it difficult (if not impossible) to think of heterosex outside of pornographic norms, a political analysis of pornography requires a simultaneous rejection of heterosex, at least in currently imaginable forms. To an extent, my initial experience of reading Dworkin's *Pornography: Men Possessing Women* bore this out: the images Dworkin described repulsed me, yet they were also at times fascinating and arousing. I felt manipulated by porn (and by Dworkin for telling me about it): I didn't want it to be about sex, but it certainly felt like it was.

When I first encountered these debates, I wanted to embrace arguments more accepting of pornography – not least because (particularly for a straight woman) it seemed a lot more fun. But having looked at the evidence amassed by anti-pornography scholars I couldn't do this in good conscience. That evidence demanded that I think of pornography as more than a group of texts that may or may not turn me on, and – to borrow a phrase from Susan Cole (1989) – that I recognized that pornography was also a *practice*, produced in a variety of contexts and conditions, many of which were explicitly abusive. A great deal of the debate at that time hinged on the testimony of individual women, and feminists on both sides incorporated the accounts of porn performers in their discussions of the industry.[2] It is easy to understand why: these voices are uniquely powerful and provide a vital grounding for academic analysis that can otherwise be abstract and disembodied. However, this strategy had a damaging impact on the debates about pornography which continues to reverberate. It pitted women against women, allowed personal accounts to drown out structural analysis and let men off the hook. We let the debate become about women's choices, and this framing continues to be seductive for mainstream media accounts of commercial sex in all its forms (Boyle 2008, 2010, forthcoming a, forthcoming b). In such a context, the textual turn in porn studies which followed Linda Williams' groundbreaking *Hard Core* (1989) was something of a relief, although it would ultimately bring its own problems (Boyle 2006).

But for me, encountering these debates in the early 1990s, there was also something personal at stake. Like Dworkin I didn't want to live my life in or through porn, but – unlike Dworkin – I did (and do) believe that heterosexual relationships do not have to be defined by pornography. Admittedly, at times during the research for this book, I have wondered whether such a belief is almost utopian today (particularly for young people) as pornography has become increasingly mainstream and its codes, conventions and values have become widely replicated. To cling to this belief requires a different way of thinking about commercial porn, a way of separating porn and sex. Clearly this is not a total or permanent separation: I am not arguing that porn performers do not perform sexual acts (this is what defines pornography, at least in its audio-visual forms), that pornography doesn't represent sex, or that it isn't experienced as sex for many (most?) consumers. However, pornography is a very particular kind of sex: it is, to return to Gail Dines, *industrial* sex.

Pornography is produced according to a principle of maximum visibility, not maximum sensation: the goal is to make sure the viewer gets a good look, not to enhance the performers' experience. As a sex education tool, even the most ethically produced pornography will always fall short in this important respect (which is not to say that ethical sexually explicit material is impossible, just to question its educative value). Indeed, the performers' experience is, in many ways, incidental to the economy of pornography: what matters is what the consumer wants and what he wants to believe about the experience and reality of the performer – if he gets what he wants, he'll keep coming (back for more). As Lisa Moore and Juliana Weissbein argue in Chapter 5, there is a relationship between seminal spending and cash spending. And as Ana Bridges, Meagan Tyler, Rebecca Whisnant and Jennifer Johnson all argue, to keep him spending in an era when porn is plentiful and often available 'free' (paid for through advertising) requires a continual upping of the ante.

If pornography is a particular kind of sex for the performer, what is represented is also a particular kind of sex. Given the diversity of sexual practices on display in porn (described in many of the chapters in this book), this argument may seem somewhat counter-intuitive, but it is again intended to remind us of the fallacy that 'anything goes' in pornography. Most obviously, no matter how ethical the production context, the one thing that pornography can never represent is the intimacy of a private sexual encounter. The sex of pornography is always, by definition, performative: even when there are only one or two people on screen, they are always addressing a viewer (even if, as in some amateur porn, that viewer is only ever intended to be their future selves). As such, pornography externalizes sex: it is to be looked at, performed; not felt, experienced. As Susanna Paasonen argues (Chapter 4), in the context of commercially produced pornography, pornographic sex is hyperbolic, generic, repetitive. Further, as both Moore and Weissbein and Sarah Neely demonstrate in their chapters, apparently more participatory modes of production do not necessarily change the range of representations.

What about the consumer? Surely, for the consumer, the relationship between pornography and sex is far more straightforward? For some consumers this is certainly true, although, as Michael Flood's review of existing research on consumption demonstrates (Chapter 11), this is not, necessarily, a good thing. Rather than expanding sexual possibilities, pornography can close them down, divorce consumers from their own imaginations and sensations, promote emotional disengagement as the price of physical pleasure and choreograph sexual practices to the pornographer's tune (which sounds a lot like the ringing of cash registers). That said, I do not assume it is necessarily a bad thing that certain sex acts have increased in the context of heterosexual practice because of their prevalence in porn. However, it is certainly not a good thing if these practices are being expected, enacted out of obligation or under pressure rather than because those involved are mutually curious or desiring. Nor is it a good thing if these – or any other sexual practices – are being performed according to the logic of commercial heterosexual pornography, where women exist simply to maximize men's pleasure.

All of this suggests that whilst choice – for both performers and consumers – is imperative, we conflate choice, desire and sexual subjectivity at our peril. Such distinctions are, unsurprisingly, rarely made in mainstream media representations of pornography or other forms of commercial sex, where women's *choices* to prostitute/perform are too easily conflated with desire and sexuality. The assumption appears to be that women involved in commercial sex are more, or differently, sexual from other women so that even evidence of serious physical injury sustained through the industrial use of their bodies for sex can be reinterpreted as a consequence of *their* sexuality. Moreover, it is striking that an explicit acknowledgement of the performativity of prostituted sex (including in pornography) does little to undermine this. The television adaptation of the blog/book *Secret Diary of a Call Girl* (ITV-2, 2007–?) is just one of many examples of this process: the protagonist regularly reminds viewers that the sex of prostitution is a performance that has nothing to do with her own sexual pleasure (which is often faked) whilst, at the same time, claiming that she prostitutes because she loves sex.[3] That this contradiction is neither recognized nor thematized within the show speaks volumes. And so it is with much mainstream discourse about pornography: on the one hand, there is a recognition that the women on screen are 'performing', yet, on the other, their choice is read as defining their sexuality.

In resisting dominant discourses of pornography we need to be clear that choice, desire and sexual subjectivity are not the same thing (Jeffreys 2009b; Miriam 2005; Whisnant 2004). One can choose things one does not desire and – whether in front of a camera or in a more intimate encounter – can choose to perform sexually in ways that are not physically and/or emotionally pleasurable and/or have nothing to do with one's own sexuality. Such choices are not immaterial and they are always better than no choice (Whisnant 2004), but they don't necessarily tell us anything about women's sexual desire or subjectivity. In short, the choice to perform in pornography – or to perform in one's own life according to the logic of pornography – does not *necessarily* have anything to do with sexual desire or pleasure.

Whilst some of these points might seem self-evident – particularly after reading the essays in this book – they are important building blocks for a contemporary anti-pornography feminism. For too long, anti-pornography feminism has been caricatured as being anti-sex, and this makes it a fairly unattractive proposition for many encountering its debates for the first time. In contrast, some contemporary academic writing about pornography which takes a stance broadly supportive of the industry and its texts uses titillation as a means of 'learning': making pornography sex(y)[4] and mirroring much mainstream media commentary on pornography.[5] Anti-pornography writing just isn't sexy. At one level, the reason for this is quite simple: feminists who take an anti-porn position don't want pornography (at least as it currently exists) to be part of our sex lives. We don't see the sexual appeal of thinking of ourselves, and our practices, in or through pornography. But that doesn't mean that we're anti-sex, it just means we're not talking about sex – at least not here, not now.

In saying I am an anti-porn feminist I am not telling you anything about my sex life or attitudes to sex. If you've picked up this book expecting it to be about sex, then this silence might be troubling. And then you go on to read what porn producers told Robert Jensen about the popularity of anal sex in heterosexual pornography in Chapter 7 and by placing the pornographer's comment in a critical context it can seem like it is the practice of anal sex *per se* which is critiqued here. But this isn't about anal sex as it might be practised between consenting curious, horny adults (which, frankly, is none of our business unless we're directly involved), but an industrialized, pornographic anal sex that carries a particularly limited (and limiting) range of meanings. This is about a product (pornography) and how it defines and delimits a particular experience. It is only about the experience itself if consumers translate that understanding into their own lives.

However, such distinctions can be easily lost in heated debates when individuals feel like their own sexual pleasure might be under scrutiny or attack. But, in my experience at least, such perceptions often seem wedded to what it is *expected* that feminists speaking on these issues will say. One of the most striking examples of this I encountered was in the debate following a conference presentation of the arguments Clare McGlynn lays out in Chapter 13 (McGlynn 2009). McGlynn was critiquing a public *debate* about *policy* about extreme *pornography* and yet her paper was angrily interpreted by some audience members as an expression of disapproval of particular sexual practices and communities. Such are the debates that often accompany speaking (out) on pornography. Because the equation of pornography and sex is so culturally embedded, any critique of porn (and even a critique of a debate about a policy about porn) can be reinterpreted as a critique of specific sexual practices or communities. And what are perceived as personal attacks are then too often responded to in a personal way (Graham 2007). We need to be smarter than that and not lose sight of the ways in which pornography is always also a representation. *Representations* of BDSM activities, particularly in commercially produced porn (enacted by performers for whom it may or may not be part of their own sexuality), do not have the same status or meaning (personally, culturally, politically) as BDSM *experiences*. Or to give another example: rape fantasies can look a lot like rape when enacted for an audience, as Neely's discussion of Second Life demonstrates (Chapter 6). To raise questions about such representations is to raise questions not about fantasy (or about sexual practice between consenting adults) but about the characteristics of that representation and the possible frames of reference for interpreting and using it, particularly once it is placed in the public sphere as a commercial product.

Of course, anti-pornography feminists have long been concerned about the ways in which that product defines experience for many in our culture. But whilst the ways in which we experience sex are certainly shaped by our culture, that culture does not speak about sex (or pornography) with one voice. Now you've read the evidence presented here *you* have a choice about whether/how you (continue to) make these examples of everyday pornography *about* sex in your own life. As Jensen acknowledges, this isn't always an easy choice, and it can be particularly difficult for men and boys who are so much more 'steeped' in pornography. But, it is a worthwhile one, because to recognize that porn isn't about sex – or doesn't have to be – opens up lots of other sexual possibilities (as well as intellectual ones) and, hopefully, gives space to think about what it is that really works for *you* sexually, without having to stick to a script or scripts written by others.

In short, there doesn't have to be a contradiction in loving (hetero)sex and hating porn.

This, in itself, is a form of resistance: the personal is, after all, political, although in our analysis, argument and activism we need to think through and beyond our own experience(s). Resisting pornography is a personal choice but making that choice public gives it an additional political character. This is particularly important at the moment, as one of the things many of us speaking and teaching about pornography have had to acknowledge is that in a pornified culture the possibility of resistance on anything other than moral or religious terms is too often unimaginable, particularly for young women. This is why organizations and campaigns such as Stop Porn Culture and Object are so important.[6] Even if you don't agree with them, their campaigns give visibility to the possibility of resistance and so provide alternatives and choice. That can only be a good thing. For those of us who do agree with them, they provide the possibility of making our voices heard in the public sphere as part of a *movement*, which provides some insulation against the kind of personal critique that too often accompanies speaking (out) on porn but also makes this work sustaining (and sustainable) as well as – sometimes – *fun*.

Academics are, of course, part of that movement and – in many cases – academics are driving and reinvigorating activist politics (see Chapter 1, this volume). However, as academics we also have a responsibility to engage with research and thinking outside our own comfort zone, to get to grips with other arguments and think through their implications for our research, teaching and activism. Obviously, this book privileges a particular position (anti-pornography feminism), just as others in the field privilege a different one. But in their disciplinary diversity, and the breadth of their scholarship, the contributors to this volume provide a range of ways of engaging with pornography's everyday within the academy, utilizing a variety of methodologies, focusing on a range of 'objects', engaging with and responding to the framing of pornography as an object of study, debate, regulation and representation.

Of course, there is much we still need to do. Even as this volume has been in preparation the nature of pornography's everyday in the 'West' has been changing: it would appear, for instance, that pornography is no longer recession-proof. It will be important to monitor the way the industry reorganizes in the wake of this economic crisis, not only in terms of the kind of content it privileges but also its modes of delivery, how it generates profit from them and what that means for performers. As more and more material becomes available for free, we may need to rethink the ways in which we have conceptualized the *commercial* nature of pornography and learn more about how such transactions are understood by consumers relative to their use of free material. We also need to know more about the diverse ways in which the industry generates money on line – work begun by Jennifer Johnson in this volume. Further, as a number of chapters in this book make clear, we need to understand better how young people – for whom the porn culture is utterly normalized – think about and use pornography (including material they make themselves) in the context of their lives. To do this most effectively requires not only that we listen to those who choose to use pornography, but also that we hear from those who choose not to, and investigate the conditions in which *not* using pornography is possible.

From my disciplinary position (film and television studies) it is not surprising that I think that textual work continues to be important. Whilst it is often the more marginal and esoteric texts which generate the most interesting questions about representation, genre, ideology and identity, we need to be alert to the broader cultural and historical contexts in which these texts are situated and be wary of generalizing about 'pornography' by analysing its fringes. Hyberbolic and generic though it may be, the importance of detailing the content of everyday pornography in academic and policy contexts which too often deal in abstractions cannot be overestimated.

One of the most distressing aspects of compiling this book and of working on mainstream representations of commercial sex over the past few years has been reading the explicit and often gleeful acknowledgement from industry insiders that everyday production practices are misogynist, abusive and destructive. There are exceptions and, of course, we should not accept what industry insiders say at face value. Nonetheless, what is striking about much of this commentary is that producers' and performers' willingness to acknowledge the abuse *whilst they are still working within the industry* suggests that we have become so jaded as to no longer hear these stories as abuse (and so actionable) *and* that these stories are part and parcel of the everyday marketing of pornography (as Tyler and Whisnant demonstrate in this volume). Finally, then, we can never lose sight of the ways in which – every day – the production of legal, pornography uses (up) the bodies of real women and men. Whatever choices performers make about entering and staying in the industry, we need to ensure that we do not conflate those choices with desire or sexual subjectivity or let such choices (where they do exist) blind us to the physical and psychological toll of industrial sex. Because that is what commercial pornography is: it is industrial sex, and it uses (up) its constituent parts in a ruthlessly efficient way.

Notes

1 Of particular relevance here are accounts considering the impact on the feminist researcher of researching sexual violence, e.g. Stanko (1997), Hippensteele (1997), Mattley (1997), Huff (1997), Hearn (1998), Hume (2007). Not surprisingly, the emphasis in much of this literature is on relationships between the researcher and those s/he researches. Because our research often involves 'texts', there has seemed to be less urgency for feminist media scholars to address these issues. However, as Jensen demonstrates, there are costs to this research, and acknowledging them helps us to support one another better. Our emotions are also a resource for understanding the material. This is not only true of work which takes an explicitly anti-porn position.
2 Anthologies which incorporate personal testimony alongside academic analysis include Russell (1993), Assiter and Carol (1993a), Elias et al. (1999) and Stark and Whisnant (2004). Such testimonies are moving and vital; nevertheless, we need to think critically about the claims we make for any individual account, understanding that they are produced in particular circumstances, for particular audiences (which is always more obvious when looking at accounts produced by people whose position on the issue is different from one's own). This is not to say they are not real, but to argue that one of the roles of the academic (and policy maker) is to *analyse* such testimony to understand its broader implications. This can put particular pressure on academics who are also activists, and keeping the demands of the different sectors in balance is an on-going challenge.
3 See Boyle (2010) for a fuller discussion of this show.
4 This is explicitly discussed in an article by Dennis Waskul (2009) in relation to using pornography in a general class about sexuality.
5 See Boyle (Chapter 9) and Jones and Carlin (Chapter 12) in this volume.
6 Stop Porn Culture: <http://www.stoppornculture.com>; Object: <http:www. object.org.uk>. Other useful on-line anti-porn resources include: One Angry Girl: <http://www.oneangrygirl.net/index.html>; Anti-porn Activist network: <http:// www.antipornactivist.com/>; Anti-porn London: <http://antipornfeminists. wordpress.com/>; Coalition against Trafficking in Women Australia: <http:// www.catwa.org.au/ > (all accessed 26 November 2009).

Bibliography

Abel, D. (2001) 'Porn is hot course on campus', *Boston Globe*, 20 August: A1.

Abel, M. (2007) *Violent Affect: Literature, Cinema, and Critique after Representation*, Lincoln: University of Nebraska Press.

Adcox, S. (2004) 'C of C professor makes project of graphic class presentation', in *The* [Charleston] *Post and Courier*, 22 February. Online. Available HTTP: < https://listserv.temple.edu/cgi-bin/wa?A2=ind0402&L=btmm_grad&D=0&F=P&T=0&P=10885> (accessed 30 October 2009).

Adult Video News (2005) 'Top 250 VHS & DVD rentals'. Online. Available HTTP: <http://www.avn.com/index.php?Primary_Navigation=Charts > (accessed July 2005).

AFL-CIO (2002) *The Service Sector Vital Statistics Fact Sheet 2002–2005*. Online. Available HTTP: <http://www.dpeaflcio.org/programs/factsheets/archived/fs_service.pdf > (accessed 17 November 2009).

Ahmed, S. (2004) *The Cultural Politics of Emotion*, Edinburgh: Edinburgh University Press.

Allen, L. (2001) 'Closing sex education's knowledge/practice gap', *Sex Education*, 1: 109–22.

——(2006) ' "Looking at the real thing" ', *Discourse*, 27: 69–83.

Allen, M., D'Alessio, D. and Brezgel, K. (1995) 'A meta-analysis summarizing the effects of pornography II', *Human Communication Research*, 22: 258–83.

Allen, M., D'Alessio, D., Emmers, T. and Gebhardt, L. (1996) 'The role of educational briefings in mitigating effects of experimental exposure to violent sexually explicit material', *Journal of Sex Research*, 33: 135–41.

Allen, M., Emmers, T., Gebhardt, L. and Glery, M. (1995) 'Exposure to pornography and acceptance of rape myths', *Journal of Communication*, 45: 5–26.

American Psychological Association (APA) (2007) *Report of the APA Task Force on the Sexualization of Girls*, Washington, DC: APA.

Amis, M. (2001) 'A rough trade', *The Guardian* (London), 17 March.

Anderson, A. (2003) 'Harder, faster, can porn get any nastier?', *Adult Video News*, October. Online. Available HTTP: <http://www.adultvideonews.com/cover/cover1003_03.html > (accessed 17 January 2006).

——(2005) Review, '*The Story of J*——', *Adult Video News*, March. Online. Available HTTP: <http://www.adultvideonews.com/editch/edch0305_06.html> (accessed 27 August 2006).

Andrews, D. (2007) 'What soft-core can do for Porn Studies', *Velvet Light Trap*, 59 (spring): 51–61.

Anon. (1991) 'Iowa students forced to watch homosexual porn films', *American Family Association Journal*, November/December: 12.

——(2003) 'Kansas Governor affirms academic freedom', *Academe*, 89 (4). Online. Available HTTP: <http://www.aaup.org/AAUP/pubsres/academe/2003/JA/NB/Kansas.htm> (accessed 30 October 2009).

——(2004a) 'Kick porn off course', *Sunday Mercury*, 25 January: 10.

——(2004b) 'Lecturer under fire as class is shown porn video', *The Mail on Sunday*, 1 February: 13.

——(2004c) 'Students watch mucky movie – for their degree', *Nuts*, 13–19 February: 14.

——(2006) *Showbiz Tonight*, CNN, 16 May, 19.00 (ET). Transcript online. Available HTTP: <http://transcripts.cnn.com/TRANSCRIPTS/0605/16/sbt.01.html> (accessed 30 October 2009).

——(2008a) 'Patch "accidentally" reduced *Age of Conan* females' breasts', *Megagames*, 2 June. Online. Available HTTP: <http://www.megagames.com/news/html/pc/patchaccidentallyreducedageofconanfemalesbreasts.shtml> (accessed 8 September 2009).

——(2008b) ' "Victim" in porn show', *News of the World*, 2 November. Online. Available HTTP: <http://www.newsoftheworld.co.uk/news/58884/Georgina-Baillie-ndash-the-innocent-victim-of-the-Sachs-scandalndash-stars-in-a-hardcore-porn-film.html> (accessed 31 August 2009)

——(2009) 'Smith's husband sorry over films', *BBC News*, 29 March. Online. Available HTTP: <http://news.bbc.co.uk/1/hi/uk_politics/7970731.stm> (accessed 31 August 2009).

Armstrong, I. (2000) *The Radical Aesthetic*, Oxford: Blackwell.

Assiter, A. and Carol, A. (eds) (1993a) *Bad Girls and Dirty Pictures: The Challenge to Reclaim Feminism*, London: Pluto Press.

Assiter, A. and Carol, A. (1993b) 'Conclusion. Women still want freedom', in A. Assiter and A. Carol (eds) *Bad Girls and Dirty Pictures*, London: Pluto.

Atlas, J. (1999) 'The loose canon: why higher learning has embraced pornography', *New Yorker*, 29 March: 60–5.

Attwood, F. (2002) 'Reading porn: the paradigm shift in pornography research', *Sexualities*, 5 (1): 91–105.

——(2009a) 'Introduction. The sexualization of culture', in F. Attwood (ed.) *Mainstreaming Sex: The Sexualization of Western Culture*, London: Tauris.

——(ed.) (2009b) *Mainstreaming Sex: The Sexualization of Western Culture*, London: I. B. Tauris.

Austin, D. J. (1999) '(Sexual) quotation without (sexual) harassment? Educational use of pornography in the university classroom', in J. Elias, V. D. Elias, V. L. Bullough, G. Brewer, J. J. Douglas and W. Jarvis (eds) *Porn 101: Eroticism, Pornography, and the First Amendment*, Amherst, MA: Prometheus.

Aydemir, M. (2007) *Images of Bliss: Ejaculation, Masculinity, Meaning*, Minneapolis, MN: University of Minnesota Press.

Babbie, E. (2009) *The Practice of Social Research*, Belmont, CA: Wadsworth.

Backlash (2007) ' "Extreme" pornography proposals: ill-conceived and wrong', in C. McGlynn, E. Rackley and N. Westmarland (eds) *Positions on the Politics of Porn*, Durham, NC: Durham University. Online. Available HTTP: <http://www.dur.ac.uk/resources/law/research/politicsofporn/PositionsonthePoliticsofPorn.pdf> (accessed 16 December 2009).

Bailey, F. (1999) 'Introduction', in I. Tang, *Pornography: The Secret History of Civilisation*, London: Channel 4.

Bancroft, L. (2002) *Why Does He Do That? Inside the Minds of Angry and Controlling Men*, New York: Putnam.

Bandura, A. (1986) *Social Foundations of Thought and Action: A Social Cognitive Theory*, Englewood Cliffs, NJ: Prentice Hall.

——(1996) 'Mechanisms of moral disengagement in the exercise of moral agency', *Journal of Personality and Social Psychology*, 71: 364–74.

——(1999) 'Moral disengagement in the perpetration of inhumanities', *Personality and Social Psychology Review*, 3: 193–209.

——(2004) 'Swimming against the mainstream: the early years, from chilly tributary to transformative mainstream', *Behaviour Research and Therapy*, 42: 613–30.

Bandura, A., Ross, D. and Ross, S. A. (1961) 'Transmission of aggression through imitation of aggressive models', *Journal of Abnormal and Social Psychology*, 63: 575–82.

Bandura, A., Underwood, B. and Fromson, M. (1975) 'Disinhibition of aggression through diffusion of responsibility and dehumanization of victims', *Journal of Research in Personality*, 9: 253–69.

Barabasi, A. L. (2003) *Linked: How Everything is Connected to Everything Else and What it Means for Business, Science, and Everyday Life*, New York: Plume Books.

Barron, M. and Kimmel, M. (2000) 'Sexual violence in three pornographic media: toward a sociological explanation', *Journal of Sex Research*, 37 (2): 161–8.

BBC (2006) 'Mother wins ban on violent porn', 30 August. Online. Available HTTP: <http://news.bbc.co.uk/1/hi/england/berkshire/5297600.stm> (accessed 16 December 2009).

——(2009) 'Honesty test "should be reviewed" ', 7 September. Online. Available HTTP: <http://news.bbc.co.uk/1/hi/sci/tech/8240985.stm> (accessed 16 December 2009).

Benwell, B. (2001) 'Male gossip and language play in the letters pages of men's lifestyle magazines', *Journal of Popular Culture*, 34 (4): 19–33.

Bernstein, A. (2006) 'Women's pay: why the gap remains a chasm', in P. Rothenberg (ed.) *Race, Class, and Gender in the United States: An Integrated Study*, New York: Worth Publishing.

Bisch, K. (1999) 'The gang's all here: hope flickers at the world's biggest gang bang', *Salon*, 31 August. Online. Available HTTP: <http://www.salon.com/health/sex/urge/1999/08/31/houston/index.html> (accessed 14 December 2008).

Blass, T. (2004) *The Man who Shocked the World: The Life and Legacy of Stanley Milgram*, New York: Basic Books.

Bockhorn, L. (2002) 'At Berkeley wild things are going on in a "Male Sexuality" class', *Weekly Standard*, 22 February. Online. Available HTTP: <http://www.weeklystandard.com/Content/Public/Articles/000%5C000%5C000%5C936bnsuz.asp> (accessed 30 October 2009).

Boellstorff, T. (2008) *Coming of Age in Second Life: An Anthropologist Explores the Virtually Human*, Princeton, NJ, and Oxford: Princeton University Press.

Bogaert, A. F., and Turkovich, D. A., and Hafer, C. L. (1993) 'A content analysis of *Playboy* centrefolds from 1953 through 1990: changes in explicitness, objectification, and models' age', *Journal of Sex Research*, 30: 135–9.

Bonino, S., Ciairano, S., Rabaglietti, E. and Cattelino, E. (2006) 'Use of pornography and self-reported engagement in sexual violence among adolescents', *European Journal of Developmental Psychology*, 3: 265–88.

Borzekowski, D. L. G. and Rickert, V. I. (2001) 'Adolescent cybersurfing for health information: a new resource that crosses barriers', *Archives of Pediatrics and Adolescent Medicine*, 155: 813–17.

Boswell, A. A. and Spade, J. Z. (1996) 'Fraternities and collegiate rape culture: why are some fraternities more dangerous places for women?' *Gender and Society*, 10 (2): 133–47.

Bowser, B. (1994) 'African American male sexuality through the early life course', in A. Rossi (ed.) *Sexuality across the Life Course*, Chicago: University of Chicago Press.

Boyle, K. (2000) 'The pornography debates: beyond cause and effect', *Women's Studies International Forum*, 23 (2): 187–95.

——(2005) 'Feminism without men: feminist media studies in a post-feminist age', in J. Curran and M. Gurevitch (eds) *Mass Media and Society*, fourth edition, London: Arnold.

——(2006) 'The boundaries of porn studies: on Linda Williams' *Porn Studies*', *New Review of Film and Television Studies*, 4 (1): 1–16.

——(2008) 'Courting consumers and legitimating exploitation', *Feminist Media Studies*, 8 (1): 35–50.

——(2009) 'Beyond the Raincoats: the Porn Consumer in Mainstream Media', paper presented at Porn Cultures conference, Leeds, June.

——(2010) 'Selling the selling of sex: *Secret Diary of a Call Girl* on screen', *Feminist Media Studies*, 10 (1): 115–18.

——(forthcoming a) 'The dark side of hard core: critical documentaries on the sex industry', in C. Hines and D. Kerr, *Hard to Swallow: Hard-core Pornography on Screen*, London: Wallflower.

——(forthcoming b) ' "That's so fun": selling pornography for men to women in *The Girls Next Door*', in G. Dines and J. Humez (eds) *Gender, Race and Class in Media*, third edition, Thousand Oaks, CA: Sage.

Bozelka, K.J. (2007) 'An Interview with Peter Lehman and Linda Williams', *The Velvet Light Trap*, 59 (spring): 62–8.

Branigan, T (2006) 'Violent porn ban "a memorial to my daughter" ', *The Guardian*, 31 August. Online. Available HTTP: <http://www.guardian.co.uk/politics/2006/aug/31/humanrights.ukcrime> (accessed 16 December 2009).

Brenner, S. (2008) 'Fantasy crime', *Vanderbilt Journal of Technology and Entertainment Law*, 11 (1). Online. Available HTTP: <http://works.bepress.com/susan_brenner/1/> (accessed 30 October 2009).

Brewster, A. (2006) 'Porn 101', *Columbia News Service*, 14 March. Online. Available HTTP: <http://jscms.jrn.columbia.edu/cns/2006-03-14/brewster-porn/> (accessed 31 August 2009).

Bridges, A., Bergner, R. and Hesson-McInnis, M. (2003) 'Romantic partners' use of pornography', *Journal of Sex and Marital Therapy*, 29: 1–14.

Brod, H. (1988) 'Pornography and the alienation of male sexuality', *Social Theory and Practice*, 14 (3): 265–84.

——(1990) 'Eros thanatized', in M. Kimmel (ed.) *Men Confront Pornography*, New York: Crown.

Brubaker, S. J. and Johnson, J. A. (2008) ' "Pack a more powerful punch" and "Lay the pipe": erectile enhancement discourse as a body project for masculinity', *Journal of Gender Studies*, 17 (2): 131–46.

Bryant, J. and Brown, D. (1989) 'Uses of pornography', in D. Zillman and J. Bryant (eds) *Pornography*, Hillsdale, NJ: Erlbaum.

Buchmann, C. and DiPrete, T. A. (2006) 'The growing female advantage in college completion: the role of family background and academic achievement', *American Sociological Review*, 71 (4): 515–41.

Buckingham, D. and Bragg, S. (2003) *Young People, Media and Personal Relationships*, London: Advertising Standards Authority.

Bureau of Labor Statistics (2009) *The Employment Situation, October 2009*. Online. Available HTTP: <http://www.bls.gov/news.release/pdf/empsit.pdf> (accessed 17 November 2009).

Burress, C. (2002) 'Cal sex class flunks out', *San Francisco Chronicle*, 19 February: A1.

Butler, J. (1990) *Gender Trouble: Feminism and the Subversion of Identity*, New York: Routledge.

——(1993) *Bodies that Matter: On the Discursive Limits of 'Sex'*, London: Routledge.

Cameron, D. (1990) 'Discourses of desire: liberals, feminists and the politics of pornography in the 1980s', *American Literary History*, 2 (4): 784–98.

Cameron, K., Salazar, L., Bernhardt, J., Burgess-Whitman, N., Wingood, G. and DiClemente, R. (2005) 'Adolescents' experience with sex on the web', *Journal of Adolescence*, 28: 535–40.

Caputi, J. (2003) 'Everyday pornography', in G. Dines and J. Humez (eds) *Gender, Race, and Class in Media: A Text-Reader*, second edition, Thousand Oaks, CA: Sage.

Care, N. (1996) *Living with One's Past: Personal Fates and Moral Pain*, Lanham, MD: Rowman & Littlefield.

Carlson, T. (2003) 'That's outrageous: Porn 101: Yep, that's *Penthouse* on the syllabus', *Reader's Digest*, March: 31–3.

Carol, A. (1993) 'Don't get fooled again: assailed in Britain', *New York Law School Law Review*, 38: 183–94.

Carpenter, L. M. (1998) 'From girls into women: scripts for sexuality and romance in *Seventeen* magazine, 1974–1994', *Journal of Sex Research*, 35: 158–68.

Carroll, J. S., Padilla-Walker, L. M., Nelson, L. J., Olson, C. D., McNamara Barry, C. and Madsen, S. D. (2008) 'Generation XXX: pornography acceptance and use among emerging adults', *Journal of Adolescent Research*, 23: 6–30.

Castells, M. (2000) *The Rise of the Network Society*, Oxford: Blackwell.

Castronova, E. (2005) *Synthetic Worlds: The Business and Culture of Online Games*, Chicago and London: University of Chicago Press.

Centers for Disease Control and Prevention (2009) *Key Statistics from the National Survey of Family Growth*. Online. Available HTTP: <http://www.cdc.gov/nchs/nsfg/abc_list_s.htm#vaginalsexual> (accessed 12 September 2009).

Check, J. (1995) 'Teenage training', in L. R. Lederer and R. Delgado (eds) *The Price we Pay*, New York: Hill & Wang.

Chun, W. H. K. (2006) *Control and Freedom: Power and Paranoia in the Age of Fiber Optics*, Cambridge, MA: MIT Press.

Cole, S. G. (1989) *Pornography and the Sex Crisis*, Toronto: Amanita Press.

Colombo, J. and Mitchell, D. W. (2009) 'Infant visual habituation', *Neurobiology of Learning and Memory*, 92: 225–34.

Connell, R. W. (1987) *Gender and Power: Society, the Person, and Sexual Politics*, Stanford, CA: Stanford University Press.

Cook, I. (2006) 'Western heterosexual masculinity, anxiety, and web porn', *Journal of Men's Studies*, 14 (1): 47–63.

Cooper, A. (1998) 'Sexuality and the internet: surfing into a new millennium', *Cyberpsychology and Behavior*, 1 (2): 187–93.

——(2002) *Sex and the Internet: A Guidebook for Clinicians*, New York: Brunner-Routledge.

Cooper A., Delmonico, D., Griffin-Shelley, E. and Mathy R. (2004) 'Online sexual activity', *Sexual Addiction and Compulsivity*, 11: 129–43.

Cooper, A., Morahan-Martin, J., Mathy, R. M. and Maheu, M. (2002) 'Toward an increased understanding of user demographics in online sexual activities', *Journal of Sex and Marital Therapy*, 28: 105–29.

Coopersmith, J. (2006) 'Does your mother know what you really do? The changing nature and image of computer-based pornography', *History and Technology*, 22 (1): 1–25.

Corneliussen, H. G. (2008) '*World of Warcraft* as a playground for feminism', in H. Corneliussen and J. Walker Rettberg (eds) *Digital Culture, Play and Identity: A World of Warcraft Reader*, Cambridge, MA: MIT.

Cornell, D. (ed.) (2000) *Feminism and Pornography*, Oxford: Oxford University Press.

Cowan, G. (2002) 'Content analysis of visual materials', in M. W. Wiederman and B. E. Whitley, Jr (eds) *Handbook for Conducting Research on Human Sexuality*, Mahwah, NJ: Erlbaum.

Cowan, G. and Campbell, R. R. (1994) 'Racism and sexism in interracial pornography: a content analysis', *Psychology of Women Quarterly*, 18: 323–38.

——(1995) 'Rape: causal attitudes among adolescents', *Journal of Sex Research*, 32: 145–53.

Cowan, G. and Dunn, K. F. (1994) 'What themes in pornography lead to perceptions of the degradation of women?', *Journal of Sex Research*, 31: 11–21.

Cowan, G., Lee, C., Levy, D. and Snyder, D. (1988) 'Dominance and inequality in X-rated videocassettes', *Psychology of Women Quarterly*, 12: 299–311.

Crabbe, M. and Corlett, D. (2008) *Reality and Risk*, Warmambool, Vic.: Brophy Family & Youth Services.

Cullen, L. T. (2006) 'Sex in the syllabus', *Time*, 3 April, 167 (14): 80–1.

Curry, R. (1996) 'Media scholars teaching pornography: stepping across Broadway', *Jump Cut*, 40 (March): 114–18.

Dahlquist, J. P. and Vigilant, L. G. (2004) 'Way better than real: manga sex to tentacle Hentai', in D. D. Waskul (ed.) *Net.seXXX: Readings of Sex, Pornography, and the Internet*, New York: Peter Lang.

Dean, L. (2007) 'Young Men, Pornography and Sexual Health Promotion', unpublished Master's thesis, University of Brighton.

Dery, M. (2007) 'Paradise lust: pornotopia meets the culture wars', in K. Jacobs, M. Janssen and M. Pasquinelli (eds) *C'Lick Me: A Netporn Studies Reader*, Amsterdam: Institute of Network Cultures.

de Visser, R. O., Smith, A. M. A., Rissel, C. E., Richters, J. and Grulich, A. E. (2003) 'Heterosexual experience and recent heterosexual encounters among a representative sample of adults', *Australian and New Zealand Journal of Public Health*, 27: 146–54.

Dial, K. (2001) 'Pornography 102', *Boundless Webzine*, 29 November. Online. Available HTTP: <http://www.boundless.org/2001/features/a0000518.html> (accessed 31 August 2009).

Dines, G. (1998) 'Dirty business: *Playboy* and the mainstreaming of pornography', in G. Dines, R. Jensen and A. Russo (eds) *Pornography: The Production and Consumption of Inequality*, New York: Routledge.

——(2006) 'The white man's burden: Gonzo pornography and the construction of black masculinity', *Yale Journal of Law and Feminism*, 18, 293–7.

——(2009a) 'Childified women: how the mainstream pornography industry sells child pornography to men', in S. Olfman (ed.) *The Sexualization of Childhood*, Westport, CT: Praeger.

——(2009b) 'Mapping Pornography: Constructing and Deconstructing the Text', paper presented at Porn Cultures conference, Leeds, June.

——(2010) *Pornland: How Porn has Hijacked our Sexuality*, Boston, MA: Beacon Press.

Dines, G., Jensen, R. and Russo, A. (eds) (1998) *Pornography: The Production and Consumption of Inequality*, New York: Routledge.

Dominus, S. (2004) 'What women want to watch', *New York Times*, 29 August. Online. Available HTTP: < http://www.nytimes.com> (accessed 19 January 2009).

Donnerstein, E., Linz, D. and Penrod, S. (1987) *The Question of Pornography: Research Findings and Policy Implications*, New York: Free Press.

Doty, A. (2000) *Flaming Classics: Queering the Film Canon*, New York and London: Routledge.

Downs, D. A. (1989) *The New Politics of Pornography*, Chicago: University of Chicago Press.

Doyle, T. C. (2000) *The Architects of Porn*. Online. Available HTTP: <http://www.crn.com/it-channel/18808197;jsessionid=URSUL34XHR0H1QE1GHOSKHWATM-Y32JVN> (accessed 17 November 2009).

Duggan, L., Hunter, N. and Vance, C. (1988) 'False promises', in Caught Looking (eds) *Caught Looking*, Seattle, WA: Real Comet Press.

Dumenco, S. (2008) 'Welcome back, asshole', *Details*, December: 114–18.

Duncan, D. F. (1991) 'Violence and degradation as themes in "adult" videos', *Psychological Reports*, 69: 239–40.

Durbin, J. (1996) 'Confessions of a feminist porn teacher', in C. Matrix (ed.) *Tales from the Clit: A Female Experience of Pornography*, Edinburgh: AK Press.

Dworkin, A. (1981) *Pornography: Men Possessing Women*, London: Women's Press.

——(1987) *Intercourse*, London: Secker & Warburg.

——(1988) 'I want a twenty-four-hour truce during which there is no rape', in A. Dworkin, *Letters from a War Zone*, London: Secker & Warburg.

——(1994) 'Why pornography matters to feminists', in A. Jagger (ed.) *Living with Contradictions: Controversies in Feminist Social Ethics*, Boulder, CO: Westview Press.

——(1997) *Life and Death: Unapologetic Writings on the Continuing War against Women*, London: Virago.

Dworkin, A. and MacKinnon, C. A. (1988) *Pornography and Civil Rights: A New Day for Women's Equality*, Minneapolis, MN: Organizing against Pornography.

Online. Available HTTP: <http://www.nostatusquo.com/ACLU/dworkin/other/ordinance/newday/TOC.htm> (accessed 30 October 2009).

Dworkin, R. (1985) *A Matter of Principle*, Oxford: Oxford University Press.

——(1996) *Freedom's Law: The Moral Reading of the American Constitution*, New York: Oxford University Press.

Edwards, S. (2003) 'Discourses of denial and moral panics: the pornographisation of the child in art, the written word, film, and photograph', in J. Rowbotham and K. Stephenson (eds) *Behaving Badly: Social Panic and Moral Outrage: Victorian and Modern Parallels*, Burlington, VT: Ashgate.

Dyzenhaus, D. (1992) 'John Stuart Mill and the harm of pornography', *Ethics* 102 (3): 534–51.

Ehrlich, S. (2002) 'Mid-1990s porn turns extra hard', *Adult Video News*, August. Online. Available HTTP: <http://www.adultvideonews.com/cover/cover0802_01.html> (accessed 18 August 2005).

Elias, J., Elias, V. D., Bullough, V. L., Brwer, G., Douglas, J. J. and Jarvis, W. (1999) *Porn 101: Eroticism, Pornography, and the First Amendment*, Amherst, NY: Prometheus.

Everywoman (1988) *Pornography and Sexual Violence: Evidence of the Links*, London: Everywoman.

Fagan, P. F. (2009) *The Effects of Pornography on Individuals, Marriage, Family and Community*, Washington, DC: Family Research Council. Online. Available HTTP: <http://www.frc.org/pornography-effects> (accessed 16 December 2009).

Faulkner, Lord (2008) Hansard, HL Vol. 699, col. 897 (3 March).

Faludi, S. (1999) *Stiffed: The Betrayal of the American Man*, New York: HarperCollins.

Fawcett Society (2009) *Engendering Justice: From Policy to Practice*, London: Fawcett Society.

Feinberg, J. (1983) 'Pornography and the criminal law', in D. Copp and S. Wendell (eds) *Pornography and Censorship*, New York: Prometheus.

Fenton, H., Grainger, J. and Castoldi, G. L. (1999) *Cannibal Holocaust and the Savage Cinema of Ruggero Deodato*, Guildford: FAB Press.

Fisher, B. S., Cullen, F. T. and Turner, M. G. (2000) *The Sexual Victimization of College Women*, Washington, DC: Bureau of Justice Statistics, National Institute of Justice, US Department of Justice.

Fisher, L. (2009) 'Protesters say it's their right to watch sadistic porn. Tell that to the mother of the girl murdered by a man addicted to it', *Daily Mail*, 3 January. Online. Available HTTP: <http://www.dailymail.co.uk/femail/article-1104523/Protesters-say-right-watch-sadistic-porn-Tell-mother-girl-murdered-man-addicted-.html> (accessed 16 December 2009).

Fisher, W. and Barak, A. (2001) 'Internet pornography', *Journal of Sex Research*, 38: 312–23.

Fleming, M. J., Greentree, S., Cocotti-Muller, D., Elias, K. A. and Morrison, S. (2006) 'Safety in cyberspace', *Youth and Society*, 38: 135–54.

Flood, M. (2007) 'Exposure to pornography among youth in Australia', *Journal of Sociology*, 43: 45–60.

——(2009) 'Bent straights', in E. H. Oleksy (ed.) *Intimate Citizenships*, New York: Routledge.

Flood, M. and Hamilton, C. (2003) *Youth and Pornography in Australia*, Canberra: Australia Institute.

Forsberg, M. (2001) 'Does pornography influence sexual activities?', in C. von Feilitzen and U. Carlsson (eds) *Children in the New Media Landscape*, Göteberg, Sweden: UNESCO International Clearinghouse on Children and Violence on the Screen.

Foucault, M. (1978) *The History of Sexuality*, Vol. 1, *An Introduction*, New York: Random House.

Frable, D., Johnson, A. and Kellman, H. (1997) 'Seeing masculine men, sexy women, and gender differences', *Journal of Personality*, 65: 311–55.

Franklin, K. (2004) 'Enacting masculinity: antigay violence and group rape as participatory theater', *Sexuality Research and Social Policy*, 1 (2): 25–40.

Free Speech Coalition (2007) 'State-of-the-industry report, 2007–2008'. Online. Available HTTP: <http://www.freespeechcoalition.com/images/pdf/FSCSOI2007. pdf> (accessed 17 November 2009).

Fritz, B. (2009) 'Tough times in the porn industry: the business, centered in the San Fernando valley, is being undercut by a growing abundance of free content on the internet', *Los Angeles Times*, 10 August. Online. Available HTTP: <http://www. latimes.com/business/la-fi-ct-porn10–2009aug10,0,4788614.story> (accessed 8 September 2009).

Garos, S., Beggan, J. K., Kluck, A. and Easton, A. (2004) 'Sexism and pornography use', *Journal of Psychology and Human Sexuality*, 16: 69–96.

Gelder, U. (2002) *Boys and Young Men*, Newcastle upon Tyne: Directorate of Health and Social Care Public Health Group North East, for the Department of Health.

Gill, R., Henwood, K. and McLean, C. (2005) 'Body projects and the regulation of normative masculinity', *Body and Society*, 11 (1): 37–62.

Gillis, S. (2004) 'Cybersex', in P. C. Gibson (ed.) *More Dirty Looks: Gender, Pornography and Power*, London: British Film Institute.

Goodson, P., McCormick, D. and Evans, A. (2001) 'Searching for sexually explicit materials on the internet', *Archives of Sexual Behavior*, 30 (2): 101–18.

Gossett, J. L. and Byrne, S. (2002) ' "Click here": a content analysis of internet rape sites', *Gender and Society*, 16: 689–709.

Government Equalities Office (2008) *Women's Changing Lives: Priorities for the Ministers for Women: One-year-on Progress Report*, London: Stationery Office. Online. Available HTTP: <http://www.equalities.gov.uk/pdf/Womenschanginglivesjuly08.pdf> (accessed 16 December 2009).

Graham, L. (2007) 'Post-positions on the politics of pornography: internet discussion of the seminar', in C. McGlynn, E. Rackley and N. Westmarland (eds) *Positions on the Politics of Porn: A Debate on Government Plans to Criminalise the Possession of Extreme Pornography*, Durham: University of Durham.

Green, R. (2001) ' "Serious" sadomasochism: a protected right of privacy?', *Archives of Sexual Behavior*, 30 (5): 543–50.

Grossman, D. (1996) *On Killing: The Psychological Cost of Learning to Kill*, Boston, MA: Little Brown.

Grunder, T. M. (2000) *The Skinner Box Effect: Sexual Addiction and Online Pornography*, Lincoln, NE: Writers Club Press.

Gumbel, A. (1999) 'Pornography is a feminist issue', *The Independent*, 1 October: 10.

Haggstrom-Nordin, E., Hanson, U. and Tyden, T. (2005) 'Associations between pornography consumption and sexual practices among adolescents in Sweden', *International Journal of STD and AIDS*, 16: 102–7.

Hald, G. (2006) 'Gender differences in pornography consumption among young heterosexual Danish adults', *Archives of Sexual Behavior*, 35 (5): 577–85.

Hald, G. and Malamuth, N. (2008) 'Self-perceived effects of pornography consumption', *Archives of Sexual Behavior*, 37 (4): 614–25.

Hald, G. M., Malamuth, N. M. and Yuen, C. (2009) 'Pornography and attitudes supporting violence against women: Revisiting the relationship in nonexperimental studies', *Aggressive Behavior*, 35 (29 September): doi: 10.1002/ab.20328 (advance access). Online. Available HTTP: <http://www3.interscience.wiley.com/journal/122665126/abstract?CRETRY=1&SRETRY=0> (accessed 30 November 2009).

Hall, A. C. and Bishop, M. J. (2007) *Pop Porn: Pornography in American Culture*, Westport, CT: Praeger.

Harding, S. (1981) 'What is the real material base of patriarchy and capital?' in L. Sargent (ed.) *Women in Revolution: A Discussion of the Unhappy Marriage of Marxism and Feminism*, Boston, MA: South End Press.

Hardy, S. (1998) *The Reader, the Author, his Woman and her Lover: Soft-core Pornography and Heterosexual Men*, London: Cassell.

——(2009) 'The new pornographies: representation or reality?' in F. Attwood (ed.) *Mainstreaming Sex: The Sexualization of Western Culture.*, London: I. B. Tauris.

Hartmann, H. I. (1979) 'The unhappy marriage of Marxism and feminism: towards a more progressive union', in V. D. Lippit (ed.) (1996) *Radical Political Economy: Explorations in Alternative Economic Analysis*, New York: Sharpe.

Hearn, J. (1998) *The Violences of Men*, London: Sage.

Hennessy, R. (2000) *Profit and Pleasure: Sexual Identities in Late Capitalism*, New York: Routledge.

Hentai, W. (2001) 'A kinder, gentler Max?', *Adult Video News*, May. Online. Available HTTP: <http://www.adultvideonews.com/bone/by0501_08.html> (accessed 20 April 2006).

Heron, D. and Shapira, N. (2003) 'Time to log off', *Current Psychiatry Online*, 2 (4). Online. Available HTTP: <http://www.currentpsychiatry.com/2003_040403_internet.asp.> (accessed 7 October 2003).

Hillier, L., Kurdas, C. and Horsley, P. (2001) *'It's Just Easier'*, Melbourne: Australian Research Centre in Sex, Health and Society, Latrobe University.

Hippensteele, S. K. (1997) 'Activist research and social narratives: dialectics of power, privilege, and institutional change', in M. D. Schwartz (ed.) *Researching Sexual Violence against Women: Methodological and Personal Perspectives*, Thousand Oaks, CA: Sage.

HM Government (2009) *Together We Can End Violence against Women and Girls: A Strategy*, London: HM Government.

Holmer, W. (2008) 'Human trafficking mansion is not just about sex: "I came here to roleplay a rape, and all the guys just want to hold my hand! Do I have to beg?" ', *Alphaville Herald*, 27 March. Online. Available HTTP: < http://foo.secondlifeherald.com/slh/2008/03/a-more-convinci.html> (accessed 12 November 2009).

Home Office (2005) *Consultation: On the Possession of Extreme Pornographic Material*, London: Home Office.

Home Office (2006a) *Consultation on the Possession of Extreme Pornographic Material: Summary of Responses and Next Steps*, London: Home Office.

Home Office (2006b) 'Cracking Down on Violent Pornography', press release, 30 August. Online. Available HTTP: <http://www.homeoffice.gov.uk/about-us/news/violent-porn-outlawed> (accessed 16 December 2009).

Huff, J. K. (1997) 'The sexual harassment of researchers by research subjects: lessons from the field', in M. D. Schwartz (ed.) *Researching Sexual Violence against Women: Methodological and Personal Perspectives*, Thousand Oaks, CA: Sage.

Huffstutter, P. J. (2003) 'Porn crackdown puts chill in *Boogie Nights* land', *Oakland Tribune*, 8 August.

Hume, M. (2007) 'Unpicking the threads: emotion as central to the theory and practice of researching violence', *Women's Studies International Forum*, 30 (2): 147–57.

Hunt, Lord (2008a) Hansard, HL Vol. 699, col. 893 (3 March).

——(2008b) Hansard, HL Vol. 699, col. 894 (3 March).

Huston, A., Wartella, E. and Donnerstein, E. (1998) *Measuring the Effects of Sexual Content in the Media*, Menlo Park, CA: Henry J. Kaiser Family Foundation.

Huston, D. (2008) Review, '*Fuck Slaves 3*', X Critic. Online. Available HTTP: <http://www.xcritic.com/review/32365/cindy-crawford-ii-fuck-slaves-3/> (accessed 17 August 2009).

Itzin, C. (ed.) (1992) *Pornography: Women, Violence and Civil Liberties*, Oxford: Oxford University Press.

Itzin, C., Taket, A. and Kelly, L. (2007) *The Evidence of Harm to Adults relating to Exposure to Extreme Pornographic Material: A Rapid Evidence Assessment*, London: Ministry of Justice Research Series 11/07. Online. Available HTTP: <http://www.justice.gov.uk/docs/280907.pdf> (accessed 16 December 2009).

Jablonski, J. (2001) 'Porn Studies latest academic fad', *Accuracy in Academia*, October. Online. Available HTTP: <http://www.academia.org/campusreport_2001.html> (accessed 31 August 2009).

Jackson, P., Brooks, K. and Stevenson, N. (1999) 'Making sense of men's lifestyle magazines', *Environment and Planning D: Society and Space*, 17: 353–68.

Jameson, J. and Strauss, N. (2004) *How to Make Love like a Porn Star: A Cautionary Tale*, New York: HarperCollins.

Janghorbani, M., Lam, T. and Youth Sexuality Study Task Force (2003) 'Sexual media use by young adults in Hong Kong', *Archives of Sexual Behavior*, 32 (6): 545–53.

Jarrard, D. (1998) 'The Porn Profs' plans for your kids', *The Morality in Media Newsletter*, November/December. Online. Available HTTP: <http://www.moralityinmedia.org/index.htm?obscenityEnforcement/pornprof.htm> (accessed 30 October 2009).

Jeffreys, S. (1990) 'Sexology and anti-feminism', in D.Leidholdt and J. G. Raymond (eds) *The Sexual Liberals and the Attack on Feminism*, New York: Pergamon.

——(2009a) 'Pornography in the Global Sex Industry', paper presented at Porn Cultures conference, Leeds, June.

——(2009b) *The Industrial Vagina: The Political Economy of the Global Sex Trade*, New York: Routledge.

Jenkins, H. (2004) 'Foreword. So you want to teach pornography', in P. C. Gibson (ed.) *More Dirty Looks: Gender, Pornography and Power*, second edition, London: British Film Institute.

Jensen, R. (1998a) 'Introduction. Pornographic dodges and distortions', in G. Dines, R. Jensen and A. Russo (eds) *Pornography: The Production and Consumption of Inequality*, New York: Routledge.

——(1998b) 'Using pornography', in G. Dines, R. Jensen and A. Russo (eds) *Pornography: The Production and Consumption of Inequality*, New York: Routledge.

——(2002) 'You are what you eat: the pervasive porn industry and what it says about you and your desires', *Clamor*, September/October: 54–9.

——(2004) 'A cruel edge: the painful truth about today's pornography – and what men can do about it', *MS*, spring: 54–8.

——(2007a) *Getting off: Pornography and the End of Masculinity*, Cambridge, MA: South End Press.

——(2007b) 'The problem with solutions', CommonDreams.org, 2 January. Online. Available HTTP: <http://www.commondreams.org/views06/0102–52. htm> (accessed 13 November 2009).

Jensen R. and Dines G. (1998) 'The content of mass-marketed pornography', in G. Dines, R. Jensen and A. Russo (eds) *Pornography: The Production and Consumption of Inequality*, New York: Routledge.

Johansson, T. and Hammarén, N. (2007) 'Hegemonic masculinity and pornography', *Journal of Men's Studies*, 15: 57–70.

Joint Committee on Human Rights (2008) *Fifth Report*. Online. Available HTTP: <http://www.publications.parliament.uk/pa/jt200708/jtselect/jtrights/37/3704. htm> (accessed 16 December 2009).

Jones, M. and Carlin, G. (2004a) 'Call this English Lit.?', *The Guardian*, 4 February, *G2*: 6.

——(2004b) 'Porn to study', *Times Online*, 17 February. Online. Available HTTP: <http://www.timesonline.co.uk/tol/comment/talking_point/article1022480.ece> (accessed 30 October 2009).

——(forthcoming) 'Pornogogy: teaching the titillating', in C. Hines and D. Kerr (eds) *Hard to Swallow: Hard-core Pornography on Screen*, London: Wallflower Press.

Jones, S. and Mowlabocus, S. (2009) 'Hard times and rough rides: the legal and ethical impossibilities of researching "shock" pornographies', *Sexualities*, 12 (5): 613–28.

Juffer, J. (1998) *At Home with Pornography*, New York: New York University Press.

Kaestle, C., Halpern, C. and Brown, J. (2007) 'Music videos, pro wrestling, and acceptance of date rape among middle school males and females', *Journal of Adolescent Health*, 40: 185–7.

Kalof, L. (1999) 'The effects of gender and music video imagery on sexual attitudes', *Journal of Social Psychology*, 139: 378–85.

Kane, K. (1996) 'Teaching the body course', *Jump Cut*, 40 (March): 123–6.

Kappeler, S. (1986) *The Pornography of Representation*, Cambridge: Polity Press.

Katz, N. (2005) '*Spent:* review', *Adult Video News,* January. Online. Available HTTP: <http://www.adultvideonews.com/editch/edch0105_13.html> (accessed 18 August 2006).

Kelly, L. (1996) 'Weasel words: paedophiles and the cycle of abuse', *Trouble and Strife* 33: 44–9.

Kernes, M. (2005) '*Neo-pornographica:* review', *Adult Video News*, May. Online. Available HTTP: <http://www.adultvideonews.com/editch/edch0505_05.html> (accessed 17 August 2006).

Kimmel, M. S. (1990) 'Introduction. Guilty pleasures', in M. Kimmel (ed.) *Men Confront Pornography*, New York: Crown.
——(1994) 'Masculinity as homophobia: fear, shame, and silence in the construction of gender identity', in H. Brod and M. Kauffman (eds) *Theorizing Masculinities*, Thousand Oaks, CA: Sage.
——(2005) 'Pornography and male sexuality', in M, Kimmel (ed.) *The Gender of Desire*, New York: State University of New York Press.
——(2008) *Guyland: The Perilous World where Boys become Men*, New York: HarperCollins.
Kingi, V., Poppelwell, E. and Paulin, J. (2004) '*I know I'm not a dirty old man': The Viewing Habits of Users of Sexually Explicit Movies*, report prepared for the New Zealand Office for Film and Literature Classification. Wellington, NZ: Crime and Justice Research Centre, Victoria University of Wellington.
Kipnis, L. (1996) *Bound and Gagged: Pornography and the Politics of Fantasy in America*, New York: Grove Press.
Kirkham, P. and Skeggs, B. (1996) 'Pornographies, pleasures, and pedagogies in UK and US', *Jump Cut*, 40 (March): 106–13.
Kitzinger, J. (1999) 'The ultimate neighbour from hell? Stranger danger and the media representation of "paedophilia" ', in B. Franklin (ed.) *Social Policy, the Media and Misrepresentation*, London: Routledge.
Klein, M. (2006) 'Pornography: what men see when they watch', in P. Lehman (ed.) *Pornography: Film and Culture*, New Brunswick, NJ: Rutgers University Press.
Kleinhans, C. (1996) 'Teaching sexual images: some pragmatics', *Jump Cut*, 40 (March): 119–22.
Koukounas, E. and Over, R. (2001) 'Habituation of male sexual arousal: effects of attentional focus', *Biological Psychology*, 58: 49–64.
Kravets, D. (2009) 'Linden lab targeted in Second Life sex-code lawsuit', *Wired*, 17 September. Online. Available HTTP: <http://www.wired.com/threatlevel/2009/09/linden/> (accessed 30 October 2009).
Kuhn, A. (1985/1994) *The Power of the Image: Essays on Representation and Sexuality*, London: Routledge.
Langman, L. (2004) 'Grotesque degradation: globalization, carnivalization, and cyberporn', in D. D. Waskul (ed.) *Net.seXXX: Readings of Sex, Pornography, and the Internet*, New York: Peter Lang.
Lanis, K. and Covell, K. (1995) 'Images of women in advertisements', *Sex Roles*, 32: 639–49.
Lassiter, G. D. and Irvine, A. A. (1986) 'Videotaped confessions: the impact of camera point of view on judgements of coercion', *Journal of Applied Social Psychology*, 16: 268–76.
Leatherman, C. (1996) 'Court finds college violated First Amendment', *Chronicle of Higher Education*, 6 September: A16.
——(1999) 'Conflict over a divisive scholar combines issues of art, sexuality, and teaching style', *Chronicle of Higher Education*, 13 August: A14–16.
Lees, J. (2006) 'Virtual prostitutes make real cash'. Online. Available: HTTP: <http://www.joystiq.com/2006/04/10/virtual-prostitutes-make-real-cash/> (accessed 8 September 2009).
Lehman, P. (2006a) 'A dirty little secret: why teach and study pornography?', in P. Lehman (ed.) *Pornography: Film and Culture*, New Brunswick, NJ, and London: Rutgers University Press.

——(ed.) (2006b) *Pornography: Film and Culture*, New Brunswick, NJ: Rutgers University Press.

Lenhart, A., Rainie, R. and Lewis, O. (2001) *Teenage Life Online*, Washington, DC: Pew Internet and American Life Project.

Leominster, S. (2008) 'Second Life news: Second Life company wins legal case against illegal copying', *SLEntrepreneur Magazine*, 19 March. Online. Available HTTP: <http://www.slentre.com/second-life-news-second-life-company-wins-legal-case-against-illegal-copying/> (accessed 8 September 2009).

Leventhal, A. M., Martin, R. L., Seals, R. W., Tapia, E. and Rehm, L. P. (2007) 'Investigating the dynamics of affect: psychological mechanisms of affective habituation to pleasurable stimuli', *Motivation and Emotion*, 31: 145–57.

Levy, A. (2006) *Female Chauvinist Pigs: Women and the Rise of Raunch Culture*, London: Pocket Books.

Liberty (2008) *Liberty's Second Reading Briefing on the Criminal Justice and Immigration Bill in the House of Lords*, January. Online. Available HTTP: <http://www.liberty-human-rights.org.uk/publications/pdfs/criminal-justice-and-immigration-bill-2nd-reading-lords.pdf> (accessed 16 December 2009).

Lifton, R. J. (1986) *The Nazi Doctors: Medical Killing and the Psychology of Genocide*, New York: Basic Books.

Lillie, J. (2002) 'Sexuality and cyberporn: towards a new agenda for research', *Sexuality and Culture*, 6 (2): 25–47.

Linden, D. (2007) 'Keeping Second Life safe, together', 1 June. Online. Available HTTP: <http://blogs.secondlife.com/community/features/blog/2007/06/01/keeping-second-life-safe-together> (accessed 7 July 2009).

Linden, T. (2009) 'The Second Life economy: first quarter 2009 in detail', 16 April. Online. Available HTTP: <https://blogs.secondlife.com/community/features/blog/2009/04/16/the-second-life-economy–first-quarter-2009-in-detail> (accessed 7 July 2009).

Lindgren, J. (1993) 'Defining pornography', *University of Pennsylvania Law Review*, 141 (4): 1153–275.

Lo, V. and Wei, R. (2002) 'Third-person effect, gender, and pornography on the internet', *Journal of Broadcasting and Electronic Media*, 46: 13–33.

——(2005) 'Exposure to internet pornography and Taiwanese adolescents' sexual attitudes and behavior', *Journal of Broadcasting and Electronic Media*, 49: 221–37.

Lo, V., Neilan, E., Sun, M. and Chiang, S. (1999) 'Exposure of Taiwanese adolescents to pornographic media and its impact on sexual attitudes and behavior', *Asian Journal of Communication*, 9: 50–71.

Loftus, D. (2002) *Watching Sex: How Men Really Respond to Pornography*, New York: Thunder's Mouth Press.

Long, J. (2009) 'Voices of Resistance: the Re-emergence of Feminist Anti-porn Activism', paper presented at Porn Cultures conference, Leeds, June.

Lord, M. G. (1997) 'Pornutopia: how feminist scholars learned to love dirty pictures', *Lingua Franca*, 7 (4): 40–8.

Luff, D. (2001) ' "The downright torture of women": moral lobby women, feminists and pornography', *Sociological Review*, 49 (1): 78–99.

Lynn, R. (2007) 'Stroker Serpentine, Second Life's porn mogul, speaks', *Wired*, 30 March. Online. Available HTTP: <http://www.wired.com/culture/lifestyle/commentary/sexdrive/2007/03/sex_drive0330> (accessed 7 July 2009).

McClintock, A. (1992) 'Gonad the Barbarian and the Venus Flytrap: portraying the female and male orgasm', in L. Segal and M. McIntosh (eds) *Sex Exposed: Sexuality and the Pornography Debate*, London: Virago.

McColgan, A. (2000) *Women under the Law: The False Promise of Human Rights*, Harlow: Longman.

Macdonald, A. [pseud. of W. L. Pierce] (1978) *The Turner Diaries*, Washington, DC: National Alliance.

MacDonald, S. (1990) 'Confessions of a feminist porn watcher', in M. Kimmel (ed.) *Men Confront Pornography*, New York: Crown.

McElroy, W. (1995) *XXX: A Woman's Right to Pornography*, New York: St Martin's Press.

McGlynn, C. (2009) 'Regulating Extreme Pornography in the UK: the Turn to Law', paper presented at Porn Cultures conference, Leeds, June 2009.

McGlynn, C. and Rackley, E. (2007) 'Striking a balance: arguments for the criminal regulation of extreme pornography', *Criminal Law Review*: 677–90.

McGlynn, C. and Rackley, E. (2009) 'Criminalising extreme pornography: a lost opportunity', *Criminal Law Review*: 245–60.

McGlynn, C. and Ward, I. (2009) 'Pornography, pragmatism and proscription', *Journal of Law and Society* 36 (3): 327–51.

McKee, A. (2004) 'The aesthetics of pornography: the insights of consumers', *Continuum: Journal of Media and Cultural Studies*, 20 (4): 523–39.

——(2005a) 'The need to bring the voices of pornography consumers into public debates about the genre and its effects,' *Australian Journal of Communication Studies*, 32 (2): 71–94.

——(2005b) 'The objectification of women in mainstream pornographic videos in Australia', *Journal of Sex Research*, 42 (4): 277–90.

——(2007a) 'The relationship between attitudes towards women, consumption of pornography, and other demographic variables in a survey of 1,023 consumers of pornography', *International Journal of Sexual Health*, 19: 31–45.

——(2007b) ' "Saying you've been at dad's porn book is part of growing up" ', *Metro* magazine, 155: 118–22.

McKee, A., Albury, K. and Lumby, C. (2008) *The Porn Report*, Melbourne: Melbourne University Press.

MacKinnon, C. (1987) *Feminism Unmodified: Discourses on Life and Law*, Cambridge, MA: Harvard University Press.

——(1993) *Only Words*, Cambridge, MA: Harvard University Press.

——(2005) 'Underrated', *Times Higher Education Supplement*, 20 May: 18–19.

MacKinnon, C. A. and Dworkin, A. (eds) (1997) *In Harm's Way: The Pornography Civil Rights Hearings*, Cambridge, MA and London: Harvard University Press.

McNair, B. (1996) *Mediated Sex: Pornography and Postmodern Culture*, London: Hodder Arnold.

——(2002) *Striptease Culture: Sex, Media and the Democratization of Desire*, London: Routledge.

——(2009) 'Teaching porn', *Sexualities*, 12 (5): 558–67.

McRobbie, A. (2009) *The Aftermath of Feminism*, London: Sage.

Maddison, S. (2009) ' "Choke on it, bitch!": porn studies, extreme gonzo and the mainstreaming of hardcore', in F. Attwood (ed.) *Mainstreaming Sex: The Sexualization of Western Culture*, London: I. B. Tauris.

Malamuth, N. and Ceniti, J. (1986) 'Repeated exposure to violent and nonviolent pornography: likelihood of raping ratings and laboratory aggression against women', *Aggressive Behavior*, 12 (1): 129–37.

Malamuth, N. and Donnerstein, E. (eds) (1984) *Pornography and Sexual Aggression*, Orlando, FL: Academic Press.

Malamuth, N. and Impett, E. (2001) 'Research on sex in the media', in D. Singer and J. Singer (eds) *Handbook of Children and the Media*, Thousand Oaks, CA: Sage.

Malamuth, N.M. and Spinner, B. (1980) 'A longitudinal content analysis of sexual violence in the best-selling erotic magazines', *Journal of Sex Research*, 16: 226–37.

Malamuth, N., Addison, T. and Koss, M. (2000) 'Pornography and sexual aggression', *Annual Review of Sex Research*, 11: 26–91.

Maltz, L. and W. Maltz. (2008) *The Porn Trap: The Essential Guide to Overcoming Problems caused by Pornography*, New York: HarperCollins.

Manganello, J., Franzini, A. and Jordan, A. (2008) 'Sampling television programs for content analysis of sex on TV: how many episodes are enough?', *Journal of Sex Research*, 45: 9–16.

Manning, J. (2006) 'The impact of internet pornography on marriage and the family', *Sexual Addiction and Compulsivity: Journal of Treatment and Prevention*, 13: 131–65.

Marks, I. and Dar, R. (2000) 'Fear reduction by psychotherapies: recent findings, future directions', *British Journal of Psychiatry*, 176: 507–11.

Matacin, M. L. and Burger, J. M. (1987) 'A content analysis of sexual themes in *Playboy* cartoons', *Sex Roles*, 17: 179–86.

Mattley, C. (1997) 'Field research with phone sex workers: managing the researcher's emotions', in M. D. Schwartz (ed.) *Researching Sexual Violence against Women: Methodological and Personal Perspectives*, Thousand Oaks, CA: Sage.

Measor, L. (2004) 'Young people's views of sex education', *Sex Education*, 4 (2): 153–66.

Mehta, M. D. and Plaza, D. (1997) 'Content analysis of pornographic images available on the internet', *Information Society*, 13: 153–61.

Messner, M. A. (1992) *Power at Play: Sports and the Problem of Masculinity*, Boston, MA: Beacon Press.

Milburn, M., Mather, R. and Conrad, S. (2000) 'The effects of viewing R-rated movie scenes that objectify women on perceptions of date rape', *Sex Roles*, 43: 645–64.

Mill, J. S. (1985) *On Liberty*, London: Penguin.

Miller, Baroness (2008a) Hansard, HL, Vol. 699, col. 896 (3 March).

——(2008b) Hansard HL, Vol. 699, col. 897 (3 March).

Miller, W. I. (1997) *The Anatomy of Disgust*, Cambridge, MA: Harvard University Press.

Millet, K. (1971) *Sexual Politics*, London: Abacus.

Ministry of Justice (2007) *Criminal Justice and Immigration Bill Regulatory Impact Assessment*, London: Ministry of Justice.

Miriam, K. (2005) 'Stopping the traffic in women: power, agency and abolition in feminist debates over sex-trafficking', *Journal of Social Philosophy*, 36 (1): 1–17.

Modine, A. (2009) 'Second Life slapped with counterfeit sextoy suit', *The Register*, 16 September. Online. Available HTTP: <http://www.theregister.co.uk/2009/09/16/secondlife_alderman_class_action_lawsuit/> (accessed 30 October 2009).

Monk-Turner, E. and Purcell, H. C. (1999) 'Sexual violence in pornography: how prevalent is it?', *Gender Issues,* 17 (2): 58–67.

Mooney, A. (2008) 'Boys will be boys: men's magazines and the normalisation of pornography', *Feminist Media Studies,* 8 (3): 247–65.

Moore, L. J. (2007) *Sperm Counts: Overcome by Man's Most Precious Fluid,* New York: New York University Press.

Morrison, H. (2008) 'Violent porn ban gets the green light', *BBC Newsbeat,* 8 May. Online. Available HTTP: <http://news.bbc.co.uk/newsbeat/hi/newsbeat/newsid_7390000/7390930.stm> (accessed 30 October 2009).

Morrison, Jack (2004) 'The distracted porn consumer: you never knew your online customers so well,' *Adult Video News Media Network.* Online. Available at HTTP: <http://business.avn.com/articles/printable/16315.html> (accessed 6 November 2009).

Morrison, Todd G. (ed.) (2004) *Eclectic Views on Gay Male Pornography: Pornucopia,* Binghamton, NY: Haworth Press.

Morrison, T. G., Ellis, S. R., Morrison, M. A., Bearden, A. and Harriman, R. L. (2006) 'Exposure to sexually explicit material and variations in body esteem, genital attitudes, and sexual esteem among a sample of Canadian men', *Journal of Men's Studies,* 14: 209–23.

Morrison, T. G., Harriman, R., Morrison, M. A., Bearden, A. and Ellis, S. R. (2004) 'Correlates of exposure to sexually explicit material among Canadian post-secondary students', *Canadian Journal of Human Sexuality,* 13: 143–56.

National Television Violence Study (1998) *National Television Violence Study: Executive Summary.* Santa Barbara, CA: Center for Communication and Social Policy, University of Santa Barbara.

Nelson X (2008) '*Fuck Slaves 3:* review', *Adult Video News,* 1 August. Online. Available HTTP: <http://www.avn.com/movies/70050.html> (accessed 19 July 2009).

Niven, D., Lichter, S. R. and Amundson, D. (2003) 'The political content of late night comedy', *Harvard International Journal of Press/Politics,* 8: 118–33.

Nock, S. (1998) *Marriage in Men's Lives,* Oxford: Oxford University Press.

Nosko, A., Wood, E. and Desmarais, S. (2007) 'Unsolicited online sexual material', *Canadian Journal of Human Sexuality,* 16: 1–10.

Nussbaum, M. (2004) *Hiding from Humanity: Disgust, Shame and the Law,* Princeton, NJ: Princeton University Press.

O'Neil, R. M. (1996) 'Protecting free speech when the issue is sexual harassment', *Chronicle of Higher Education,* 13 September: B3–4.

Orford, A. (1994) 'Liberty, equality and pornography: the bodies of women and human rights discourse', *Australian Feminist Law Journal,* 3: 72–102.

O'Toole, L. (1998) *Pornocopia: Porn, Sex, Technology and Desire,* London: Serpent's Tail.

Paasonen, S. (2006) 'Email from Nancy Nutsucker: representation and gendered address in online pornography', *European Journal of Cultural Studies,* 9 (4): 403–20.

——(2007a) 'Strange bedfellows: pornography, affect and feminist reading', *Feminist Theory,* 8 (1): 43–57.

——(2007b) 'Viidakkokuume polttaa: internet-porno ja rodun spektaakkeli', in L-M. Rossi and A. Seppä (eds) *Tarkemmin katsoen. Visuaalisen kulttuurin lukukirja,* Helsinki: Gaudeamus.

——(2010) 'Disturbing, fleshy images: close reading and close looking at pornography', in M. Liljeström and S. Paasonen (eds) *Working with Affect in Feminist Readings: Disturbing Differences*, London: Routledge.

——(forthcoming a) 'Online pornography: ubiquitous and effaced', in M. Consalvo and C. Ess (eds) *The Handbook of Internet Studies*, Oxford: Wiley-Blackwell.

Paasonen, S., Nikunen, K. and Saarenmaa, L. (2007a) 'Pornification and the education of desire', in S. Paasonen, K. Nikunen and L. Saarenmaa (eds) *Pornification: Sex and Sexuality in Media Culture*, Oxford: Berg.

Paasonen, S., Nikunen, K. and Saarenmaa, L. (eds) (2007b) *Pornification: Sex and Sexuality in Media Culture*, Oxford: Berg.

Palmer, C. E. (1979) 'Pornographic comics: A content analysis', *Journal of Sex Research*, 15: 285–98.

Palmer, S. (1996) 'Critical perspectives on women's rights: the European Convention on Human Rights and Fundamental Freedoms' in A. Bottomley (ed.) *Feminist Perspectives on the Foundational Subjects of Law*, London: Cavendish Press.

Palys, T. S. (1986) 'Testing the common wisdom: the social content of video pornography', *Canadian Psychology*, 27: 22–35.

Parvez, Z. F. (2006) 'The labor of pleasure: how perceptions of emotional labor impact women's enjoyment of pornography', *Gender and Society*, 20 (5): 605–31.

Pascoe, C. J. (2007) *Dude, You're a Fag: Masculinity and Sexuality in High School*, Berkeley and Los Angeles: University of California Press.

Patterson, Z. (2004) 'Going on-line: consuming pornography in the digital era', in L. Williams (ed.) *Porn Studies*, Durham, NC: Duke University Press.

Patton, C. (1988) 'The cum shot: three takes on lesbian and gay sexuality', *Outlook*, 1: 72–7.

——(1991) 'Visualizing safe sex: when pedagogy and pornography collide,' in D. Fuss (ed.) *Inside/out: Lesbian Theories, Gay Theories*, New York: Routledge.

Paul, P. (2005) *Pornified: How Pornography is Transforming our Lives, our Relationships, and our Families*, New York: Times Books.

Petley, J. (2007) 'To the censors we're all Aboriginals now', *Spiked*, 2 July. Online. Available HTTP: < http://www.spiked-online.com/index.php?/site/article/3556> (accessed 16 December 2009).

——(2008a) 'Legislating in haste', *Index on Censorship*, 11 March. Online. Available HTTP: <http://www.indexoncensorship.org/2008/03/11/legislating-in-haste/> (accessed 16 December 2009).

——(2008b) 'Britain: matters of decency', *Index on Censorship*, 18 January. Available HTTP: <http://www.indexoncensorship.org/2008/01/18/britain-matters-of-decency/> (accessed 16 December 2009).

Pollack, W. S. and Pipher, M. (1999) *Real Boys: Rescuing our Sons from the Myths of Boyhood*, New York: Owl Books.

Pook, S. (2005) ' "The internet normalised Graham Coutts's peverse [sic] impulses. That is the danger" ', *The Telegraph*, 15 August. Online. Available HTTP: <http://www.telegraph.co.uk/news/uknews/1496224/The-internet-normalised-Graham-Couttss-peverse-impulses.-That-is-the-danger.html> (accessed 16 December 2009).

Poole, O. (2002) 'Orgy puts stop to degree courses in sex', *Daily Telegraph*, 20 February: 14.

Potts, A. (2000) ' "The essence of the hard-on": hegemonic masculinity and the cultural construction of "erectile dysfunction" ', *Men and Masculinities*, 3 (1): 85–103.

Poynor, R. (2006) *Designing Pornotopia: Travels in Visual Culture*, New York: Princeton Architectural Press.

Primack, B. A., Gold, M. A., Schwarz, E. B. and Dalton, M. A. (2008) 'Degrading and non-degrading sex in popular music: a content analysis', *Public Health Reports*, 123: 593–600.

Prince, S. (1990) 'Power and pain: content analysis and the ideology of pornography', *Journal of Film and Video*, 42: 31–41.

R v. Coutts (2006) UKHL 39.

Ramone, M. (2005a) '*Service Animals 18:* review', *Adult Video News*, January. Online. Available HTTP: <http://www.adultvideonews.com/editch/edch0105_11.html> (accessed 27 August 2006).

——(2005b) '*Service Animals 20:* review', *Adult Video News*, October. Online. Available HTTP: <http://www.adultvideonews.com/editch/edch1005_07.html> (accessed 27 August 2006).

——(2005c) '*Tales from the Crack:* review', *Adult Video News*, January. Online. Available HTTP: <http://www.adultvideonews.com/editch/edch0105_14.html> (accessed 27 August 2006).

——(2005d) '*Butt Blassted!*' review', *Adult Video News*, December. Online. Available HTTP: <http://www,adultvideonews.com/editch/edch01205_01.html> (accessed 22 August 2006).

——(2005e) '*Mouth 2 Mouth:* review', *Adult Video News*, December. Online. Available HTTP: <http://www.adultvideonews.com/editch/edch0305_04.html> (accessed 22 August 2006).

Ramone, M. and Kernes, M. (2003) '*AVN* directors roundtable: old school/new school smackdown', *Adult Video News*, January. Online. Available HTTP: <http://www.adultvideonews.com/cover/cover0103_01.html> (accessed 22 August 2006).

Rea, A. (2004) 'University row over soft porn film study', *Express and Star*, 26 January: 5.

Reading, A. (2005) 'Professing porn or obscene browsing? On proper distance in the university classroom', *Media, Culture and Society*, 27 (1): 123–30.

Reisman, J. (2003) 'Are campus pornography courses sexual abuse?', *Human Events*, 1 June. Online. Available HTTP: <http://www.humanevents.com/article.php?id=754> (accessed 30 October 2009).

Reist, M. T. (ed.) (2009) *Getting Real: Challenging the Sexualisation of Girls*, Melbourne: Spinifex.

Rich, E. (1999) 'Learning stripped bare for some students, Wesleyan a pornographic experience', *Hartford Courant*, 8 May: A1.

Richardson, D. (1996) 'Heterosexuality and social theory', in D. Richardson (ed.) *Theorising Heterosexuality: Telling it Straight*, Buckingham: Open University Press.

Richters, J., Grulich, A. E., de Visser, R. O., Smith, A. M. A. and Rissel, C. E. (2003) 'Autoerotic, esoteric and other sexual practices engaged in by a representative sample of adults', *Australian and New Zealand Journal of Public Health*, 27: 180–90.

Roberts, S. (2007) '51 percent of women are now living without a spouse', *New York Times*, 16 January. Online. Available HTTP: <http://www.nytimes.com/2007/01/16/us/16census.html?pagewanted=print> (accessed 17 November 2009).

Robinson, J. and Brook, S. (2009) 'Censors revolt at plan to make them watch porn alone', *The Guardian*, 23 February: 7.

Rogala, C. and Tyden, T. (2003) 'Does pornography influence young women's sexual behavior?', *Women's Health Issues*, 13: 39–43.

Ross, A. (1989) *No Respect: Intellectuals & Popular Culture*, New York: Routledge.

Ross, L. (2007) *Money Shot: Wild Days and Lonely Nights Inside the Black Porn Industry*, Philadelphia: Thunder Mouth Press.

Ruberg, B. (2007) 'Peeking up the skirt of online sex work: Topless and proud, Second Life escorts sidestep gender discrimination', *The Village Voice*, 28 September. Online. Available HTTP: < http://www.villagevoice.com/2007-08-28/columns/peeking-up-the-skirt-of-online-sex-work/> (accessed 30 October 2009).

Rubin, G. (1993) 'Misguided, dangerous and wrong: an analysis of anti-pornography politics', in A. Assiter and A. Carol (eds) *Bad Girls and Dirty Pictures: The Challenge to Reclaim Feminism*, London: Pluto Press.

Russell, D. (ed.) (1993) *Making Violence Sexy: Feminist Views on Pornography*, New York: Teachers College Press.

——(1998). *Dangerous Relationships: Pornography, Misogyny and Rape*, Thousand Oaks, CA: Sage.

Rutter, J. (2005a) '*Secrets of the Karma Sutra:* review', *Adult Video News*, July. Online. Available HTTP: <http://www.adultvideonews.com/editch/edch0705_02.html> (accessed 27 August 2006).

——(2005b) '*Ass Quake:* review', *Adult Video News*, January. Online. Available HTTP: <http://www.adultvideonews.com/editch/edch0105_04.html> (accessed 27 August 2006).

——(2005c) '*Service Animals 21:* review', *Adult Video News*, December. Online. Available HTTP: <http://www.adultvideonews.com/editch/edch1205_08.html> (accessed 27 August 2006).

——(2005d) '*Who Fucked Rocco:* review', *Adult Video News*, December. Online. Available HTTP: <http://www.adultvideonews.com/editch/edch1205_09.html> (accessed 27 August 2006).

Rymaszewski, M., Au, W. J., Wallace, M., Winters, C., Ondreika, C., Batstone-Cunningham, B. and Rosedale, P. (2008) *Second Life: The Official Guide*, Indianapolis, IN: Wiley.

Sabina, C., Wolak, J. and Finkelhor, D. (2008) 'The nature and dynamics of internet pornography exposure for youth', *CyberPsychology and Behavior*, 11: 691–3.

Sarler, C. (2006) 'Please get interfering government ministers out of our bedrooms', *The Observer*, 3 September. Online. Available HTTP: < http://www.guardian.co.uk/commentisfree/2006/sep/03/comment.politics> (accessed 16 December 2009).

Sarracino, C. and Scott, K. M. (2008) *The Porning of America: The Rise of Porn Culture, What it Means, and Where we go from Here*, Boston, MA: Beacon Press.

Schneider, J. P. and Irons, R. (1996) 'Differential diagnosis of addictive sexual disorders using the DSM-IV', *Sexual Addiction and Compulsivity*, 3: 7–21.

Schneider, J. and Weiss, R. (2001) *Cybersex Exposed*, Hazelden, MN: Hazelden Information Education.

Schooler, D. and Ward, L. M. (2006) 'Average Joes', *Psychology of Men and Masculinity*, 7: 27–41.

Schunk, D. H. (1987) 'Peer models and children's behavioral change', *Review of Educational Research*, 57: 149–74.

Scott, J. E. and Cuvelier, S. J. (1987) 'Sexual violence in *Playboy* magazine: a longitudinal content analysis', *Journal of Sex Research*, 56: 534–9.

Scott, J. E. and Cuvelier, S. J. (1993) 'Violence and sexual violence in pornography: is it really increasing?', *Archives of Sexual Behavior*, 22: 357–71.

Sedgwick, E. K. (2003) *Touching Feeling: Affect, Pedagogy, Performativity*, Durham, NC: Duke University Press.

Segal, L. (1998) 'Only the literal', *Sexualities* 1: 43–62.

Shaw, W. (2008) *Business Ethics*, sixth edition, Belmont, CA: Thomson Wadsworth.

Silverman, J. and Wilson, D. (2002) *Innocence Betrayed: Paedophilia, the Media and Society*, Cambridge: Polity Press.

Skeggs, B. (1997) *Formations of Class and Gender: Becoming Respectable*, London: Sage.

Smith, C. (2009) 'Pleasure and distance: exploring sexual cultures in the classroom', *Sexualities*, 12 (5): 568–85.

——(2007a) 'Designed for pleasure: style, indulgence and accessorized sex', *European Journal of Cultural Studies*, 10 (2), 167–84.

——(2007b) *One for the Girls! The Pleasures and Practices of Reading Women's Porn*, Bristol: Intellect.

Smith, D. D. (1976) 'Explicit sex: liberation or exploitation? The social content of pornography', *Journal of Communication*, 26: 16–24.

Soble, A. (1986) *Pornography: Marxism, Feminism, and the Future of Sexuality*, New Haven, CT: Yale University Press.

Sontag, S. (1967/2002) *Styles of Radical Will*, New York: Farrar Straus & Giroux.

Stack, S., Wasserman, I. and Kern, R. (2004) 'Adult social bonds and use of internet pornography', *Social Science Quarterly*, 85: 75–88.

Stanko, E. A. (1997) ' "I second that emotion": reflections on feminism, emotionality, and research on sexual violence', in M. D. Schwartz (ed.) *Researching Sexual Violence against Women: Methodological and Personal Perspectives*, Thousand Oaks, CA: Sage.

Star, M. (2005) '*Go Fuck Yerself 3*: review', *Adult Video News*, September. Online. Available HTTP: <http://www.adultvideonews.com/editch/edch0905_02.html> (accessed 27 August 2006).

Stark, C. and Whisnant, R. (eds) (2004) *Not for Sale: Feminists Resisting Prostitution and Pornography*, Melbourne: Spinifex.

Stebbins, R. A. (1992) *Amateurs, Professionals and Serious Leisure*, Montreal: McGill-Queen's University Press.

Steinem, G. (1980) 'Erotica and pornography: A clear and present difference', in L. Lederer (ed.) *Take Back the Night*, New York: Morrow.

Straayer, C. (1994) 'Sexual representation in film and video', in D. Carson, L. Dittmar and J. R. Welch (eds) *Multiple Voices in Feminist Criticism*, Minneapolis, MN: University of Minnesota Press.

Strager, S. (2003) 'What men watch when they watch pornography', *Sexuality and Culture*, 7: 50–61.

Strasburger, V. and Wilson, B. (eds) (2002) *Children, Adolescents, and the Media*. Thousand Oaks, CA: Sage.

Straw, Jack (Secretary of State for Justice and Lord Chancellor) (2007) Hansard, HC Vol. 464 (137), col. 60 (8 October).

Strossen, N. (1993) 'A feminist critique of "the" feminist critique of pornography', *Virginia Law Review*, 79 (5):1099–190.

——(1995) *Defending Pornography: Free Speech, Sex and the Fight for Women's Rights*, New York: Scribner.

——(1999) 'In defense of pornography', in J. Elias, V. Elias, V. Bullough, G. Brewer, J. L. Douglas and W. Jarvis (eds) *Porn 101: Eroticism, Pornography and the First Amendment*, New York: Prometheus.

Strouse, J., Goodwin, M. and Roscoe, B. (1994) 'Correlates of attitudes toward sexual harassment among early adolescents', *Sex Roles* 31: 559–77.

Summers, C. (2008) 'When does kinky porn become illegal?', *BBC News Magazine*, 29 April. Online. Available HTTP: <http://news.bbc.co.uk/1/hi/magazine/7364475.stm> (accessed 30 October 2009).

Sun, C., Bridges, A. J., Wosnitzer, R., Scharrer, E. and Liberman, R. (2008) 'A comparison of male and female directors in popular pornography: what happens when women are at the helm?', *Psychology of Women Quarterly*, 32: 312–25.

The Sun (2006) 'New porn offence laws', 30 August. Online. Available HTTP: <http://www.thesun.co.uk/sol/homepage/news/61497/New-porn-offence-laws.html> (accessed 16 December 2009).

Sussman, S. (2007) 'Sexual addiction among teens', *Sexual Addiction and Compulsivity*, 14: 257–78.

Sutherland, J. (2000) 'Gospels of hate that slip through the net', *The Guardian*, 3 April, *G2:* 5.

Taylor, Jerome (2008) 'Battle lines drawn over Bill to ban "extreme porn" ', *The Independent*, 30 December. Online. Available HTTP: <http://www.independent.co.uk/news/uk/politics/battle-lines-drawn-over-bill-to-ban-extreme-porn-1216231.html> (accessed 16 December 2009).

Taylor, Katy (2008) 'Criminalising extreme porn', *New Statesman*, 28 October. Online. Available HTTP: < http://www.newstatesman.com/uk-politics/2008/10/extreme-porn-violence-women> (accessed 16 December 2009).

Tecson, B. J. (2005) 'Porn class exciting students, arousing politicians' ire', *MTV*, 19 May. Online. Available HTTP: <http://www.mtv.com/news/articles/1502632/20050519/index.jhtml> (accessed 30 October 2009).

Thomson, R. (1999) ' "It was the way we were watching it": young men negotiate pornography', in J. Hearn and S. Roseneil (eds) *Consuming Cultures*, Basingstoke: Macmillan.

Thornburgh, D. and Lin H. (eds) (2002) *Youth, Pornography, and the Internet*, Washington, DC: National Academy Press.

Tiefer, L. (1994) 'The medicalization of impotence: normalizing phallocentrism', *Gender and Society*, 8 (3): 363–77.

Turkle, S. (1995) *Life on the Screen: Identity in the Age of the Internet*, London: Phoenix.

Tyden, T., Olsson, S-E. and Haggstrom-Nordin, E. (2001) 'Improved use of contraceptives, attitudes towards pornography, and sexual harassment among female university students', *Women's Health Issues*, 11: 87–94.

Tyden, T. and Rogala, C. (2004) 'Sexual behaviour among young men in Sweden and the impact of pornography', *International Journal of STD and AIDS*, 15: 590–3.

Wagner, M. (2007) 'Sex in Second Life', *Information Week*, 26 May. Online. Available HTTP: <http://www.informationweek.com/news/software/hosted/showArticle.jhtml?articleID=199701944> (accessed 11 September 2009).

Waller, J. (2002) *Becoming Evil: How Ordinary People Commit Genocide and Mass Killing*, New York: Oxford University Press.

Wallmyr, G. and Welin, C. (2006) 'Young people, pornography, and sexuality', *Journal of School Nursing*, 22: 290–5.

Walsh, A. (1999) 'Life history theory and female readers of pornography', *Personality and Individual Differences*, 27: 779–87.

Ward, L. M. (2002) 'Does television exposure affect emerging adults' attitudes and assumptions about sexual relationships?', *Journal of Youth and Adolescence*, 31: 1–15.

——(2003) 'Understanding the role of entertainment media in the sexual socialization of American youth', *Developmental Review*, 23: 347–88.

Ward, L., Hansbrough E. and Walker, E. (2005) 'Contributions of music video exposure to black adolescents' gender and sexual schemas', *Journal of Adolescent Research*, 20: 143–66.

Warren, P. (2005) '*Squealer:* review', *Adult Video News*, November. Online. Available HTTP: <http://www.adultvideonews.com/editch/edch1105_07.html> (accessed 27 August 2006).

Waskul, D. D. (2009) ' "My boyfriend loves it when I come home from this class": pedagogy, titillation, and new media technologies', *Sexualities*, 12 (5): 654–61.

Waskul, D. D., Douglass, M. and Edgley, C. (2004) 'Outercourse: body and self in text cybersex' in D. D. Waskul (ed.) *net.seXXX: Readings on Sex, Pornography and the Internet*, New York: Peter Lang.

Wasserman, S. and Faust, K. (1994) *Social Network Analysis: Methods and Applications*, Cambridge: Cambridge University Press.

Wells, T. (2004) 'Students study hard porn' and 'What the Dickens are they teaching?', *Sunday Mercury*, 25 January: 1, 6.

West, R. (1987) 'The feminist–conservative anti-pornography alliance and the 1986 Attorney General's Commission on Pornography report', *American Bar Foundation Research Journal*: 681–712.

Whisnant, R. (2004) 'Confronting pornography: some conceptual basics', in C. Stark and R. Whisnant (eds) *Not for Sale: Feminists Resisting Prostitution and Pornography*, Melbourne: Spinifex Press.

Whissell, C. (1998) 'Linguistic, emotional and content analyses of sexually explicit scenes in popular fiction', *Canadian Journal of Human Sexuality*, 7: 147–59.

Williams, B. (1979) *Report of the Committee on Obscenity and Film Censorship*, Cmnd 7772, London: HMSO.

Williams, L. (1989) *Hard Core: Power, Pleasure, and the 'Frenzy of the Visible'*, Berkeley, CA: University of California Press.

——(1991) 'Film bodies: gender, genre, and excess', *Film Quarterly*, 44: 2–13.

——(2004a) 'Proliferating pornographies on/scene: an introduction', in L. Williams (ed.) *Porn Studies*, Durham, NC: Duke University Press.

——(ed.) (2004b) *Porn Studies*. Durham, NC: Duke University Press.

Williams, T. (1961) *The Night of the Iguana*, in M. Gussow and K. Holdich (eds) *Tennessee Williams: Plays, 1957–1980*, New York: Library of America.

Wilson, B. J., Smith, S. L., Potter, W. J., Kunkel, D., Linz, D., Colvin, C. M. and Donnerstein, E. (2002) 'Violence in children's television programming: assessing the risks', *Journal of Communication*, 52: 5–35.

Wilson, E. (1992) 'Feminist fundamentalism: the shifting politics of sex and censorship', in L. Segal and M. McIntosh (eds) *Sex Exposed: Sexuality and the Pornography Debate*, London: Virago.

Wilson, R. (1994) 'Colo. regents reject promotion of erotic-literature scholar', *Chronicle of Higher Education*, 28 September: A24.

Wingood, G., DiClemente, R., Harrington, K., Davies, S., Hook, E. and Oh, M. (2001) 'Exposure to X-rated movies and adolescents' sexual and contraceptive-related attitudes and behaviors', *Pediatrics*, 107 (5): 1116–19.

Winick, C. (1985) 'A content analysis of sexually explicit magazines sold in an adult bookstore', *Journal of Sex Research*, 21: 206–10.

Winkler, K. J. (1989) 'Research on pornography gains respectability, increased importance among scholars', *Chronicle of Higher Education*, 14 June: A4–A5, A8.

Wolak, J., Mitchell, K. and Finkelhor, D. (2007) 'Unwanted and wanted exposure to online pornography in a national sample of youth internet users', *Pediatrics*, 119: 247–57.

Wood, A. (2007) *Digital Encounters*, London and New York: Routledge.

World Health Organization (2006) *Defining Sexual Health: Report of a Technical Consultation on Sexual Health, 28–31 January 2002*, Geneva: World Health Organization.

Wosnitzer, R. and Bridges, A. J. (2007) 'Aggression and Sexual Behavior in Best-selling Pornography: A Content Analysis Update', paper presented at the annual meeting of the International Communication Association, San Francisco, May.

Yagielowicz, S. (2007) 'WAAT Media selects Vantrix for mobile video delivery', *X-Biz*. Online. Available HTTP: <http://www.xbiz.com/news/87960> (accessed 6 November 2009).

Yang, N. and Linz, D. (1990) 'Movie ratings and the content of adult videos: the sex–violence ratio', *Journal of Communication*, 40 (2): 28–42.

Young, C. (2003) 'Skin flicks 101: what Porn Studies profs don't get about sex', *Reason*, 1 May: 20–1.

Young, S. (2008) 'Internet sex addiction', *American Behavioral Scientist*, 52: 21–37.

Zillmann, D. (1989) 'Effects of prolonged consumption of pornography', in D. Zillman and J. Bryant (eds) *Pornography*, Hillsdale, NJ: Erlbaum.

Zimbardo, P. (2004) 'A situationist perspective on the psychology of evil: understanding how good people are transformed into perpetrators,' in A. Miller (ed.) *The Moral Psychology of Good and Evil*, New York: Guilford Press.

——(2007) *The Lucifer Effect: Understanding how Good People turn Evil*, New York: Random House.

Zimmerman, B. (2006) 'Professor known for class on porn says he won't be teaching it at ISU', *Tribune Star* (Terre Haute, IN), 25 October. Online. Available HTTP: <http://www.tribstar.com/archivesearch/local_story_298000431.html> (accessed 30 October 2009).

Index